BRAHMANAS OF SOUTH INDIA

BRAHMANAS OF SOUTH INDIA

Nagendra Rao

Publications

KALPAZ PUBLICATIONS

DELHI-110052

Brahmanas of South India

Rs. 690

ISBN: 81-7835-300-8

Published in 2005 in India by
Kalpaz Publications,
C-30, Satyawati Nagar, Delhi-110052
E-mail : Kalpaz@hotmail.com

Laser Typesetting at : Shree Vaishnavi Creations, Delhi
Printed at : Salasar Imaging System, Delhi

Contents

Foreword

It is with immense pleasure, and a certain amount of pride, that I present this book by Dr. Nagendra E. Rao to the world of scholarship. I may have to start by dispelling certain misgivings about the subject matter of the book. A book on the history of *the Brahmanical groups in South Kanara* is likely to raise the question whether it is about a particular caste group, and a limited geographical area. The answer is both "yes" and "no". Dr. Rao does deal with the Brahmanical groups; and his primary concern is geographically limited to the southern parts of coastal Karnataka. However, the study he has undertaken does open out into something more than that, taking up questions related to the social function of historical tradition, patterns of group migrations and settlement, types of domination and its linkages with forces and relations of production, the role of ideology in it and the memories - whether remembered or legislated- of group experience cherished by sections of society. Hence I believe that a word or two, bringing out this transcendental character of this book on a small caste within a limited geographical area, may not be out of place.

Historiography of coastal Karnataka cannot quite boast that it has grown beyond the elementary levels. The giant strides that historiography has taken in recent years in India have left this part of the country largely unaffected. In fact, many primary "facts" remain to be ascertained; many documents pertaining to the past await publication, let alone interpretation and generalization. When, in the nineteenth century, historical writing on "modem" lines began in this region, the pioneering attempts were to find out the historicity or otherwise of legends, of which there were many. Thus, scholars tried hard to historicise the weightless stories that floated in an air of fancy -stories about Parasurama, Mayuravarman, Bhutala

Pandya and others - thus trying to concoct a strange mixture of two traditions with entirely different functions. The colonial masters, who were convinced that "the master knew better", dismissed what is available in the indigenous tradition as legend, superstition and nonsense. Their mission to create a new knowledge, which would suit the regime of power that they presided over, demanded such a rejection: it was in fact a precondition for it. They had their willing ally in the missionaries, primarily of the Basel Mission, who studied not only the cults and practices and the oral literature associated with it in the region but also characterized them as so much of devil worship and folk tradition, obviously implying that the "natives" were less than their masters who had a "standard" religion, a book and a literate literature. The Utilitarian and Evangelical agendas of the two coalesced only too well. It was this that was carried forward in the manuals and Gazetteers, which pronounced the official version of the history of this region.

The colonial state, it should be stated in all fairness, engaged itself in a project of collecting and publishing documents pertaining to the past, whatever the purpose behind it. A large number of inscriptions were so published and many monuments were documented. This could replace the old kind of telling tales about the past - perhaps the distance covered from Sheenappa Hegdes and Ganapathi Rao Aigals to a more 61 scientific" way of writing about the past. The Rankean method of history had come to stay, where going by evidence was the credo. B.A. Saletore made the best statement of this arrival in *Ancient Karnataka,* vol. 1. However, attempts to proverbially drive the square peg of historical evidence into the round hole of legend and popular tradition did not quite stop; in fact it continued even in the "professional" histories produced after that, Participating in the Freedom Movement, at least in a vicarious way, historians celebrated the past of South Kanara, making so many swans of its geese. The post-Independence freshness that we see th historiography in relation to the rest of India, unfortunately, somewhat by-passed Karnataka in general and South Kanara in particular. It is against this background that I will look at Dr. Rao's new book.

Dr. Rao takes up an examination of the traditions of the Brahmanical groups in South Kanara in its various forms and at its various levels and looks for traces of the existence of the groups in the places suggested by these traditions. He, however, resists the temptation to boil in the same stew and pin such weightless traditions down to points in space and time. He goes beyond that, to place these historical traditions within the context of early Indian historical tradition and raise questions related to the social function of such traditions within the framework in which they took shape. He takes up the *Grāinapaddhati* and *Sahyadrikhanda,* two narratives of mythological recovery of the past of coastal Karnataka. Dissimilarities in form and content notwithstanding, both of them were produced by similar groups and served similar purposes.

An examination of this kind, to be sure, was possible with the insights available in the recent development of historiography in India. One can see that Dr. Rao has benefited from it at two levels. Colonial scholarship on Indology had rejected any possibility of India having had a sense of the past or a tradition of historical writing. Recent work, however, has not only proved this to be wrong but also tried to show the form in which such consciousness was expressed and the reasons for that. The work of Romila Thapar on the *itihasa-purana* tradition, for instance, has raised many refreshing questions on this. Benefiting from such discussion, Dr. Rao attempts to see how expressions of historical consciousness contained in the Brahmanical chronicles from South Kanara can be used as a case study to answer the question regarding the existence or otherwise of a sense of the past in India. He sees that the answer has to be in the affirmative; he also shows that, being the expressions of particular groups, they had their own function. The Brahmanical element in the society of South Kanara sought its ideological legitimation through such expressions.

It is here that Dr. Rao's extensive reading in the social history of early India has stood him in good stead. Work on the migrations of Brahmanical groups along the west coast of India, done particularly in relation to Kerala, had demonstrated that the Parasurama tradition is not something which is exclusive about one or the other part of the west coast. It was cherished from Sourashtra to Kanyakumari with emphasis laid on different aspects. B.A. Saletore had seen this earlier in the case of South Kanara; but to place this in the larger context of the whole west coast required experience from further south, which was denied to Saletore. Dr. Rao has made use of the researches of M.G.S. Narayanan and the present writer into the history of Kerala in this regard and has shown that the experience in South Kanara indicates that that region formed part of a long chain stretching from Gujarat to Kanyakumari. At the same time, Dr. Rao has not failed to see the distinctive features of the South Kanara tradition: the relatively weak character of the Brahmanical groups and the rather subdued political tones of the narratives are points which can be seen here.

What makes this contribution valuable is also the extensive field work that has been carried out to support the arguments. Even if all the findings that Dr. Rao has drawn were to be discredited - which is not going to happen - this work has a claim to remain on account of the rich data from epigraphy and ethnography that the scholar has presented. Thus, I have absolutely no hesitation in commending this book to the reader for both its empirical richness and the theoretical validity. It will be embarrassing for me to say anything more about this book as I had the good fortune to associate myself with the preparation of this monograph in the capacity of the supervisor. I leave the rest of it to the reader.

Kesavan Veluthat

1
Introduction

This work attempts to study the traditional chronicles of South Kanara and see how these traditions were utilised by brahmanical groups to justify their already superior social position and status.[1] The traditional histories of South Western India, *Grāmapaddhati* and *Sahyādri Khanda* are authored by brahmanas who made use of a particular version of history which benefited their own community. The traditions are utilized to uphold the caste status of brahmanas in the region. Both the chronicles, *Grāmapaddhati* and *Sahyādri Khanda*, speak about the tradition of *Paraśurāma* creating the land on the west coast and donating it to brahmanas. These two works speak also about the arrival of various brahmanical groups into the region. Thus, these texts noticed the migration of different brahmanical groups into South Kanara. The emphasis given to brahmanical details in the chronicles, the level of sense of history expressed in these traditions, the link maintained between *Parasurāma sṛiṣti* or creation and the ownership of land claimed by brahmanas are highlighted in this monograph.

A study of the contents of *Grāmapaddhati* shows the importance given by its authors to certain events. The events are narrated in the form of episodes without giving importance to chronological accuracy. This exhibits the feature of a traditional history of a region and the traditional chronicles on the west coast maintained some link with the history of the region. In the case of South Western India, the traditional histories, *Grāmpaddhati* and *Sahyādri Khanda*, reveal the sense of history of their authors, thus proving the existence of a historical tradition in this region. These authors provided certain pieces of information which can be compared with the evidences from other sources available to us such as epigraph and the continuing traditions of families. The present work proposes to make an attempt by searching for evidences for the family names and the villages which are mentioned in different versions of *Grāmapaddhati*. The author, through the fieldwork, has been able to confirm the identity of villages, most of which continue to exist even today.

An attempt is also made here to investigate the function of the tradition of Paraśurāma creating the land on the West Coast. The *Paraśurāma* tradition was used in various regions of West Coast including Kanara region and Kerala. Both these regions exhibited cultural affinity, if not political unity and continuity[2], at least in the case of the brahmana settlements. As the tradition goes, thirty-two villages were donated to brahmanas of Kerala, while the same number of villages were given to the brahmanas of Tulunadu[3]. An analysis of traditional chronicles of both the regions confirms the assumption of cultural linkage that existed between Kerala and Tulunadu, which is also indicated in *Grāmapaddhati*. Regarding the traditional chronicles of Kerala, Kesavan Veluthat has done studies on the brahmana settlements of Kerala with the help of *Kēralotpatti*.[4] The present author has tried to extend the work in Kerala to Tulunadu of South Western India.

The British colonial rulers who emerged in the scene of Indian history in 19th century started looking at oriental traditional history and they tried to interpret what was narrated in the traditional chronicles. In the case of South Western India, Sturrock wrote regarding the traditional history of Tulunadu.[5] He did notice the existence of *Grāmapaddhati* but did not find the necessity to study it in great detail.

Among the Indian authors, Polali Sheenappa Heggade studied the contents in *Grāmpaddhati* but he did not consider this work as of any importance and rejected its value as a source for writing any history.[6] Ganapati Rao Aigal also used it while writing the history of South Western India, but he gave only a list of villages and households and did not study it further.[7]

B.A. Saletore adopted a new methodology of studying the social history of the region with the help of traditional chronicles like *Grāmapaddhati* and *Sahyādri Khanda*.[8] He studied in great detail the occurrences of Paraśurāma tradition in different regions of India and noticed the migration of the legend from Gujarat to other parts of the West Coast. He also tried to judge the historicity of *Grāmapaddhati* with the help of the contents included in *Grāmapaddhati*. He asserted that, "...the *Grāmapaddhati* is a source which cannot be dismissed as an instance of Brahmanical fabrication".[9] Thus, Saletore recognized the importance of use of *Grāmapaddhati* for reconstructing social history of South Western India. However, he did not put forward the question as to why certain of the events were considered as more relevant by the brahmanical authors.

B.A. Saletore, even though studied the minute details found in *Grāmapaddhati,* he had certain problems regarding the date of this text. He says that this text does not give uniform details in all the versions. Thus in one version, Mayūra Varma is introduced abruptly; while in others his parentage is given. In some he is made the son of Manivarma; in others son of Sushila and Hemangada. But in some versions, Hemangada is described to be issueless. Saletore further states that *Grāmapaddhati* contains certain statements which cannot be accepted. In one version the ministers who go in search of ruler are described to have proceeded to northern Varakula or Barakuru, while there never existed northern and southern Barakūru. Further, *Grāmapaddhati* was represented as a portion of *Skanda Purana.* This, according Saletore, detracts its value as a piece of independent historical work.[10] Thus, this statement made by Saletore exhibits the fact that he did not believe that Puranas could be used as a reliable source for studying the social history of a region. However, many scholars, like Pargiter and D.C. Sircar, have showed that a cautious study of Puranas reveals certain interesting details. Regarding the date of *Grāmapaddhati,* Saletore states that this text may belong of middle of 15th century A.D. He justifies this theory by giving following details[11] :

1. The text mentions controversy between Shankaracharya and Mandana Pandita. There it belongs to a period later than 8th century A.D.
2. There is a reference to spread of Jainism, which happened in the case of South Kanara, after 9th century A.D. Hence it was written after 9th century A.D.
3. It speaks about Barahakanyapura which emerged only in 10th century A.D. So it is argued that this text was composed after 10th century A.D.
4. One version mentions king Vasu, who is identified with the Alupa king, Vibudhavasu, who ruled during 13th century A.D.
5. Since there is reference to Madhwacharya who lived during 13th century A.D., it is suggested that this text may belong to period after 13th century A.D.
6. There is reference to Vira Bhupa who is identified with Vijayanagara viceroy Vira Bhupati who ruled the region during 14th century A.D.

Based on the above, it is argued by Saletore that the text was written after 14th century A.D. However it is problematic to accept this calculation of date of any text, as it consists of both old events and events which took place during the later period. It is possible, like any other text like Kautilya's *Arthashastra*, it was composed during an earlier period and additions were made by the different authors during later period. For example there are certain Hindi terms in this text like 'battisa' which indicates the influence of Hindi language on this text. Thus, it is quite plausible that it did not remain a static text from the period when it was composed for the first time to the modern times. Perhaps, this led to creation of many versions of the text which is found in different households of South Kanara. The need to create so many versions of the text was precisely to add recent data. Perhaps it obtained religious sanction as many of these versions are found in religious institutions like Puttige Mutt, Udupi and Balekudru Mutt near Barkur.[12]

Saletore tried to compare references in *Grāmapaddhati* with details found in the epigraphs. For instance, there is reference to the family of Nidamburu and the people of this village both in the literature as well as in the inscriptions. Both the sources also mention the brahmana families like Naduvantillaya, Maduvantillaya, Koditillaya and various other families. In the sources there is reference to God Markandeshwara of Barakuru and the families of Holla, Hande, Mayya, Karanta and Mudila Nidamburu Ballala. Some of them belonged to Kota while others belonged to Shivalli village. The members of Mayya and Holla families were cited as witnesses to public grants made by the prominent citizens of Barakuru in the first half of 15th century A.D. According to Saletore, Chittupadi and Nidamburu households of Udupi wielded considerable influence in their own locality. In *Grāmapaddhati,* they are called Pakshanathas. Both the families were mentioned in the inscriptions and they were given grant of land by the kings.[13]

The other historians of the region like Gururāja Bhat, K.V. Ramesh and K.G. Vasanthamadhava seldom recognized the significance of traditional histories, even though their contribution to the history of South Western India in other fields is impressive. P. Gururāja Bhat tried to give a rational explanation for the tradition regarding settlement of brahmanas on the western coast. He mentions that according to the traditional story, the Kadamba king Mayūra Varma brought brahmanas from North India and settled them in different parts of South Kanara. We do not have any reliable historical evidence in substantiation of this tradition. According to him, the advent of Brahmanism and brahmanical culture may be traced to the beginnings of the political rise of Kadambas of Banavasi. It is possible that South Kanara was brought under the control of the Kadambas who had their capital at Banavasi in the district of North Kanara. The introduction of brahmanical culture into this region was a very significant stride in the cultural growth. The earlier non Vedic cultural pattern was brought under Vedic influence and the Vedic system of worship incorporated into its many elements alien to it. This kind of synthesis and transformation is strikingly seen in temple worship and worship of local deities called *bhutaradhana*. Thus, Bhat accepts that it was the Kadambas who brought brahmanas and made them to settle here.[14] He says that according to one version of tradition brahmanas were introduced into the region in 8th century A.D. Barkur was one of the places at which a brahmana governor is said to have been appointed. However, he does not agree with the historicity of this tradition. The Havika brahmanas of Haive relate to the introduction of brahmanas into the land by Kadamba ruler, Maūra Varma. Likewise, brahmanas of South Kanara attribute their first arrival owing to certain families being brought from Ahicchatra on a special request, made personally by Maūra Varma, the ruler of Barakuru. This account is found in *Grāmapaddhati.* But there is no reliable evidence to support this tradition. Inscriptions of South Kanara do not mention about the introduction of brahmanas by Maūra Varma. Bhat says that it is unhistorical to say that any ruler of name Maūra Varma or Maūra Sharma ever ruled Barakuru. This analysis allowed Bhat to mention the following:

1. They were immigrants to South Kanara some times in the past, although we are uncertain about the date of their arrival.
2. There had been some kind of proliferation amongst the brahmanas after their immigration and settlement in the region. For instance, *Grāmapaddhati* mentions that there existed different grades of brahmana families.[15]

It is argued that the story narrated by brahmanas may be a reflection of a memory of what was recorded in Talagunda epigraph which mentions the agrahara of Kuppaturu of Shimoga district. Brahmana settlement was established in this region with the initiative of Maūra Varma in the 4th century A.D. Gururaj Bhat further argues that there was migration of brahmanas from Shimoga district to South Kanara district during the rule of Alupas who ruled South Kanara during the period 1st century A.D. to 14th century A.D. Vaddarse inscription belonging to 7th century A.D. mentions the existence of brahmanas in this region. It cannot, however be, said that all brahmanas migrated simultaneously to this region. With greater and increased contact with Karnataka, different sections of them may have been attracted to this region for settlement. Hence, the Havikas settled in Haive and formed their own group. The brahmanas of South Kanara comprising different branches sought settlement in different places and developed their individuality. Gururaja Bhat mentions that among brahmanas of South Kanara there were five subdivisions, Sivalli, Kota, Koteshwara, Kandavara and Panchagrama. We find that these names are derived from the names of the different places where they perhaps settled initially.[16] Bhat argues that religious differences and social conflicts must have been responsible for a schism among them. He pointed out the importance of Shivalli brahmanas as mentioned in Udyavar inscription of 8th century A.D. At the same time, it is pointed out that Kota was one of the biggest centres of Brahmanism as evidenced by inscriptions which refer to 10000 mahajagattu which was an assembly of brahmanas in Kota. Gururaj Bhat says that Brahmanism was popular in South Kanara by 7th century A.D. There is reference to arrival of disciple of Shankaracharya to Kumaradri and Kolluru in South Kanara. In South Kanara there are number of other sections of brahmanas such as the sthanika, the chitpavana, the karad, the konkanastha and the sarasvata.[17] We should accept that the above evidences furnished by Gururāja Bhat are very useful in discovering the origin and growth of brahmana settlements in South Kanara.

Based on study of inscriptions he presented the following list of brahmana families with their surnames. They are Adiga, Acharya, Ahitagni, Amna, Asrana, Ayitala, Ballala, Basuri, Bhatta, Bhattatila, Goli, Hande, Hatvara, Hebbaruva, Herala, Hosala, Joisa, Kalembi, Kalkura, Kadekara, Karanta, Kedila, Kodacha, Kodakalanaya, Kunjatava, Kramita, Madacha, Marinaya, Mattinaya, Mayya, Mitanta, Navada, Oja, Padiraya, Puranika, Sabhayita, Somayaji, Tantri, Tunga, Udupa, Upadhya, Ugrani, Ungurapalli, Urala, Vaidya, etc.[18] We may note that some of these families are mentioned in different versions of *Grāmapaddhati*. Thus Gururāja Bhat tried to analyse the brahmanical tradition on the basis of epigraphical evidences, which was unfortunately not forthcoming. Hence, he thought that one cannot depend on this traditional history narrated in *Grāmapaddhati*.

K.V. Ramesh did not give much importance to the tradition of South Kanara. However, he suggested that the tradition of Paraśurāma creating land out of sea may indicate the beginning of Iron Age in the region as the weapon used by Paraśurāma was axe. According to him the faint recollections of what had happened in the remote past induced later generations to coin this legend.[19] At another context, he says that *Sahyādri Khanda* gives a legendary history of Tuluva. Apart from these statements, Ramesh did not give much importance to these works.[20]

The literary figures of the region also noticed importance of traditional chronicles. For instance, Shivarama Karantha emphasized the need for the cautious study of *Grāmapaddhati* and Sahyādri Khanda[21] Padmanabha Kekunnaya[22] made a linguistic study of family names appearing in *Grāmapaddhati*. His work is useful to discover the origin of some of the brahmana family names.

The present author has attempted to continue the work of both B.A. Saletore and Kesavan Veluthat in the Kanara and Kerala coasts. The traditions of these two areas present these regions as a single cultural unit. There are certain similarities between *Grāmapaddhati* and *Kēralotpatti*. The *Kēralotpatti* uses the Parasurama tradition as is seen in *Grāmapaddhti*. The *Kēralotpatti* also speaks about the donation of thirty-two villages to brahmanas and it links the brahmanas with the king Mayūra Varma. Between the above two works, there are dissimilarities too. The brahmanical details such as the family names found in *Grāmapaddhati* are not found in *Kēralotpatti*, which gives more importance to political details.

The primary sources used in this work are traditional chronicles *Grāmapaddhati* and *Sahyādri Khanda*. The author has used three versions of *Grāmapaddhati*, which are named GP1, GP2 and GP3 respectively. A comparative study of the contents of these three versions was made by taking GP1 as master narrative. This work also uses a Sanskrit *Sahyādri Khanda* and a Kannada *Sahyādri Khanda*. Here a comparison is made between the contents in *Sahyādri Khanda* (Sanskrit) and *Grāmapaddhati*. Inscriptions are the next important source. They are used to cross check the information available in the above mentioned traditional chronicles. Following are some of the finding of the author:

1. The author, through field work, was able to identify and locate the villages mentioned in *Grāmapaddhati*. He has shown that some of the villages do not continue to exist. In other existing villages, the continuing family traditions have been identified.
2. He has noticed the inscriptional references to brahmana family names and the survivals of traditions. This has been presented with the help of tables and a map listing the brahmana settlements in South Western India as mentioned in *Grāmapaddhati*.
3. He has also shown the links maintained by these traditions with Madhva traditions which would prove the post Madhva dating of the Brahmanical texts.

4. The author has shown how there were additions made in different versions of *Grāmapaddhati* which date to different periods. These additions are generally regarding family names and list of villages. This will be an index to the growth of historical tradition.
5. This study shows that the brahmana settlements consisted of temples and agraharas and that these settlements were established on fertile river valleys. It is possible to identify clusters of villages in different parts of South Western India.

References

1. It is suggested by Veena Das that one important social context in which a caste could be called upon to submit their Purana was in the courts of kings or important political heads, who were vested with the power to settle disputes relating to rank, privileges, or disabilities of the castes within their respective jurisdictions. The caste Puranas would have to provide evidence of caste group's claim to a particular status. They first established the conceptual order of Hinduism by the use of categories taken from the *varna* scheme and *ashrama* scheme, and only proceeded to discuss the position of the caste within this order. See Veena Das, *Structure and Cognition Aspects of Hindu Caste and Ritual,* Delhi, 1997, pp. 14-15.
2. Kesavan Veluthat, *Aryan Brahman Settlement of Ancient Kerala,* Unpublished M.A. Dissertation, Calicut University, 1974.
3. In early period the present day region comprising South Kanara was known as Tulunadu. The people who inhabited in this region are called Taulavas; language spoken was called Tulu; and there were brahmana categories called Tulu brahmanas, most of whom spoke Tulu in their locality. Tulu was the language of both brahmanas and non-brahmanas. However, Tulu spoken by brahmanas seems to be more sanskritised than the latter.
4. Kesavan Veluthat, *Brahman Settlements in Kerala: Historical Studies,* Calicut, 1978.
5. Sturrock, J., *Madras District Manuals South Kanara, Vol. I,* Madras, 1894.
6. A. Balakrishna Shetty (ed.), *Sheenappa Heggade Samagra Sahitya* (Kan.), Udupi, 1991.
7. Ganapathi Rao Aigal, *Dakshina Kannada Jilleya Prachina Itihāsa,* (Kan.), Mangalore, 1923.
8. B.A. Saletore, *Ancient Karnataka, Vol. I, History of Tuluva,* Poona, 1936.
9. *Ibid.*, p. 342.
10. *Ibid.*, p. 341-342.

11. *Ibid.*, pp. 341-347.
12. It is interesting to note that, among these two mutts, Puttige mutt belongs to Vaishnava tradition initiated by Madhwacharya, while Balekudru mutt belongs to Smarta tradition which follow the teachings of Shankaracharya.
13. *Ibid.*, pp. 335-336.
14. P. Gururaj Bhat, *Studies in Tuluva History and Culture*, Kallianpur, 1975, p. xi.
15. *Ibid.*, pp. 2-3.
16. Similar situation is mentioned in Gujarat by Veena Das. It is stated that there was a close association between caste-name and the name of a locality. Thus Shrimali brahmanas are those brahmanas who come from Shrimal, Modh brahmanas are those who come from Modhera and Nagar brahmanas come from Vadnagar. See Veena Das, *Structure and Cognition*. p. 11.
17. *Ibid.*, pp. 237ff.
18. *Ibid.*, p. 255.
19. K.V. Ramesh, *A History of South Kanara*, Dharwar, 1970, p. xxiii.
20. This lack of interest in literary sources may be due to the fact K.V.Ramesh himself was an epigraphist and obviously he gave much prominence to inscriptions.
21. B. Malini Mallya, (ed), *Shivarama Karantara Lekhanagalu, Vol. II*, (Kan.), Mangalagangotri, 1994.
22. Padmanabha, K, "Shivalli Brahmanara Kulanamagalu-Ondu Adhyayana", (Kan.) Unpublished M.A. dissertation, University of Madras, 1982.

2

Early Indian Historical Tradition

The most fashionable view regarding the early history of India, current among the early European writers of India has been that India had no sense of the past. Al-Biruni, the Muslim scholar who studied the ancient Indian literature, was one of the first persons to remark on the lack of historical sense among the Indians.[1] Regarding Hindus Al-Biruni made certain decisive observations. He referred to the self-conceit of Hindus as their most important flaw. Hindus consider that there is no country but theirs, no nation like theirs, no kings like theirs, no religion like theirs, no science like theirs. They are haughty, foolishly vain, self-conceited, and stolid. At the same time Al-Biruni states that if they travelled and mixed with other nations they would soon alter their mind, for their ancestors were not as narrow-minded as the current generation is.[2] He says that the Indian scribes are careless, and do not take care to produce correct and well-collated copies. In consequence, the highest results of the author's mental development are lost by their casualness, and his book becomes already in the first or second copy so full of faults, that the text appears as something entirely new, which neither a scholar nor one familiar with the subject, whether Hindu or Muslim, could any longer understand. Besides, the scientific books of the Hindus are composed in various favourite metres, by which they intend, considering that the books soon become corrupted by additions and omissions, to preserve them exactly as they are, in order to facilitate their being learned by heart, because they consider as canonical only that which is known by heart, not that which exists in writing.[3] Al-Biruni criticized the Indian approach towards history and historical facts. He says that unfortunately the Hindus do not pay much attention to the historical order of things, they are very careless in narrating the chronological succession of their kings, and when they are pressed for information and are at a loss, not knowing what to say, they invariably take to tale-telling.[4] In spite of this criticism of Indian sense of history, Al-Biruni mentions the knowledge of Indians regarding different eras like those of Sri Harsha, Vikramaditya, Saka, Vallabha and Gupta.[5] The common people of India date by the years of a *centennium,* which they call *samvatsara.* If a *centennium* is finished, they drop it, and simply begin to date by a new one.[6] Thus Al-Biruni was conscious of the fact that Indians had the knowledge of different eras which may represent a sense of history. It is these alleged limitations which were criticized by Al-Biruni. He says that the heathen Greeks, before the rise of Christianity, held much the same opinions as the Hindus, their educated classes though much the same as those of the Hindus; their common people held same idolatrous views as those of Hindus. The Greeks, however, had philosophers who, living in their country, discovered and worked out for them the elements of science not of popular superstition. He states that the Hindus had no men of this stamp both capable and willing to bring sciences to a classical perfection. Therefore even the so-called scientific theorems of the Hindus are in a state of utter confusion, devoid of any logical order. He compares their mathematical and astronomical literature to a mixture of pearl shells and sour dates, or of pearls and dung or of costly crystals and common pebbles. Both kinds of thing are equal in their eyes, since they cannot raise themselves to the methods of strictly scientific deduction.[7] Thus Al-Biruni was not much overwhelmed by the Indian scientific literature. The above criticisms leveled against ancient Indians should be regarded as those by a foreigner who was trying to get accustomed to alien conditions. During those days it was not very easy to get accustomed to a alien culture and strange atmosphere. It is possible that Al-Biruni was not able to study all the texts of ancient India and whatever texts he studied did not deal with explicit history. This may be because of the fact that he was not in a position to comprehend the implicit nature of Indian historical tradition. In the modern period the studies made by Pargiter has showed us how in the Purānas one can cull data regarding historical events and personalities.

The European scholars who came to India during the 18th and 19th centuries perhaps took the clue from Al-Biruni and put forward the theory that Indians lacked a reasonable sense of history, a consciousness of the past, when compared to other contemporary societies. History was written with a rationale, with a particular ideology. During various points of time history has been used and misrepresented. Hence it was very natural that the British, perhaps willfully, tried to diminish the import of Indian culture. By doing that they could validate the superiority of the British administration when compared to the early Indian political institutions. Some British historians wrote with political purpose and some others, like James Mill, wrote with ideological purpose. In the process they analysed the Indian history and culture and tried to construe the past in the light of current circumstances.

They noticed, following their meticulous study of Indology, i.e., Indian literature, culture, philosophy and religion, that Indians wrote on virtually all subjects, on science, astronomy, mathematics, even human anatomy; but they intriguingly discovered a lack of scientific mindedness as far as the discipline of history is concerned. This failing was particularly curious since they had acknowledged the scientific mind-set of Indians in other fields like astronomy and that too when in contemporary western societies scientific attitude was nearly equated with offense[8]. Philips suggests that the Hindu peoples of ancient India had no sense of history as there was remarkable dearth of historical writing in the period down to the close of the first millennium A.D. Further he says that we are struck by the absence in the voluminous general and religious literature of the period not only of manuscripts of ancient historical works but also of references to them. He does not agree with the view that many historical works were destroyed by the invaders of the middle ages. Philips states that, "Contact with peoples possessing a stronger historical sense than is discernible in India, for example, with the Islamic, Central Asian, and Chinese peoples, may well have encouraged the growth of historical writing in Kashmir".[9] Apparently, what appeared for the Europeans was the subsistence of copious material which gave details about religion and not regarding the history of the state and the people.

In a way the above suggestion to some degree was approved by a nationalist historian like R.C. Majumdar when he mentioned that, "It is well-known fact that with the single exception of the *Rājatarangini* (History of Kashmir) there is no historical text in Sanskrit dealing with the whole or even parts of India".[10] However, he goes on to argue that even though there are no references to historical text, still there existed ideas regarding history as is found in the *Narasamsi* or hero-lauds which formed an essential feature in the preparatory ceremonies of the year-long celebration of horse-sacrifice.[11] Majumdar tries to give explanation for the lack of historical literature in ancient India. He states that the absence of real historical literature is regarded so very unusual that even many distinguished Indians seriously entertain the belief that there were many such historical texts, but that they have all perished. Majumdar further argues that the loss of historical chronicles in Kashmir is due, in a large measure, to the *Rājatarangini* itself which superseded them and, to ordinary readers, rendered them superfluous. Kautilya's *Arthashastra* furnishes a similar instance. It refers to many previous works on the subject, which have entirely disappeared, presumably because nobody cared to read them after the masterly treatise of Kautilya was composed. When a good literary work superseded previous texts on the subject, the latter were no longer studied and therefore fell into disuse and perished, in most cases, beyond recovery.[12] Thus, R.C. Majumdar tried to present a clarification for the lack of discovery of historical literature in ancient India as compared to other branches of knowledge.

He also states that the various theories put forward to explain the absence of history in India fail to take note of the fact that the problem that we have to solve is not the lack of historical writings, of which we have a fair number of specimens, but the absence of finished products like the *Rājatarangini.* We have historical writings about Kumarapala, about Ramapala, Vikramaditya VI, and Sindhuraja, but no history of the Chaulukyas, the Palas, the later Chalukyas and the Paramaras. Majumdar says that none of the extant theories can sufficiently explain this phenomenon. India lacked neither historical materials nor historical chronicles, and even the popular demand for, or interest in, historical knowledge was not altogether absent, but still no other first-rate writer like Kalhana appeared in this branch of literature. This fact, to Majumdar, seems more an accident than the result of any definite causes. The absence of such a writer diminished, or led to the lack of, popular interest in history, and these two factors acted and reacted on each other. It is mentioned that Kalhana had four successors who carried the history of Kashmir from the point where he left it to some years after its annexation by the Mughal Emperor Akbar.[13]

Another scholar who discussed the nature of Buddhist Pali chronicles suggested that the main difference between the historical ideas of this time and those of our own lies not so much in content or even in historiography but in the conception of historical truth. The chroniclers had no clear notion of historical accuracy and there is no mention of historical verification, although in some parts of the chronicle they set town factual data. However, truth for them lay not so much in the correspondence between the event and the record but in the intention, which might be religious, aesthetic, or emotional. This scholar argues that the overriding motives of the literary forms adopted tended to take the writer away from the correspondence between the fact and the record.

According to him, the intention of the *kavya* veered from truth and accuracy. The motive was literary. The main interest here was aesthetic and directed to the emotions rather than intellect. If the theme was historical it was quite permissible to change, modify and even add to and reconstruct the facts for literary effect.[14] This statement indicates that the *kavya* literature, although it was a historical work, could not be depended upon, as many non-historical facts were associated with historical events.

A few historians are of the opinion that it was with the emergence of Muslim rule in India that there was the commencement of new historical tradition. For instance, Professor Dodwell mentioned that the dawn of Islam begins a great series of Indian chronicles. The Muslim chronicles are far superior to even the English medieval chronicles. They were written for the most part not by monks but by men of affairs. He further states that the Muslim period is one of vivid living men whereas the Hindu period is one of shadows.[15] It is known fact that Muslim societies have maintained historical records, but most of their records do not give information regarding the earlier period of their civilization. It is problematic to accept the supposition that a civilization which existed several centuries before the Islamic culture, imbibed the tradition of maintaining record from only the medieval period.

Pargiter made a detailed study of ancient Indian historical tradition consisting of Vedas, Purānas and other traditions. His work is noteworthy for the simple reason that he was one of the first western scholars to realise the proper worth of ancient Indian historical tradition. At the same time, he attacked the brahmanical traditions for their certain weaknesses. He says that ancient India has bequeathed to us no historical works. The total lack of the historical sense is so characteristic, that the whole course of Sanskrit literature is darkened by the shadow of this defect, suffering as it does from an entire absence of exact chronology. This is especially true of the brahmanic literature, for it has been truly said that the Vedic texts, the Samhitas and the Brahmanas, are not books of historical purpose is notorious, nor do they deal with history. Regarding the historical value of vedic literature he argues that the evidence in the Rigveda, whether contemporary notices or matter concerning the past borrowed from tradition, consists of statements more or less isolated; they are merely allusions and, make up no connected account. Even the contemporary notices, though having all the trustworthiness of first-hand evidence, yet fix little or nothing definitely of themselves, because they have no certain chronological setting with reference to other events. The same remarks hold good for the brahmanical literature later than the Rigveda.

This may be illustrated by the contemporary information about king Sudas in the Rigveda. It tells us of his battle with the ten kings, but that event can not be assigned to any definite time unless we know when he lived and there is the widest difference, whether it took place when the Aryans were in the Panjab conquering their way into India, and was a battle between them and the hostile races who opposed their eastward advance; or whether it took place long after the Aryans had established themselves in North India, and was a battle between Sudasa (Sudas) king of North Pancala, and other Aryan and non-Aryan king who opposed his westward conquests. There is nothing in the Rigveda to fix his position chronologically, but there are plain statements in the genealogies and tradition which assign him definite place in the scheme of Aryan expansion in North India. Even contemporary historical notices in the Rigveda therefore remain chronologically vague, and by themselves yield little information that can be co-ordinated for historical purposes. Statements of an historical kind in the Vedic literature become serviceable. They can be linked up with other statements from elsewhere, and that can be only from tradition. It is tradition that gives many of them a chronological position; hence the soundness and force of the counsel given in the verses prefixed to this chapter are manifest. Tradition therefore becomes all-important. It is the only resource, since historical works are wanting, and is not an untrustworthy guide. In ancient times men knew perfectly well the difference between truth and falsehood, as abundant proverbs and sayings show. It was natural therefore that they should discriminate what was true and preserve it; and historical tradition must be considered in this light[16]. Further he says that Vedic literature is not always to be trusted in matters that concerned brahmanical claims and pretensions.[17] It is suggested by him that great importance has been attached to historical statements in the Vedic literature, even when not contemporaneous and when based on tradition, and epic and puranic tradition has been discredited, however numerous and clear may be its statements about any particular matter. He says that such exaltation of Vedic literature and depreciation of epic and puranic literature has led to surprising conclusions.[18]

In certain sections thus Pargiter seems to be more critical of certain sections of ancient Indian historical tradition. He discussed the two kinds of traditions, brahmanical traditions and ksatriya traditions. According to him the difference between the two kinds of tradition is best brought out where fortunately.both the ksatriya and the brahmanic versions exist. That is found in the stories about Trisanku, Vasistha and Visvamitra. The ksatriya ballad gives a simple and natural account of Trisanku's fortunes as affected by those two rishis, while the brahmanical versions are a farrago of absurdities and impossibilities, utterly distorting all the incidents. But it is rare that the two aspects of a story are presented so characteristically, and what is found very often is a story which suggests that it was a ksatriya version which has been subsequently revised according to brahmanic ideas, that is, a story of the third or intermediate class. The legend of Sunasepa presents different stages of this process. Thus ksatriya tales sometimes exist without brahmanic counterparts, such as the above story of king Sagara, many brahmanic tales exist without ksatriya counterparts, and the intermediate class is abundant. Another marked difference appears between ksatriya tales on the one hand, and brahmanical tales and tales of an intermediate character on the other hand. In ksatriya tales there is generally some historical consistency, but the two other classes are generally deficient in the historical sense, often revealing a total lack of it. This lack of the historical sense in ancient Indian literature is a commonplace, but it does not hold entirely good as regards ksatriya tradition. Before the invention of writing, genealogies, ballads and tales are practically the only literature of an historical kind that can exist. Genealogies are essentially chronological; and the old tales, especially those narrated in the course of the best versions of the genealogies, have also an historical character. Royal genealogies certainly do not lack the historical sense, and those ksatriya tales and ballads are generally consistent in their historical conditions. Since the brahmans did treasure up and hand down the ancient hymns, there is nothing impossible in holding that the sutas also displayed similar care in preserving traditions committed to their charge, until the purana was compiled, and there were men and brahmans who made old tales and genealogies their special concern.[19]

Pargiter further suggests that the lack of the historical sense was a special characteristic of the brahmans. The Vedic texts, notoriously, are not books of historical purpose, nor do they deal with history. Before the introduction of writing the brahmans had, like everyone else, to rely on tradition when referring to preceding times, and, even after writing was introduced, they discountenanced it so far as their religious books were concerned. There is no want of references to prior events in the Rigveda as well as some to contemporaneous occurrences, and allusions to bygone men and events were necessarily drawn from tradition, such as those to Nahusa, Yayati and others, who were ancient even then. So also the mention of Yadu, Turvasa (Turvasu), Druhyu, Anu and Paru is generic, referring to the families and kings descended from them, and not to the progenitors themselves, who had passed away into tradition even then. Similarly as regards Bharata, his descendants are introduced, but he himself was a by gone figure.

The lack of the historical sense, especially among brahmans, while on the one hand it failed to compose genuine history or fabricated incorrect stories and fables, on the other hand has been of valuable service in that it often neglected to revise or harmonize historical tradition. Positively it was a defect, negatively it was often a safeguard, with the result that the Puranic brahmans preserved a large mass of ksatriya and popular tradition, which was inconsistent with brahmanic stories and tenets, and the bearing of which thereon they did not perceive. Thus not seldom they unconsciously passed on traditions which are a check on brahmanic statements and often refute much of them. When we seek for explanations of the lack, differences of opinion arise. It was not for want of history. There were plenty of historical events in the earliest times. A reason assigned for the lack is that the Brahmans, whose task it would naturally have been to record great deeds, had early embraced the doctrine that all action and existence are a positive evil, and could therefore have felt but little inclination to chronicle historical events. But, as already pointed out, that was not the task of the brahmans but of the sutas, and what they preserved was incorporated in the Purānas. When the literature of tradition passed into brahmanic custody later, the brahmans were prevented in two ways; first, since the Purānas dealt with ancient tradition, they could not incorporate into them the doings of later kings; and secondly, the above reason applied from the time when the brahmans embraced that doctrine, namely, in and after the age of the Brahmanas and Upanisads, when, according to tradition as already explained, Purānas had been compiled. Thenceforward they added no fresh historical events beyond incorporating the account of the dynasties of the Kali age. That doctrine, and its consequence that men should strive to be rid of further existence, was later than the Rigvedic age. The primitive doctrine was different. Asceticism has been practised ardently in India at all times, but its object varied. Under that doctrine it became the means of training the body and mind to a condition which ended virtually in non-existence; but in ancient times the rishis aimed at acquiring superhuman faculties and powers or the reputation of possessing them, and asceticism was the means by which that could be attained. During all that time it was the sutas who preserved tradition.[20]

Pargiter also argues that there have been, broadly speaking, three classes among brahmans throughout Indian history, namely, (1) the ascetic devotee and teacher, the rishi or muni; (2) the priest and spiritual guide of kings, nobles and people; and (3) the minister of state, royal officer, and those who followed secular employments. The first was the brahman *par excellence,* the saint; the second, the priest and preceptor; and the third, the semi-secular brahman and sometimes wholly a layman. The first class, devoting itself to an ascetic life, lived apart in secluded hermitages. The second dwelt in cities and towns, ministering to their royal and other patrons, and conversant with what went on around them; they were not ordinarily religious thinkers. The third class were busied chiefly or altogether with mundane affairs, and were practically brahmanas only by caste, they do not concern here. Kings performed sacrifices through their own priests, but invoked the aid of celebrated rishis also on special occasions as various stories show. Both the first and second classes appear to have composed the Rigvedic hymns, but the Brahmanas and Upanisads were the product of the meditations and speculations of the first class. These men lived away from the world, immersed in spiritual problems and in close relation to the influences of Nature. Their religious rites, meditations and questionings were deeply and continuously concerned with the divine; the gods were very real to them. Mythology therefore was not an abstract subject, but as real to them as Nature. On the other hand, kings and political life belonged to a sphere with which they had nothing to do and of which they knew little or nothing personally; and political vicissitudes did not affect them. All that they knew of such matters was what penetrated into their seclusion through popular report and tale, mere hearsay, often less real to them than mythology and of far less importance. There was no vivid distinction between history and mythology, and naturally there was a constant tendency to confuse the two, to mythologize history and give mythology an historical garb. We can thus see why there was a total lack of the historical sense among the brahmans who composed the brahmanical literature. It is of course authoritative on the religious matters of which it treats, but one cannot extend its authority to secular matters.[21] Pargiter makes a difference between Vedic and Puranic literature. In the preface to his book he writes: "The views about ancient India now held by scholars are based upon examination of the Veda and Vedic literature, the neglect of Puranic and epic tradition; that is, ancient Indian history has been fashioned out of compositions, which are purely religious and priestly, which notoriously do not deal with history, and which totally lack the historical sense. The extraordinary nature of such history may be perceived, if it were suggested that European history should be constructed merely out of theological literature..."[22]

Pargiter analysed certain characteristics of brahmanical traditions. He presented the following features of brahmanical traditions: [23]

1. The brahmanas confused kings, rishis and others with mythological persons of the same names.
2. They did not always distinguish different periods, and so often misplaced persons chronologically and brought together as contemporaries persons who were widely separated in time.
3. The historical sense being lacking, the difference between reality and mythology became obliterated. So history was mythologized.
4. The brahmanas freely misapplied historical or other tradition to new places and conditions to subserve religious ends.
5. They took some person or incident from historical tradition and freely fabricated edifying religious tales.

According to Pargiter there are three categories of brahmanical traditions. They are: (1) those that extol rishis and brahmanas, (2) those that advocate or describe the merits of tirthas and (3) those that commend religious rites and observances. He says that such tales too often indulge in marvels or impossibilities, and it is not always easy to divide the quasi-historical tales from fables that are mythological, for the former have a tendency to treat their subject-matter in a mythological way or to introduce mythology. For him brahmanic tales generally are untrustworthy for traditional history, because of lack of historical sense; yet sometimes they introduce allusions of an historical kind incidentally, as well as geographical particulars and notices of other matters, and these are useful and sometimes even valuable. However according to Pargiter the historical allusions cannot be trusted of themselves, and should not be relied on unless they are corroborated from elsewhere.[24] He further states that it is mainly the brahmanical mistakes and absurdities that have discredited the Purānas. However there are certain traditions preserved by brahmanas through the medium of Purānas which give valuable information regarding history of the kings and other aspects.[25]

The scholars could identify only *Rājatarangini,* written by Kashmiri scholar Kalhana as having some historical value. They deliberated that the reason for the lack of historical literature was either that the historical works, written by Indians about their kings and political developments, must have been lost us on account of the devastation of original manuscripts or that the Indians had never attempted to record their past. Since they found no reference to these historical literatures in other contemporary and later works, unlike Kautilya's *Arthashastra,* they rejected the first possibility and accepted the latter. This approval is best represented by the European scholar Macdonell who said, "History is one weak spot in Indian literature. It is in fact non existent".[26]

However, before reaching the above conclusion, these scholars did not consider the likelihood of differences between the Indian sense of the past and the sense of the past in western society. The sources for the reconstruction of the history of western society and the history of Indian society are different from each other. The scholars did not, for instance, consider the fact that each society or the same society in different periods may look at its own past in a different way and that the form which the expression of the past takes in the one may be so indistinguishably different from the other that it may be totally missed in looking for a record of the past. The divergence of cultures in different societies makes it impossible for the historian to look for similar kind of attitude towards the past in different societies. Thus, the expressions of history in Indian and western societies would naturally vary.

The predicament with the earlier scholars, who wrote on ancient Indian history, was that they tried to evaluate the Indian and western societies on the basis of the models which were borrowed from the west. But they were trying to compare the historical senses of two societies on the basis of faulty logic that both societies should have the same kind of historical consciousness; they overlooked this point and the result was their argument that Indians lacked a sense of history.

This kind of outlook towards Indian history is because of the appearance of British colonialism. To begin with, the British colonial masters tried to comprehend the institutions of the conquered country. Within colonial framework there was the emergence of different schools of thought, some of which were very critical of everything Indian. There were some schools of thought within British colonialism which showed certain contempt towards the Indian culture and heritage. We find the writings of British administrator historians like James Mill, Elphinstone, V.A. Smith and others. The main attempt of the historians was the defend the British empire and the various institutions of British empire. There was a general criticism of the Hindu institutions. The Indians were looked upon as backward when compared to the progressive Europeans. The greatest representative of this kind of historians was James Mill.

James Mill was one European who was certainly critical of everything Indian and obviously he did not exclude history of ancient India in this black list. In his study of history of India he begins by saying "Rude nations seem to derive a peculiar gratification from pretensions to a remote antiquity".[27] A archetypal colonial administrator historian that he was, Mill did not suppose that India had either sense of history or any history at all. Regarding the value of Hindu traditions, he says that they are the products of wild and ungoverned imagination. They mark the state of a rude and credulous people, who cannot estimate the use of a record of past events. To the monstrous period of years which the legends of the Hindus involve, they ascribe events the most extravagant and unnatural: events not even connected in chronological series; a number of independent and incredible fictions. According to him Hindus did not possess historical records. Their ancient literature affords not a single production to which historical character belongs. In all, actions of men and those of deities are mixed together; in a set of legends, more absurd and extravagant, more transcending the bounds of nature and of reason. He states that the brahmanas are the most audacious, and perhaps the most skilful fabricators, with whom the annals of fable have yet made us acquainted.[28] He further quotes from the work of Rennel that 'There is no known history of Hindoostan (that rests on the foundation of Hindu materials or record) extant, before the period of Mohemadan conquests'. He adds that the Hindus have no ancient civil history. He also quoted from the work of Wilford who stated that 'the Hindu system of geography, chronology, and history, are all equally monstrous and absurd'[29] James Mill further avers that no historical composition existed in the literature of the Hindus; they had not reached that point of intellectual maturity, at which the value of a record of the past for the guidance of the future begins to be understood.[30] Thus James Mill did not believe that Indians had any history or that their ancient literature deserved any respect. These ideas of James Mill impressed the British scholars like David Ricardo who praised it. The East India Company's directors appointed Mill to a senior post on their London staff. Macaulay referred to this work in the House of Commons as the greatest historical work to appear since that of Gibbon. Professor of Sanskrit at Oxford Hayman Wilson, though critical of Mill, said that it is still the most valuable work upon the subject which has yet been published.[31] Obviously, the British government was happy with the history constructed by Mill which justified the British administration in India since it was superior to the previous administrative structure that existed prior to the arrival of the British in India. However, it is pointed out that sources of Mill were flawed. He relied on the evidence of Buchanan and others who were prejudiced against Indians. He was committed to view that Indian society was barbarous. Mill was highly selective in his use of evidence. The testimony of Dubois, Tytler and others is cited when hostile to the Hindus, ignored when it is favourable. The massive evidence on the character of Indians, collected in the Parliamentary investigation of 1813, on the whole favourable to them, went unnoticed.[32] Based on these defective sources Mill attempted deliberate and conscious interpretation of Indian history. During this period other evidences studied by other European scholars, like for example by William Jones, the great Orientalist, were available. Nevertheless, deliberately their writings were either ignored or refuted.

These notions and theories found in the writings of colonial historians regarding history of India has been analysed by Romila Thapar. According to her, in these writings, Indian civilization was said to lack the qualities that Europe admired. For instance, the perceived emphasis on the values of rational thought and individualism was said to be absent, and India's culture was seen as stagnant. This attitude was perhaps best typified in Macaulay's contempt for things Indian, especially traditional Indian education and learning. The political institutions of India, visualized largely as the rule of Maharajas and Sultans, were dismissed as despotic and totally unrepresentative of public opinion. And this, in an age of democratic revolutions, was about the worst sin. Mill's *History of British India,* in which he argued these propositions, became a hegemonic text in the nineteenth century which influenced many commentators and administrators associated with India. Mill's views were echoed in aspects of colonial policy, increasingly concerned with the conquest of the subcontinent and the restructuring of its economy to suit colonial requirements. The Utilitarian critique of India argued that backwardness can be remedied through appropriate legislation, which could be used by the British to change the stagnant nature of Indian society that had prevented its progress.[33] Romila Thapar says that Mill's assertion that the Indian past had been unchanging, static society dominated by despotic rulers was reflected in various philosophies of history current in the nineteenth century.

A.B. Keith was a scholar who studied different aspects of Sanskrit literature. He pointed out that in spite of suggestion that Indians lacked a sense of history, there is a certain amount of writing and a number of facts attesting a degree of sense for history. However, he says that despite the abundance of its literature, history is so miserably represented that in the whole of the great period of Sanskrit literature there is not one writer who can be seriously regarded as a critical historian. The most ardent admirer of Kalhana would not for a moment claim for him that he could be matched even with Herodotus, and it must be remembered that no other writer approaches even remotely the achievement of Kalhana. Keith suggests that the causes of this phenomenon are found in peculiarities of Indian psychology aided by environment and the course of events. It may be that India failed to produce historians because the great political events which affected her during the period up to A.D. 1200 did not call forth popular action in the sense in which the repulse of the Persian attacks on Greece evoked the history of Herodotus. Keith suggests that the national feeling, which is at least a powerful aid to the writing of history, was not evoked in India. He says that foreign attacks on India in the period of the first four centuries B.C. were probably not such as to excite deep national feeling.[34]

Keith also suggests that from the standpoint of psychology it is not difficult to understand the view that history had any meaning or value was one unlikely to receive acceptance in India. The existing doctrines told distinctly against any such estimate of events. According to doctrine of karman all men's action were the outcome of actions done in previous births; they were therefore wholly uncalculable, for no one could tell what deed in the remotest past might not spring up to work out its inevitable end. Added to this was the view that all things were brought about by fate, working in a manner wholly unintelligible and beyond all foresight. In addition, the Indian mind had accepted the miraculous in the shape of divine intervention, magic and witchcraft. According to Keith, the scientific attitude of mind which seeks to find natural causes for events of nature is not normal in India. Buddhists and Jains were as little inclined to abandon popular superstitions as were brahmanas. The philosophies of every kind taught there was no progress in our sense in the world.[35]

Another reason for this lack of historical sense, according to Keith, was that Indians had a tendency to prefer the general to the particular, which is shown in widely different spheres of knowledge. He says that throughout the history of Indian philosophy the same thing is seen; no one seems to be in the least interested in the history of doctrines, no one writes a history of philosophy as contrasted with summaries of opposing doctrines; no one even attempts a real history of politics or medicine. Keith argues that the indifference to chronology is seen everywhere in India, and must be connected with the quite secondary character ascribed to time by the philosophies.[36] He states that the Purānas contain vast masses of details, but their value is of the most limited description. According to him, the Buddhists made some more serious approach to history in their legends of Buddha. But during the passage of the centuries the monks had not acquired any real historical sense. For example, no attempt is made to treat life and efforts of Asoka in an historical spirit. He states that eulogies of saints are common to the sects, but serious historical work is quite unknown.[37] Keith thus tries to give certain explanations for the lack of pure historical works in India. However, we may not accept all the judgments made by this scholar. For instance, even though in Indian philosophy we find reference to doctrine of karma and other principles, that does not mean that they did not take interest in materialistic pursuits.

Another aspect discussed by the European scholars related to the nature of Indian institutions. This analysis was connected with the critique of Indian sense of history and culture of India. They put forward the theory of oriental despotism and the Asiatic Mode of Production. The latter theory suggests that while for other regions of the world there existed different modes of production, in the case of orient or Asia, there existed a mode of production which was different from that mode of production found in other regions of the world. As Romila Thapar says this visualized a system of government consisting of a despotic ruler with absolute power, said to be characteristic of Asian societies. Such societies featured the existence of isolated, self sufficient village communities, whose surplus produce was creamed off by the despotic ruler and his court, governing through an autocratic bureaucracy. The latter controlled irrigation, which was a prerequisite for agriculture dependent on water management, and also organized the collection of surplus produce. Much of Asia was thought to be arid and dry, irrigation being provided by the state and controlled by the bureaucracy to ensure a surplus agricultural income providing revenue for the despot. The peasant was kept subjugated and had little freedom; cities were largely administrative centres and there was hardly any commercial exchange; the association of divinity with kingship strengthened the status of the king. According to this theory, Oriental Despotism encapsulated the political economy of Asian empires. Thapar further argues that this view can be traced to early Greek sources perceiving the Persian Achaemenid Empire of the mid-first millennium BC as despotic. The Greeks themselves were not averse on occasion to despotic behaviour, but their view of Asian societies as culturally alien led to exaggerated accounts. To this was added the vision of luxurious Oriental courts, a vision deriving in part from the luxury trade with the east since early times, and partly on the fantasy world of the east as described by Greek visitors. The Greek physician Ktesias at the Persian court, for instance, let his imagination run riot in describing the marvels, mysteries and wealth of the eastern lands. The Crusades and the ensuing literature on the Turks would have strengthened these notions, many of which were exaggerated to impress European audiences. Given the concerns of eighteenth-century France and England, the central question was seen as private ownership of land. The theory of Oriental Despotism, according to Thapar, assumed that there was no private ownership land in Asia and that the king owned all the land. "There had been a controversy between Voltaire, supported by the Physiocrats, arguing against the state ownership of land in Asia and Montesquieu, who held the contrary opinion. The standard text on the traditional economy of India used in Haileybury College, where administrators were trained before going to India, was that of Richard Jones who endorsed the theory. The standard history was that of James Mill who also did not question this idea. Those who came to administer India assumed the essential viability of the theory, and some among them were also the pre-eminent historians of the period writing on India. The theory became axiomatic to the interpretation of the Indian past in the nineteenth century, particularly that aspect which concerned land relations and the rights of the state over the cultivator. The nature of ownership of land was debated, as was the question of who was the owner - the king/ state, the individual cultivator or the village community. The village community was sometimes projected as an autonomous republic or as a collective for gathering and paying taxes. These debates were reflected in the writings of administrators and historians, such as, Henry Maine, Baden-Powell, Munroe and Montstuart Elphinstone".[38] This analysis indicates the Europeans, being alien to basic principles of Indian culture, could not understand the real nature of Indian civilization. Instead, they presented the theory that Indians did not have history and that history of Indians was static and not dynamic. Montesquieu first stated the concept that despots always administered people in the orient. This suggestion that oriental people were ruled by despotic rulers justified the rule of the British which was assumed to be superior to the earlier rule of Indian kings. Karl Marx evolved the idea of Asiatic Mode of Production. The analysis made by Ronald Inden shows that these scholars represented the peoples of Asia as irrational and defective versions of their western equivalents. They argue that Asiatic institutions are the outcome of racial conquests and original adaptations to the environment peculiar to Asia. The outcome of this argument is the suggestion that despotism, the arbitrary rule by fear of an all-powerful autocrat over a docile and servile populace, is the normal and distinctive political institution of the East. It is argued that Europe continued to develop and change while Asia remained more or less static. Changes in Asia were repetitive and not as in the west cumulative or directional. Ronald Inden further states that although most of the earlier orientalists believed that Chinese and Indian civilizations had arisen at about the same time as the Near Eastern, they also held that only the civilizations of the Near East had a major contributions to make to world, that is Western civilization.[39] These details clearly show us the kind of the assumptions the western historians imbibed regarding history and culture of the orient. Ronald Inden made a significant statement that, "...what Marx and Engels had to say about Asian villages was supposedly based on evidence provided by British administrators of India..."[40] Since Marx used sources supplied by British administrators it is very natural that he endorsed their views regarding various institutions of India. The above discussion has indicated, to us, the attitude of pro-imperialist historians towards Indian history and its culture.

It is suggested that the idea that the British administration brought to an end the tradition of oppressive despots, is a belief, which is found in the writings of the administrator historian V.A. Smith. His pro-Greek bias is shown in attempts to suggest the great qualities of Indian civilization were derived from Greece.[41]

It is pointed out that in the late eighteenth century the belief in progress through the use of common reason put India in a new category of static cultures, doomed to fall further and further behind the ever-advancing west. Thus, India was thought to belong to the category of semi barbarism. The conclusions of the eighteenth-century conquistador were that Indian society was corrupt and rotten. There emerged various views of India among the colonial authors. Thus, we have the view of Clive and his school, that India exists mainly to produce pagoda trees for shaking.[42]

Ballhatchet argues that the main theme in the historical writing of Christian missionaries was a bitter criticism of all things Indian. Their views are best represented by Charles Grant. His criticisms of Hinduism are typical of the period of hostility. He says that the people of India are in a degenerate condition and the Hinduism is the chief cause of this.[43] Romila Thapar states that the emphasis on village communities and despotic rulers was found in many works related ancient Indian history. Many of the historians of this period were administrators who were convinced that the pattern of British administration was acting as a catalyst in changing Indian society. Source material pertaining to the ancient period of Indian history was now interpreted to fit these preconceptions.[44]

Regarding the German medieval chronicles it was suggested by Herbert Grundmann that 'For the historian these rhymed chronicles have too little 'source value', for the literary historian too little literary value, but contemporaries appreciated them and drew from them their idea of history'.[45] It is maintained by Hermann Kulke that this statement applies to most works of early Indian historiography. He says that among the great civilizations of Asia and Europe, India seems to be the only culture without a tradition of indigenous historiography which took the decisive step beyond a mythological and legendary idea of history. This situation is particularly perplexing for Kulke because India was surrounded by regions like Arab-Persian world and China which possessed well developed historiography. However, Kulke was able to find certain evidences to say that Indians did not lack the sense of history.[46] Herman Goetz challenged this almost dogmatic view of his time about India's alleged lack of historican writing. Goetz states that: 'In science there exist sometimes certain theories which arose from insufficient knowledge of the subject at the beginning of research and which remain ineradicable in spite of contradictory evidence gathered subsequently. One of the misunderstandings is the view that Indians possessed no real historiography and also no interest in history.'[47] Goetz made a study of large list of early medieval chronicles. On the basis of this study he came to the conclusion that there was no lack of historical sense and writing but that instead one has to assume an almost total destruction of old chronicles.[48] These statements made by German historians indicate that they were more sympathetic towards the problem of Indian sense of history when compared with the British colonial historians. Obviously, the German historians did not have any political or any other agenda when they evinced keen interest in indological research.

This kind of criticism of Indian history and culture did not go unchallenged by the Indian historians and the western historians sympathetic towards Indian culture. Not that all the Europeans criticized the Indian sense of history. There were many who appreciated, like A.L. Basham, the contribution of Indians to world civilization.[49] Thus, evidence to prove that there existed sense of history among Indians is not lacking. In the colonial context, the school of nationalist historians took the lead to challenge the rigid imperialist notions regarding Indian culture and history. Among these nationalist historians we may mention the names of H.C. Rayachaudhury, K.P. Jayaswal, R.C. Majumdar, R.K. Mookerjee, etc. R.C. Majumdar was one Indian historian who did not take lightly the criticism heaped on history of ancient Indians. Majumdar stated that the

Hindus gained their first knowledge of the history of their own country from treatises which gave evidence of prejudice against the Hindu culture and civilization. Now they began to study their culture and history to cull evidence to challenge those preconceived notions. According to him the nationalist history of India was a reaction against British histories of India. Mill's view, as stated by Majumdar, was primarily due to ignorance. However, it is impossible to absolve James Mill altogether of a deep-rooted prejudice against the Hindus. Speaking from the historical point of view, he committed the great blunder of reading the present into the past. This sort of prejudice or blunder marked the average Englishman in India and clouded the visions of subsequent English historians of India. Majumdar further says that conscious and deliberate effort was made to minimize the importance of Hindu culture. Indian culture was belittled by suggesting that Indians borrowed most of their culture from the Greeks. Another method was to belittle the value of Indian culture by selecting or stressing only its weak points and ignoring its better aspects. As result of these prejudices, the Indians decided to accept the challenge and give a fitting reply. They studied the ancient Indian history with help of literary and archaeological evidences and proved the real worth of their history and culture.[50] The nationalist historians tried to glorify the Indian past. This was, as Romila Thapar says, 'in part a reaction to the criticism of Mill and other writers and in part a necessary step in the building of national self-respect.'[51] To authenticate their arguments the nationalist historians took quotations from the German scholar Max Mueller and other orientalists.

It is a fact accepted by scholars like Veena Das that it is possible to study myths, traditions with a different perspective which would allow the scholars to analyse and interpret them. Veena Das argues that there were different kinds of motives that lay behind the tradition of having the history of castes recorded in the form of Purana. Analyzing the caste Purānas of Gujarat, it is suggested that in the period of rising Muslim power, the brahmana and bania groups felt it necessary to have such texts which should affirm their separate identity.[52] According to Veena Das Purānas were group documents which expressed the caste group's perception of itself. The Purānas of sects and localities expressed the identity of sectarian and local groups.[53]

The argument of the Colonial writers failed to take into consideration the basic nature of historical consciousness of the Indians which was different from the historical attitude expressed by the western societies. The Indian historical tradition was different from that of the west because people living in each of these societies chose to record only such events as were regarded by them as relevant. In so recording the events, the people may have had certain purposes. The historiographical tradition in pre-colonial India was not influenced by that of the west – the concerns of Indian tradition and those of the west were different from one another. The Indian historical tradition maintained its own method of expressing its attitude towards the past events. This aspect has been studied in detail by Romila Thapar.[54]

In discussing the tradition of historical writing in pre-modern India, Romila Thapar makes a distinction between what she calls "embedded history" and "externalized history".[55] "Embedded history" refers to forms of expression the central purpose of which is not the recording of the past but a consciousness of the past can be still prised out of them. Analyzing the different situations described, the historians can still reflect on the past. The best example of embedded history is origin myths which have the significant function of justifying a particular section in the society.[56] At the same time they are the carriers of information about happenings in the society. A critical analysis of such myths reveal their purpose and significance of their propagation.

In "externalized history", on the other hand, one can notice rather explicit narration of events. The puranic genealogies represent such types of history. But even these historical narratives are not devoid of the function of legitimizing a particular group or groups in the society. The distinction between "embedded history" and "externalized history" indicates the changes that take place not only in different societies but also in the same society over a period of time.

As a proof of the changes taking place in the society, we find variations in the expression of historical consciousness in the form of oral and literate means. We find the representation of oral tradition in the Vedic and epic literature. The oral means of expression of historical consciousness is an important characteristic in all pre-modern societies.

The oral tradition is used in societies which found no use for writing their lore down. When the art of writing was introduced in the society which gradually started having the need for it, the historical consciousness also started getting reduced in writing. This transformation is represented by what is termed as itihāsa-purana tradition by Romila Thapar.[57]

The itihāsa-purana tradition represents the transition from oral tradition to literate tradition. Its starting point can be found in the Vedic literature which is oral in nature and its culmination we find in the puranic literature which was also oral to start with but was later put into writing. This transition of methods of expressing their attitudes toward the events exhibit the changes that were taking place in the society.

The earliest form of oral tradition we find during the period of Vedic literature is in *gāthas*, *narasasmsis, akhayana* and *purānas*. These were composed by the priest-poets who recited them during sacrificial gatherings. This function of the priest-poet fetched him rewards from chief of the tribe. The praising of the chief or the king in the later period took the form of kathas which developed into the epic literature like *Mahābhārata* and *Rāmāyana*. To start with both of them had oral origin and it was sung by the priests. In the later times they got converted to kavya tradition sung by the poets in their king's court.[58]

The next important stage of expressing historical consciousness in early India is found in the *Purānas*. For several years it remained in its oral form and was reduced into writing in the mid-first millennium A.D.[59] Pargiter has demonstrated how some of the *Purānas* were translated from oral Prakrit to literate Sanskrit.[60] This shows that they represent transition from the oral tradition to the literate tradition. The firm establishment of literate form of expressing the historical consciousness could be found in the *Purānas*.

These Purānas recorded not only the events but also dynastic lists. This list was not contemporary to the gāthas, ākhyānas and nārasamsis. The genealogical details of different dynasties were composed in the later period. The Purānas preserved the names of those who were supposed to have ruled in the past and they reflected not only a transition of historical consciousness but also the changing nature of the administrative organ in the form of the emergence of the state with its territory being defined. Thus the puranic literature, its literary form, the genealogical section represent the changes that took place in the historical tradition due to alterations in the socio-political conditions of the time.

In the post-Gupta period we find further changes in the historical tradition. There emerged smaller states in the different regions of the subcontinent like Central India and South India. Added to this, there was a social movement stressing on bhakti ideology. The consequence of this change is reflected in and charitas of the post-Gupta period. While the vamsāvalis were the chronicles of the families, charitas were the biographies of individual rulers. In these works the earlier connections with itihāsa-purana tradition were maintained and the king was connected with the genealogical lists mentioned in the purānas. The vamsāvalis, which were the chronicles of the king and the territory looked after by him, utilised the sthala-purānas, upa-purānas, tirtha-purānas, caste-purānas and māhātmyas. These sources, as Romila Thapar puts it, were the texts, "recording the past and evolution of places, sects and deities, locations of pilgrimage, dominant castes and local history".[61]

Even though the vamsāvalis were a part of the larger puranic text the details of local purānas were also included. Thus, these vamsāvalis give less importance to the earlier purānas and more importance to the local Purānas which maintained connections with the events recorded in the greater Purānas. These events referred to the local rulers as well as caste groups. Thus with the vamsāvalis we find the crystallization of itihāsa-purana tradition. It was a transition from the "embedded" form of history to the "externalized" form of history.

This itihāsa-purāna tradition was the creation of particular social groups in the society which wished to establish their authority over the society in the earlier times and to maintain this authority in the later times. The earlier oral traditions during the Vedic period represented the relations between the priest-poet and the chief of the tribe. The priests sung gāthas regarding the previous exploits of the chiefs and these gāthas were intended to make the chief to bestow generous grants to the priestly class. In ākhyānas we find the first elements of genealogy, the purpose of which was to legitimize the king. These "embedded" forms of historical tradition are usually associated with the ritual sacrifices, the *yajna*. In the yajna, there will be redistribution of wealth accumulated during cattle raids. Whatever remains after redistribution is given to the brahmans who praised the king for this *dana* or gift.

During the later period we find the emergence of state which consisted of the king, Rsis, and Brahmanas at its central organisation. Legitimacy and validation were the primary objective of epic literature. The ksatriya dynasties sought legitimacy which was provided by the brahmanas by connecting these ksatriya families with genealogies of earlier texts. In return the brahmanas are rewarded with wealth and social recognition.

During the next stage of historical tradition, i.e., the stage of the composition of the purānas, we find that the oral tradition of the earlier poets called suta and magadha were appropriated by the brahmanas and that they realized the value of the literary adaptation of this oral literature and by using it they intended to enhance their position in the society. In these purānas, a systematic list of dynasties is given so that their lineages could be connected with the historic lineages. But the emergence of non-ksatriya dynasties reduced the importance of such writings and now history came to be written in a more externalized form. The ruling families now tried to achieve legitimacy to control unoccupied areas or newly occupied areas by making land grants to the brahmanas who influenced other sections in society.[62]

Instead of the use of force, the influence of brahmanas was relied more in order to gain legitimacy. The genealogical constructions of the brahmanas facilitated the ruling class with the title of ksatriyas which was very essential for the rulers in order to maintain supremacy over other sections in the society. During this period still greater importance was given to genealogy because of the emergence of new groups of rulers who wanted legitimacy. However, they could attain legitimacy only after obtaining ksatriya status for which they had to perform brahmanical sacrificial rituals by paying sacrificial fee, dakshina, to the brahmanas.

The transition from oral tradition to literate tradition of historical writing represented the transfer of ownership of knowledge from the earlier professional groups of memorizers to those who appropriated the facility for formal education, the brahmanas. These brahmanas realized the importance of the historical knowledge and began to record the events. These brahmanas were the social base of the purānas and it was they who altered the purānas, added and deducted the things from the puranas as the situation demanded. The brahmanas through these writings desired to establish their identity in the society. And with the expansion of agriculture we find the desire to hold large tracts of land, and with their help the kings also wanted to extend their territories and influence those people in newly occupied areas who respected the brahmanas for their knowledge. Thus during the post-Gupta period, we notice the brahmanas appropriating both social and economic prerogatives.

It was during this period that there occurred a change in the historical traditions in the form of charitas and vamsāvalis. Such forms of historical writing were necessitated by the emergence of the local ruling families and the decentralization of power. Instead of earlier Mauryan or Gupta empire, now there were smaller local kingdoms in Rajasthan and South India. The smaller states emerged in Rajasthan during the seventh century A.D. As Brajadulal Chattopadhyaya says, "All ruling dynasties became regional..."[63] and during this time there was a necessity for inclusion of all these extra lineages into the mainstream. Some of the Rajasthani tribes became 'Rajputs' after they were regarded by the brahmanas in the charitas and vamsāvalis as belonging to Agnikula race. The tribes of Bhils and Gond ruling families claimed as belonging to Chandravamsa and Suryavamsa.[64] In South India the Cholas claimed to be Suryavamsi and the Pandyas claimed to be Chandravamsi. Still interesting is the case of the Pallavas who claimed to be Brahma Kśātra for their vamsāvalis averred that they were originally brahmanas prior to the assumption of powers. All these claims were made with the help of local purānas which maintained its links with the earlier purāna references and genealogies.

These local purānas, sthala māhātmyas and caste purānas were linked with each other by the use of common myths and symbols. This technique is used in the case of western India. We find the reference to Paraśurāma in Skanda Purāna and this motif of Paraśurāma is used by all the local puranas in the west coast. They use the common tradition of Paraśurāma creating land in the west coast by pushing the sea backwards. Sahyādri Khanda, which claims to be a part of Skānda Purāna, mentions the story of Paraśurāma creating the land in Konkan, Karnataka and Kerala coasts. It also narrates the story of Paraśurāma donating the newly created land to brahmanas thereby justifying ownership claims of brahmanas over Paraśurāma ksetra. It also mentions the story of Kadamba king Maūra Varma bringing the brahmanas afresh from Ahicchatra and making them settle in different parts of the western coast, as the old brahmanas to whom Paraśurāma had gifted the land had lost their caste and the land. We find such stories with variations being included in the local purānas of western India.

The local purānas and sthala māhātmyas like Sahyādri Khanda (Sanskrit), Grāmapaddhati, Gokarna Mahātme, Velapura Mahātme, Visvadarshana, Kūralotpatti and Kannada Sahyādri Khanda use the common motifs of Paraśurāma, Maūra Varma and Ahicchatra. They relate the donation of land by Paraśurāma and Maūra Varma to the brahmanas and also the brahmanas praising Maūra Varma. The authorship of these local purānas is ascribed to Rsis who are supposed to be the authors of greater purānas like Skanda purāna. Thus the literary traditions of the earlier purānas was maintained and continued even in the regional purānas. The main intention of this continuity of the puranic tradition is legitimacy and validation of both brahmanas and the local ruling families. This intention is clearer in the accounts of brahmanas of south western India, Grāmapaddhati, which is supposed to narrate the story of brahmanas of south western India who claim descent from Ahicchatra. Grāmapaddhati makes a claim to give the vamsavali of Maūra Varma, although in reality no such vamsavali is given. Thus these regional histories constitute another part of Indian historical tradition and they maintain links with the earlier puranic genealogies.

The linking of these regional histories with the larger puranas exhibits the purpose of the brahmana community to claim ownership rights of the agricultural tracts on the west coast. The land hungry brahmanas received patronage during Gupta and post-Gupta period through the land grants, brahmadeyas and devadānas[65] and these land grants began to be issued not only in North India but also in South India by the dynasties like the Kadambas, the Pallavas, the Rashtrakutas, the Cholas and other major and minor dynasties. For one thing, land grants and creation of agrahāras and brahmapuris[66] went a long way in legitimizing the regional dynasties that had emerged during the post-Gupta period. Secondly, the land grants satisfied the land hungry brahmanas who respected the temporal authority by including the genealogies of these local rulers in the larger puranas. We find the details of Rajput rulers being included in Skanda Purāna[67]; the same practice we can observe in South India. The Kadambas of Banavasi had established agrahāras in Talagunda and Kuppatturu[68] and Talagunda inscription states that Mukkanna Kadamba established thirty-two brahmana families in the agrahara of Sthānagunda.[69] There are evidences to prove that a branch of Kadambas had established their power in other regions of west coast like Goa and North Kanara.[70]

Thus, the practice of creation of agrahāras was carried on effectively by the dynasties like Alupās and Kadambas. In South Western India starting from 7th – 8th century A.D., we find the grant of land to brahmanas as well as temples[71], the property of which was ultimately appropriated by the brahmanas. These inscriptions suggest that there occurred the expansion of brahmana control of land in South Western India. During the period of Alupās, Shivalli was an important brahmanical centre[72] and during the later period, i.e., by 12th century A.D. the neighbouring villages like Brahmavara and Nilavara also acquired importance.

Thus the above details go to prove that there was ownership of large tracts of land by the brahmanas in South Western India. In order to justify this claim it was felt necessary to include this aspect of land being given to the brahmanas from an authority which is unquestionable and unchallengeable. This is one purpose we can notice in the traditional chronicles like Grāmapaddhati and Sahyādri Khanda.

The above two works mention that land, after created by Paraśurāma, was given to the brahmanas of this region and even in the years to come we find the brahmanas claiming that they are the real owners of this land since it was given to them by Sage Paraśurāma himself. This sacred authority was supported by the land grants by the temporal authority, Maūra Varma. Francis Buchanan who came to India during the initial years of 19th century says that the Tuluva brahmanas consider themselves as the "Proper lords of the country".[73] He also says that the brahmanas "pretend that the country was created expressly for their use by

Paraśurāma...".[74] In another context Buchanan says that the brahmanas of South Kanara like the Namburis pretend that the region was created for their use by Paraśurāma, and that they are the only persons entitled to be called proprietors of the soil. Buchanan says however, that it would not appear that this story was ever so successful as it has been in Kerala. The brahmanas indeed say that they did not like the country, and were always running away to a city named Ahicchatra, which seems to be in Telangana. Further it is stated by Buchanan that brahmanas say that Mayura Varma reinstated them again in the whole property of Tuluva.[75] Thus, these traditions, apart from being the pieces of imaginary talents of the brahmanas, serve the purpose of justifying the land ownership rights.

References

1. Ahmad, Qeyamuddin (ed.), *India by Al-Biruni*, 1992.
2. *Ibid.*, pp. 10-11.
3. *Ibid.*, p. 8.
4. *Ibid.*, p. 193.
5. *Ibid.*, p. 190.
6. *Ibid.*, p. 192.
7. *Ibid.*, pp. 11-12.
8. C. H. Philips, *Historians of India, Pakistan and Ceylon*, 1961, p. 4.
9. *Ibid.*, p. 5.
10. *Ibid.*, p. 14.
11. *Ibid.*
12. *Ibid.*, p. 25.
13. *Ibid.*, pp. 27-28.
14. L.S. Perera, 'The Pali Chronicle of Ceylon', C.H. Philips, *Historians*, pp. 37-38.
15. Dodwell, *India*, Vol. 1, 1936, pp. 22-23.
16. F.E. Pargiter, *Ancient Indian Historical Tradition*, Delhi, Reprint, 1997, pp. 2-3.
17. *Ibid.*, p. 9.
18. *Ibid.*, p. 11.
19. *Ibid.*, p. 61.
20. *Ibid.*, pp. 61-62.
21. *Ibid.*, pp. 62-63.
22. *Ibid.*, p. v.

23. *Ibid.*, pp. 66-71.
24. *Ibid.*, pp. 73-74.
25. *Ibid.*, p. 75.
26. Macdonnell, *History of Sanskrit Literature,* 1900, p. 10.
27. James Mill, *The History of British India,* Vol. I, New Delhi, 1972, p. 24. The objectionable use of the word 'rude nations' indicate the contempt he had for ancient history of India. When compared to other European scholars his criticism has been most direct and precise. This same contemptuous attitude he exhibited towards other Asian civilization like the Persians, whom he thought did not possess any history or historical records.
28. *Ibid.*, p. 28.
29. *Ibid.*, p. 40.
30. *Ibid.*, p. 373.
31. C. H. Philips, 'James Mill, Mountstuart Elphinstone and the History of India', idem, *Historians,* p. 219.
32. *Ibid.*, p. 221.
33. Romila Thapar, *Early India From the Origins to A.D. 1300,* California, 2002, pp. 5-6.
34. A.B. Keith, *A History of Sanskrit Literature,* Delhi, 1993, pp. 144-145.
35. *Ibid.*, p. 146.
36. *Ibid.*, p. 147.
37. *Ibid.*, pp. 147-148.
38. Romila Thapar, *Early India,* pp. 6-7.
39. Ronald Inden, *Imagining India,* Massachusetts, 1990, pp. 52-53.
40. *Ibid.*, p. 135. In fact, many Marxist historians, like for example D.D. Kosambi, do not agree with the views of Marx on India, in spite of the fact that they accept the Marxist tool of analysis for the study of Indian history.
41. Romila Thapar, *Ancient Indian Social History Some Interpretations*, p. 8.
42. T.G.P. Spear, 'British Historical Writing in the Era of the Nationalist Movements', C.H. Philips, *Historians,* p. 405.
43. Ballhatchet, 'Some Aspects of Historical Writing on India by Protestant Christian Missionaries during the Nineteenth and Twentieth Centuries', in C.H. Philips, *Historians,* p. 344.
44. Romila Thapar, *Ancient Indian Social History Some Interpretations*, p. 9.
45. H. Grundmann's statement quoted in Hermann Kulke, 'Historiography in Early Medieval India', Georg Berkemer, Tilman Frasch, Hermann Kulke and Jurgen Lutt (eds.), *Exploratıons in the History of South Asia Essays in Honour of Dietmar Rothermund,* New Delhi, 2001, p. 71.

46. *Ibid.*, pp. 71-72.
47. Quoted in *Ibid.*, p. 72.
48. *Ibid.*, pp. 72-73.
49. In fact, many present day historians of India like Romila Thapar and S.K. Maity were trained and guided by A.L. Basham.
50. R.C. Majumdar, 'Nationalist Historians', C.H. Philips, *Historians*, pp. 416-421.
51. Romila Thapar, *Ancient Indian Social History*, p. 10.
52. Veena Das, *Structure and Cognition Aspects of Hindu Caste and Ritual*, Delhi, 1997, p. 14.
53. *Ibid.*, p. 15.
54. Romila Thapar, *Ancient Indian Social History Some Interpretations*, 1978, pp. 268-293.
55. Romila Thapar, *Interpreting Early India*, 1994, p. 137.
56. *Ibid.*, p. 142.
57. Romila Thapar, *Ancient Indian Social History Some Interpretations*, 1978, p. 297.
58. Sabyasachi Bhattacharya and Romila Thapar (eds.), *Situating Indian History for Sarvepalli Gopal*, 1986, p. 361.
59. *Ibid.*, p. 365.
60. Pargiter, *Ancient Indian Historical Tradition*, 1972, p. 77.
61. Sabyasachi Bhattacharya and Romila Thapar (eds.), *Situating Indian History for Sarvepalli Gopal*, 1986, p. 380.
62. Romila Thapar, *The Past and Prejudice*, 1993, p. 29.
63. Brajadulal Chattopadhyaya, *The Making of Early Medieval India*, 1994, p. 9.
64. Romila Thapar, *The Past and Prejudice*, p. 31.
65. Brahmadeyas and devadānas were the land and monetary grants given to brahmanas and temples by elite sections in the society.
66. Agrahāras and Brahmapuris were the brahmana settlements.
67. Brajadulal Chattopadhyaya, *The Making of Early Medieval India*, p. 61.
68. P. Gururaja Bhat, *Studies in Tuluva History and Culture*, 1975, p. 238.
69. *Epigraphia Carnatica*, Vol. 7, p. 186.
70. B.R. Gopal, *Minor Dynasties of South India, Karnataka Vol. I*, 1982, pp. 74-75.
71. K.V. Ramesh, *A History of South Kanara*, 1970, p. 274.
72. *Ibid.*, p. 292.

73. Francis Buchanan, *Journey from Madras through the Countries of Mysore, Canara and Malabar*, Madras, 1870, p. 213.
74. *Ibid.*, p. 224.
75. Francis Buchanan, *A Journey From Madras Through the Countries of Mysore, Canara and Malabar,* Vol. III, New Delhi, 1988, p. 31.

3

A Study of Grāmapaddhati

The *Grāmapaddhati* is a traditional chronicle, containing the history of the brahmana settlements in the Tuḷu Country. There are different versions of this work. It is a text in Kannada, but there are a few Sanskrit versions also.[1] The script used in the manuscripts is generally Kannada although the Tulu-Malayalam script is also used in certain cases.[2] The present study is based on three versions which the author has been able to consult. One of them is a printed version, the source of the original manuscript of which is not acknowledged by the editor[3], and this version we label as GP1. A second version, which we label as GP2, is preserved in the University of Tubingen, found among the papers of the Basel missionaries who worked in the Tulu country, a copy of which was procured by the kind courtesy of B.A. Vivek Rai of the Department of Kannada, Mangalore University. A third version, which we label as GP3, in palm leaf manuscript is available in the collection of Department of Kannada, Mangalore University (No. 79). This Department has collected other versions of *Grāmapaddhati* in palm leaf. They are: (i) No. 44 in Nandinagari script, *Grāmapaddhatiya Kelavu Manetanagalu* (ii) No. 78, *Grāmapaddhati* (iii) No. 59, *Vyasa et.al, Sahyādri Khanda Mattu Itara Viḷhayagaḷu.*

There are a few other versions preserved by the families which the present writer wsa able to come across; but owing to limitations of time, he could not make use of them.

There are different versions found in the religious institutions like mutts. This author, for instance, has been informed by the authorities of Balekudru mutt that they had a copy of *Grāmapaddhati* which is now preserved in the palm leaf document Museum, Dharmasthala. B.A. Saletore claims that he has used the Puttige version for his study of *Grāmapaddhati* and, as the name suggests he must have procured it from the Puttige mutt.[4]

Grāmapaddhati claims to form part of *Sahyādri Khanda* which is again considered to be a part of Skanda Purāna. This indicates the attempts of the authors of *Grāmapaddhati* to claim authenticity on account of puranic origins.

The *Grāmapaddhati* is broadly divisible into three parts. The earlier parts belong to the realm of mythology, dealing with the creation of the land and its early settlement by *Paraḍurāma* as well as with the role of Shiva in the origin of kingship and state in this region. In the earlier part we find the narration of *Paraśurāma* creating the land. Subsequently when the *brahmans* from other regions refuse to go to this newly created land on any occasion on the plea that this land is not peopled by brahmans, Parasurāma becomes angry and decides to create brahmans by himself. Thus he converts the local fishermen into brahmans by investing them with the threads of jute and donates them land. Further on in the same part is the narration of the origin of state where monarchy is the form of government. The story is concerned with the birth of Trinetra Kadamba and it gives, during the narration of events, a list of different rulers who ruled the Paraḍurāma *Kṣetra*.

In the second part there are details of the rule of kings, some protests and even rebellions, floating in a weightless air, the spatial and temporal coordinates of which cannot be pinned down. This part gives the details of the rule of different kings like Mayura Varma, Candrangada and Lokaditya. It also mentions the rebellions by the original inhabitants under the leadership of then "Candala" chief Hubbasiga[5]. It also mentions the protests from the side of the earlier brahmans who were estranged by the decision of Mayura Varma to bring brahmans from Ahicchatra. While the rebellions of the 'holeyas' is suppressed ruthlessly, the protests of the brahmans is met with compromise. In this part there is atleast one instance which goes to suggest that the author of the text was certainly influenced by the system of inheritance obtaining in South Kanara. Mayura Varma, the Kadamba king is stated to be the son of the Kadamba princess Susila, and a prince of the solar dynasty, Hemangaraya. Mayura Varma, obviously traces descent from his mother's dynasty of the Kadambas. Later on in the text, is also stated that as this was how Mayura Varma came to the throne, he ordered that the entire country should follow the matrilineal system (*dauhitra dharma*).[6]

In the third part of this work there are statements which can be tested against other documents. This part refers to settlement of brahmans in thirty-two villages along with their family names being mentioned. It is possible to identify these different villages. There are continuing traditions in these villages, where the brahmana families and their continuing traditions survive to this day. We follow the narrative of one version, GP1, with additional information from the other two versions.

Parasurāma after slaying the *kṣatriyas* twenty-one times, gave away the entire land to Kaṣyapa as the fee for sacrifice performed to expiate for the sin. Kasyapa told Paraḍurāma that it is wrong to live in the land donated by him to others. So Paraḍurāma came to Sahya hills and wrested fresh land from the western sea. In the newly created land there was no brahmana population and brahmans from outside would not go there on any account as it was an *abrāhmanya deṣa* (land without brahmans). So he converted *dasas, Revaras-Kaivartas*, type of Moger caste people, into brahmana caste and assured them prosperity. Then he retired to mount Mahendra, telling the brahmans that if they faced any danger they could call him for help and that he would come immediately. In order to test Parasurāma the brahmans called him without any reason. Realising this Parasurāma became angry and cursed them to become Śudras.

The next part of the story narrates the birth of Kadamba. When Śhiva and Parvati came to Sahya hills, a baby was born to them under a Kadamba tree. The child had three eyes. Since he was born under a Kadamba tree, he was named Kadamba and was blessed to become a king. He was succeeded by Vasu Chakravarthi whose daughter Susile married Hemangaraya of Suryavamśa. They gave birth to Mayūra Varma. When Mayura Varma became the king he was advised by the Ṛṣis to bring brahmans from Ahicchatra, on the banks of River Godavari. As per the suggestion of the Ṛṣis, Mayura Varma went to Ahicchatra and brought brahmans from there. Previously Parasurāma had divided Paraḍurāma *kṣtra*, into the following territories: 1. Karāta 2. Varāta 3. Marāta 4. Konkana 5. Haiva 6. Touḷava and 7. Kerala. The brahmans brought by Mayura Varma were made to settle at Haiva, Touḷava and Kerala.

The brahmans were settled in eighteen villages of Haiva, thirty-two villages of Touḷava and sixty four villages in Kerala. Along with the brahmans were also brought Śudras to work for them and they were named nāyars. They were kept under the control of the brahmans. When such arrangements were being made, the fallen brahmans, who were earlier converted as brahmans and later cursed, protested against it. Mayura Varma as a matter of charity did not punish them and instead, devised a

Sanketa Paddhati by giving them the following villages: 1. Nāguru grāma 2. Mattina grāma 3. Kushasthaḷi grāma 4. Svasthi grāma. They were named in accordance with the village in which they settled. But they were only brahmans in name and their position was in reality, that of the Śudras.

In order to make the sudras co-operate with brahmans Mayura Varma gave two territories to śudras and those who settled in these nādus became the nādavas. These nādus were divided into Kelanādu–Nalavattanādu–Halasanādu–Yaradunādu[7] and the śudras were settled there as nādavas to enable them to assist the brahmans at agrahāras. In these agrahāras the brahmans were expected to study the Vedas, perform Isvara *pūja*, Mahavishna pūja and Mahagaṇapati *āradhane*.

During this time Mayūra Varma had a son called Candrangada. When he was still a minor Mayūra Varma went to do penance leaving the administration in the hands of ministers. In the absence of Mayura Varma, the brahmans lost the earlier patronage and returned to their home land, Ahicchatra. Candrangada, after assuming power realised this and gave them agraharas.

After some time Candrangada had a son called Lokaditya. While Lokaditya was still very young, Candrangada passed away. When the state had become king-less, a Candala called Hubbasiga together with several of his fellowmen, harassed Lokaditya whose mother took him and fled to another country. Hubbasiga gave a series of troubles to *brahmans* who left for Ahicchatra. But some of them remained in the region and coalesced with Hubbasiga. The property of the *brahmans* were appropriated by the non-brahmana peasants who were called nāyars.

In the meantime, Candasena of Gokarna wanted to give his sister Kanakavati in marriage to Lokaditya. But Hubbasiga threatened Candasena and asked him to give Kanakavati to him in marriage. Candasena worked a plan and with the help of Lokaditya killed Hubbasiga. Later Lokaditya occupied his lost territory and married Kanakavati. Here different types of 'holeya' caste are mentioned. 1. Bākka 2. Bakuda 3. Meera 4. Goddi 5. Bile 6. Hasaḷava and 7. Koraga. They were made to work under the brahmans.

Lokaditya decided to bring brahmans from Ahicchatra and approached Bhattacharya who accepted his request and persuaded the brahmans to proceed to Parasurama *kṣetra*. In Gokarna, with the objective of donating land to brahmans a sacrifice was performed in front of god Mahabaleshwara. Along with land donations, two brahmans from Kota village were given the right to administer the perform pūja at Mahabaleshwara temple.

GP1 goes on to give the details of thirty-two settlements in Tuḷunādu, which were divided into sixteen western villages and as many eastern villages. The households which constitute each of these settlements are also described. Lokaditya, after donating land made these details to be written in native language. Bhattacharya asked Lokaditya to make the Śudra and holeyas as subordinates of nāyars. All business activities were to be transacted through nāyars. The *brahmans* should occupy themselves in activities like *agnihotra*, pancha mahāyajña, study of Vedas, etc. The division of villages and the details regarding different households came to be called *sanketa pāddhati.*

The last part of GP1 gives a list of different brahman households, their grades, their duties and their powers. It mentions *Bhattas, Agnihotris, Smārtas, Sabhāpatis, Panditās, Prabhus, Tantris, Gramanis, Adhivasis, Pakshanathas* and *Jannis.*

Sabarāya and Tiburāya were the Sabhāpatis. Kallurāya and Uparannāya were the Panditās. Netrattāya, Icchalttāya, Putrāya, Pangannāya. Udupa and Brahmakāranta were the Tantris. Mudilaya and Nidamburāya were the Paksanāthas. Chauta, Banga, Mudilāya and Nidamburāya were the Prabhus. Munnūrāya, Arināya, Kovināya, Perannāya, Koyamegettāya, Kudurāya, Majjittāya, Talattāya, Pijittāya, Paturāya, Induvaḷittāya, Koyakodanāya, Simanturāya, Punchannāya, Machanturāya, Mogerāya, Mitrantāya, Alevoorāya, Tunga, Brahma Kāranta, Kallurāya, Udupa. Baipadittāya, Atradittāya, Appanttadittāya, Belannāya, Armanettāya, Idapadittāya, Sabarāya, Uparannāya, Korgināya, Ametadittāya, Sambāraya, Kolatāya, Mudampaditāya, Baiittāya, Koranāya, Sagurittāya, Madantillāya, Patturāya were the Bhattās. Simanturāya, Muchanturāya, Munnurāya, Alevoorāya, Kodencha, Manjittāay, Saralāya, Madapalittāya, Jadanvakuttāya, Kuñjitāya, Naduvantilāya, Sagurittāya, Tenkilāya, Putrāya, Tekudenāya, Bayiritāya, Kallurāya, Baipaditāya, Vappantāya, Idepadittāya, Kornāya, Maraditāya, Udupa, Brahmakāranta, Banninjitāya, Sivatāya, were the agnihtris. Nujitāya, Kidenāya, Naralatāya, Talantrāya, Ayapināya, Mannakalatāya, Alevoorāya, Brahmakāranta, Kallurāya, Udupa Baipadittāya, Kornginnāya, Muṇḍapādittāya, and Kodañca were the smārtas. Pāturāya, Poyeyettāya, Sullannāya, Kidekidenāya, Kotanjittāya, Tennarāya, Kannarannāya, Madantillāya, Naduvantilāya, Kunjittāya, Hērala, Kāranta, Nārittāya, Edabettānāya, Hebbāra, Sampigettāya, in Niiravara, Ambaraṇṇāya, Aramanettāya, Madappināya, Putrannāya, Kakaraṇṇāya, Kinakalattāya, Udupa and Urambaḷi were the gramaṇis. Alevoorāya, Pagampināya, Tāretāya, Aṇṇākunjittāya, Baśakaṇṇāya,

Kedatirāya, Arbirāya, Peladitāya, Kannarāditāya, Kambaraṇṇāya, Uliyaraya, Kabekodināya, Malampādittāya, Erinkatāya, Bartoditāya, Punjukannāya, Kuduraya, Ninijrāya, Iravatturāya, Nambunittāya, and Jotoditāya, were the adhivāsis. Madikudilāya, Sidikudilāya, Tinakalatāya, Madumaṇṇāya, Kapunjāya, Vailāya. Manjittāya, Kemmundenāya, Vodambaditāya, Kabetodianāya, Hebbāra, Ungarapaḷḷi, Yedebettināya, Kokodenāya, Raipattāya, Koditillāya, Babetilāya, Madilāya, Uurāla, Kudurettāya, Tenkattāya, Kuntarāya, Maratāya, Ammaṇṇāya, Bayattāya, Pudenāya, Mūlatāya, Ardundāya, Ambaraṇāya, Ulitāya, Paddilāya, Edepulitāya, Uurāya, Padilāya, Irakadittāya, Ponettāya, Uḍupa, Hērala are the Jannis (they are also referred as chinnas in P. 46-47. GPI).

Apart from giving details of the above households the text also mentions the designations like Ballāla, Dore. Sāvanta, Nādu, Biidu, Divana, Simhasana and Rājasthāna. Talepādi, Manjanāya, Nidambūru and Mūdila are the Ballaḷs. Kunda Heggade, Mūda Heggade, Maramba Heggade, Bidareś Oomanjura, Ramanatha, BØḷadadeśingattāya, and hundreds of Heggades and Bellaḷas were the Dores. Iravattūra Bạsava Sāvanta and Mūlike Kinnika Sāvanta were the Sāvantas. Nalavattanādu and Kelanādu were the Nādus. Baindūru and Bhatkala were the Biidus. Kadari and Kārkala were the Divanas. Bārakūru and Mangaḷūru were the Simhāsanas. Bārkūru, Mangalūru, Kadaba and Honnāvara were the Rājasthānas. Kaḍari and Karkala which were the two Chavadis were Mannegaru Bhairava. Bharata-Maryādes, Bārkaru Halaru are given frist Maryade. Hidiva Hachchada Maryāde is given to Kotesvara, Kandavaru māduva Sammāna, Kelanādavas are given Siddhāya.

It also states the Maryādes given to Jannis. They are atta murida akki (rice that has fallen from the ceiling), aidu mole mme (a cow which has come losing its way), Keggoda (?), Jōdumara (double tree), Kūpa (well). Kulāshrunkhila (?), Manākale shringavadya (?), Nadamadi (Cloth put on te floar on which the respected person should walk), Pakshakavāta (?), Makara tØrana (decoration), diipamalasthamba (a pillar like lamp with garland), Dolamañji (?), Ratnagambali (High quality carpet), Cchatra (Umbrella)- these sixteen maryādes or usages were given to some villages. Haratattạ, Kāratattu, Kodatattu, Handattu and Kārukaḷa.

GP2 consists of two parts; the details regarding the division of villages, the names of the brahman families and their designation etc. are found in the first part. It is written in Kannada. The second part of this document is named 'Mayura Varma vamḍāvaḷi' and it is written in the Sanskrit language, in Kannada script.

GP2 does not explain elaborately the creation of Parāsurama ksētra.

So the elaborate mythological narration found in GP1 and GP3 is missing. It gives more importance to the different villages and different brahmana households. These brahmana families are graded into atyuttamaru (highest grade), *yerdāne uttamaru* (second grade), *madyamuttamaru* (middle grade) and *viprottamaru* (good brahmans). *Shrotris* and *Smārtas* belong to the first grade. *Bhatta, Tantri* and *Pandita* belong to the second grade. The middle grade the *Paksanathas, Sabhapatis, Ballalas, Annagramānis, Grāmanis, Janni, Adhivāsi. Louikās belong to the last grade.*

GP2 also mentions that *Chittupādi Ballaḷas* were Paksanāthas for eastern sixteen villages and Nidambūru Ballaḷas are *paksanātha* for western sixteen villages. *Śabarāya* and Śibarāya were the Sabhapatis for eastern and western villages respectively. Vappantāya and Pijattāya are *panditās* for eastern and western villages respectively. The function of the *pakshanāthas* or *Pakshanāyakas* is to look after the *cāturvarna* system of the country. Their assembly was regulated the *Sabhāpatis.* These Sabhapātis were given suggestions by *Panditas* regarding *smriti, śāstra, prāyacitta* and *krama* (action). It mentions four Ballaḷas who were the heads of eight villages each. Kunhimaṇṇāya Kavudambāditāya Talepāditāya and Manjanāditāya are Ballālas. There were eight *Aṇṇagrāmaṇis* each of whom were the heads of four villages. There were sixteen *grāmanis* and thirty two *Aṇṇamaṇis*. Each of these designations had their superior officers. There were twenty four sroutāgnihōtris and sixty four *Bhattās*. The *Tantris* were responsible for management of the temples, *kśetras,* Nāgabrahmabhūtas, Aagama, Mantra śāstra, Kalāsstra fares and festivals. *Jannis* are heads of the temples. They were expected to be served by *adhivāsis* and *adhivamśi*. All these *brahmans* would meet at *Kuta Narasimha* temple and *Śhivaḷḷi Ananteśhwara* temple.

GP2 at the end mentions the *Birudāvaḷḷis* given by Mayura Varma to thirty two villages. They are *iḷidu hōda heṇṇu* (a girl who has passed puberty)[11], *basuru banda heṇṇu* (a girl who is pregnant), *Kūdapaśu* (an animal), *aidu mole paśu* (an animal with an udder that has five teats), *gati muttidavana baduku* (life of one whose fate is not good), *anathana odavi* (ornament of an orphan), *atta murida akki* (rice that has fallen down from the ceiling), *nade vadhya* the musical instrument played to show respect for persons like *swamis*), *nade madi* (cloth spread on the way on which the honoured is expected to walk), *nade chappara* (shelter), *nadenṛitya* (dance), *hagalu dīvatige* (a lamp lighted in day time), *ubhaya chamara* (*Chamara* with two sides), *jōduvejanā* (a pair of particular type of fan known as *Chamara*)[12], *ubhaya chāvadi* (?), *Shankhadhwani* (voice of a cronch), *shwētachatri* (white umbrella), *Gājāshwa* (elephant horse), *andalādi vāhana* (chāvadi (?), *Shankhadhwani* (voice of a cronch), *shwētachatri* (white umbrella), *Gajāshwa* (elephant horse), *andalādi vāhana (chāvadi) (?), Shankhadhwani* (voice of a cronch), *Shwētachatri* (white umbrella), *Gajāshwa* (elephant horse), *andalādi vāhana* (palanquin), *simhvāsana* (throne), *madena kai* (hands of wood fitted to wall), *gaja dwāra* (a door through which an elephant can pass through), *dhwaja kśetra* (place of flag).[13]

The second part of GP2 known as 'Mayura Varma vamśāvali' purports to give the genealogy of the Kadamba dynasty. However, the succession is not always established. In many cases, only the names of the rulers and the length of their reigns are given, without even a mention of the relationship in which one ruler stood his predecessor. So rather than describing it as a genealogy we may regard it as a list of rulers belonging to Kadamba family and other families as well. This list can be reproduced as follows:

Nanda Nandana Rāya (85 years)
Nandana Rāya (70 years)
Vijayanandana Rāya (40 years) (These three rulers ruled for 195 years)
Vahika Rāya (72 years)
Kunttirāya (77 years)
Koyata Rāya (18 years)
Jayantika Kadamba Rāya (45 years)
Hemanga Rāya
Lokaditya Mayura Varma (72 years)
Candrāngada (45 years)
Citravirya Varma (64 years)
Jayavarma Rāya (50 years)
Deva Varma Rāya (43 years)
Name lost (72 years)
Jayachanda Rāya (80 years)
Chikka Viirya Varma Rāya (50 years)
Angaravarma Rāya (95 years)
(Mayura Varma and his successors ruled for 539 years)
Bhutala Pāndya Rāya
Achyūta Rāya of Anegundi
Krishna Rāya
Basappa Nayaka of Nagara

Thus this version not only mentions the rulers belonging to the Kadamba family but also gives a list of other rulers. It states that in Tulunadu there were thirty-two rulers, in Haiga there were three rulers and in Malayala there were thirty-two rulers. This version mentions Bhutaḷa Pāndya Rāya which is absent in GP1.

GP3 is stated as written by Varaha Timmappa in Kavya form and copied by Somayaji in Ṣalivāhana ṣaka, 1768, i.e., A.D. 1846. It is written in a more conventional form starting with all the necessary formalities for writing a sacred work. It starts by invoking the Goddess Parvati. It also states that it should be heard in secret and should not be questioned.

The mythological part goes back in time and it starts with the story of Jamadagni, his relations with his wife and his son *Paraśurāma*. It explains in detail the desire of Kartaviryarjuna to appropriate the invaluable cattle wealth of Jamadagni and the revenge taken by Paraśurāma. This part is absent in GP1 and GP2. In the next part it explains elaborately the donation of land by Paraśurāma to brahmans and Mayura Varma's patronage to strengthening of brahmana settlements.

GP3 contains certain interesting details regarding the traditions of fallen brahmans, the story of Koteṣvara brahmans and certain important terms which are absent in the earlier two versions. It states that there was a controversy between the brahmans of Koteṣvara and Kota regarding the ownership of land. The Koteṣwara brahmans used cunning methods by digging the ground and hiding a *Koteṣvara* brahmana there and when the earth (*bhūmi*) was questioned as to who owned the land, the brahmana answered that it belonged to Koteṣvara brahmans. But an *aṣarira vāṇi* a voice not emanating from any physical body revealed the cunningness of the Koteṣvara brahmans and cursed them to become fallen brahmans.[14] While referring to Hubbasiga, GP3 mentions that Candasena killed Hubbasiga with the help of candrāyudha and he cursed the fellowmen of Hubbasiga to become slaves of others and they will have no unity among themselves. This work also mentions Brahmāvarta, Aryavarta, Padmāvarta and Nāgāvarta. It refers to Pancha drāvidas. It also mentions Maharastra drāvidas, Andhra dravida, Karnātikas and Cola drāvidas. It also mentions Battisa (thirty-two), which is curiously a Hindi word. It also mentions *hattu Sāvira Jagattu*[15] and the process of building Narasimha temple at Kota.

In these three versions we find certain geographical details. GP1 states that Haiva is situated between *Gangāvali* in the south, Sahya hills in the east and sea in the west. *Touḷava* is situated between *Gangāvali* in the north, river Nileṣvara in the south, Sahya hills in the east and sea in the west. Kerala *deṣa* is situated between river *Nileṣvara* in the north, Kanyakumari in the south, sea in the west and Sahya hills in the east. These details provide geographical descriptions of Haiva, *Touḷava* and

Kērala. Geographically, *Grāmapaddhati* is set in South Kanara including the present day district of Kasaragod in *Kērala*. It contains a geographical division of South Kanara into thirty two big villages which consisted of several *adhivāsas*, the smaller units. A study of place names occurring in these texts enable us to identify the antiquity of these places.

In the earlier part, which can be designated as the mythological section, the text refers to a number of places and other geographical identities. GP1 mentions river Godavari, Ahicchatra, Sahya hills, Mahendra hill, Kanyakumari, Kerala, Varata, Marāta, Konkana, Haiva, *Toulava*, Kerala, river Gangavaḷi, river Nileṣvara, Nāgūru grāma, Mattina grāma, Kusasthaḷi grāma, Svasthi grāma, Gokarna deṣa, Kota, Kandāvara and Ṣivaḷḷi.

The places mentioned in GP2 are Ahikśetra, Ṣivalli, Kota, Tuḷu, Maleyāḷa, Haviga, Jayantika, Bārkur, Nagara. GP3 refers to Gajapura, Koteṣwara, Sāligrāma, Venupura, Vatapura, Śivabeḷḷi, Nittur, Taḷitode, Mangaḷūru, Bārakuru, Kukku and Machivūru.

The later part of the different texts of Grāmapaddhati gives details regarding the thirty-two villages where the brahmans settled and the boundaries of certain important villages like Kota and Sivalli. GP3 gives details regarding brahmana population in Sivalli and mentions its different *adhivāsas*.

These three versions mention the names of thirty-two villages in which the brahmans settled. GP1 refers to Tareūru, Varkādi, Marane, Kolyanādu, Pādi, Kūdalu, Mogebailu, Mittanādu, Nirumarga, Simanturu, Tenekaḷa, ḷivabelli, Brahmapura, Nirāvara, Kūta and Skandapura. These are categorised as wesern *grāmas*. The eastern grāma are *Ḷripadi, Odilu, Nāla, Kāranduru, Ujire, Kunyamārga, Kokkada, Rāminja, Pude grāma, Belapa, Airnadu, Idakedu, Kemminja, Pādinja*, Siriyadi and Kudipādi.

In GP2 in the western grāma section Tāreuru is referred as Kāruru, Tenekaḷa is called Kanakkaḷa, Koḷyanādu is referred as Koḷavinādu and Skandapura is referred as Skandāvara. Instead of Mogebailu GP2 mentions Mogrālu. In the eastern *grāma* section GP2 refers to Kareya, Kavāḷa and Manikaḷa which are not mentioned in GP1. But GP2 leaves out Airnādu, siriyādi and Kudipādi which are mentioned in GP1. GP2 refers to Karanduru as Karānjuru, Kunyamārga as Kunjimārga, Rāminja as Rāmanjuru, Beḷapa as Beḷavya and Pādinja as Pālinjā.

GP3 mentions all the sixteen western villages mentioned in GP1, but instead of Mogebailu it refers to Moganādu. Kūta is referred as Gajapura and Skandapura is called Skanda *grāma*. In the western *grāma* section it calls Śripādi as Sirripādi.

The discrepancies are generally of two varieties. One of them related to the identity of the *grāmas* mentioned. In a few cases, while the number sixteen is kept sacred, a few villages mentioned in one list are altogether absent in another list. The identity is therefore, completely different. In certain other cases, the villages mentioned in different lists are the same although either it is spelt differently or a different name itself is given. A more detailed examination of the different villages mentioned in the *Grāmapaddhati* and an attempt to identify them in modern geography will through more light on this problem. We turn to such an exercise in the next chapter.

References

1. This author was able to find one version of *Grāmapaddhati* in the house of Harikrishna Tantri, Udupi, is in Sanskrit language.
2. The above mentioned version is written in Tulu-Malayalam script.
3. It is published by Holla Krishniah, Balanadu in 1924.
4. B.A. Saletore, *Ancient Karnataka Volume I, History of Tuluva*, Poona, 1936, p. 324.
5. For traditions regarding Hubbasiga cf., Purushothama Bilimale, *Koragara Samskriti*, (in Kannada) Bangalore, 1993, pp. 29-33.
6. GP 1, p. 22. Even those who are presented as antagonistic to the Kadambas, namely, the Koragas followed the same type of inheritance. c.f., Purushothama Bilimale, *op.cit.*, p. 37.
7. According to a list given by P. Gururaja Bhat, three out of these four figure in inscriptions, cf. P. Gururaja Bhat, *Studies in Tuluva History and Culture*, Kallianpur, 1975, p. 147. He has prepared a list of *nadus* on the basis of SII VII and IX Pt. II and KI Volumes I and III Pt. I.
8. This translation is taken from B.A. Saletore, *Ancient Karnataka*, Vol. 1, *History of Tuluva, op.cit.*, p. 304.
9. Author's translation.
10. S.S. Malavada (ed.), *Kaavya Pada Mānjari*, Bangalore, 1970, p. 98.
11. Some of these translations are taken from B.A. Saletore, *Ancient Karnataka*, p. 304.
12. I would like to thank Dr. Subrahmanay Bhat, Kannada Department, Mangalore University for providing some of the above translations.
13. Most of the above usages are still practised, e.g., in Udupi during processions where *Swamis* and deity are involved.
14. Cf. Ko. Sha. Karanta, Kuta Maha Jagattu, Saligrama, 1958, pp. 25-26. Some of the families of Koteśhwara brahmans have now settled in a place

called Iddya. It is said that the Koteśwara brahmans were made the followers of the Sode Mutt Vadiraja Swami cf. P. Kuppannacharya, *Sri Guruvara Vaadiraajaara Charitaamrita,* Kinnigoli, 1983, pp. 44-45.

15. An inscription dated A.D. 1520 refers to ten thousand *mahaajagattu.* A.R. No. 515 for 1928-29.

4
The Identification of the Places and their Antiquity

The *Grāmapaddhati*, as the very title indicates, is concerned with the details of *grāmas* in which the brahmanas are said to have settled originally. To trace the identity and antiquity of these *grāmas*, therefore, will be significant in two ways: for one thing, it can show to what extent the text has historical validity and secondly it can tell us something about the antiquity of these groups with a conscious identity of their own. Both are very important. We now turn, therefore, to this exercise of identifying the *grāmas*.

The Brahmans of South Kanara are stated to have been established in thirty-two *grāmas*, sixteen of them designated as western and the other sixteen as eastern. They are as follows:

Western grāmas

1. Kandāvara 2. Kūta 3. Brahmāvara 4. Varkādi 5. Karavor 6. Pādi 7. Mogrāl 8. Kūdalu 9. Mittanādu 10. Tenakala 11. Sīmantūru 12. Marane 13. Kolavinādu 14. Nilāvara 15. Śivalli 16. Nīrumārga.

Eastern grāmas

1. Sripadi 2. Vodila 3. Nāla 4. Kareya, 5. Ujire 6. Kārandura 7. Kāvala 8. Kuñjimārga 9. Kokkada 10. Rāmañjura 11. Pude 12. Balpa 13. Idekkeddu 14. Palinje 15. Kimmiñje 16. Aivarnādu[1]

Western grāmas

1. Kandāvara Known differently as Skandapura, and Skanda *grāma*, Kandāvara is situated near Basarūru in the Kundapura taluk.

GP1 gives the names of Udupa and Hebbāra. Both are expected to indulge in *adhyāyana* and *agnihotra* which indicates Vedic tradition.

GP2 mentions Udupa as *agnihotri,* Hebbara as grāmaṇi, Aṇṇa Hebbāras as *Jannis, Upparu Udupa* and *Kandāvara Udupa as adhivāsis.*

The association of this village with the worship of Skanda, as its name suggests, is supported by the existence of the Ulluru Subrahmanya temple. Dr. P. Gururaja Bhat believes that Kandāvara is named after Skanda.[2] According to him the image at Subrahmanya temple may be dated to 11th-12th Century A.D.[3] The Udupās consider Skanda as their family deity. The Vaidy as a community specialised in the performance of *Nāga Mandala*[4] a practice typical of South Kanara, before travelling to other areas of South Ḳanara, worship this deity. This pūja is performed the day before Subrahmanya *ṣaṣthi.*[5] This village also consists of hundreds of Nāga banās.[6] where the nāga stones are worshipped by the brahmans. This village also has two Janārdana temples which may suggest that it was a strong brahman settlement during the earlier times.

Both the families mentioned in GP1 could be identified here and they still exist in this village. To the south of the temple we have a Hebbāra *katte* and to the north of the temple there exists an Udupara *katte.* According to the tradition during the car festival the main deity must visit these two places. This practice which indicates that these indeed were the sites on which the original houses of these families stood. Uḷḷūru Subrahmanya temple has connections with Bālekudru mutt,[7] which has its branch called Hutturu mutt at Kandāvara.

The antiquity of this village is further proved by the discovery of nine inscriptions from the precincts of Ulluru Subrahmanya temple. Among them one inscription belongs to the modern period. Other inscriptions are dated A.D. 1358, A.D. 1409, A.D. 1433, A.D. 1456, A.D. 1467, A.D. 1476 and A.D. 1522. One undated inscription is supposed to be belonging to the middle of 16th century.[8]

The inscription belonging to A.D. 1358 mentions Kandavara and the temple by stating *Kandāvurada grāmadoḷage* Uḷūra *devālāya..* The inscription dating A.D. 1409 mentions the Brahman families Udupās and Hebbāras. It also refers to an assembly of brahmans called *grāma hadināru.* One line of this inscription is in Tuḷu script. So till A.D. 1522 inscriptional evidence is available regarding Kandāvara and Udupas and Hebbāras.

GP2 mentions Anna Udupa and Aṇṇa Hebbara. Inscriptions belonging to A.D. 1409 and A.D. 1433 refer to Anna Udupa.

The above details show that Kandāvara was an important brahmanical centre with the existence of *agrahāras* which enjoyed royal patronage. In the later period the brahmans of this village, mostly with the surname Udupa, came to be called Kandavara brahmans.[10]

2. Kōta (Kūta). Kota village is situated between Kundapura and Brahmāvara in the Udupi taluk.

GP1 mentions the following families: Hande, Basari, Tunga, Nāvada, Hoḷḷa, Mayya, Hebbāra and Kāryavanta.[11]

GP2 divides the families into Aruru *aṡtagraha* and Mururu *astagraha*. The families belonging to the first section are Tunga, Hoḷḷa, Kāranta, Hērala, Hande, Nāvada, Bāsari, Hebbāra, Hande Mayya and Uūrala.[12] These families are assigned different functions. Tunga is a *Smārta*, Holla and Kāranta are *Bhattās*, Hērala is *grāmani*, Hande, Nāvada and Bāsari are *Jannis*, Hebbāra, Mayya and Uuraḷa are *adhivāsis*.

These families are stated to have been distributed in the different *adhivāsas* of Kota.[13]

1. Kāratattu (Chitrapadi) -Kāranta.
2. Pārampaḷḷi -Hebbara and Holla.
3. Kārakādu (Karkada) -Nāvada
4. Hāratattu -Mayya, Hēraḷa
5. Kotatattu -Tunga
6. Handattu -Bāsari, Hande.

Mūrūru astagrha of Kōta village are mentioned as below: Aadināya, Mādināya, Alsattāya, Dotsattāya, Ammanittāya, Manikattāya, Koṇakattāya, Rudguṇattāya.[14] These are referred *as Narasimha dēvara sēvadivasigalu* which means that these households were supposed to serve God Narasimha at Kota. However, these families do not exist in Kota any more.

Aaruru and Mūruru could be identified. Aaruru is near Koteśvara and Mūruru is near a place called Kunjālu. Both are situated in two different directions of Kota. We have also inscriptional evidence for Mūruru. An inscription dated 1431 A.D. refers to Mururu *grāma*.[15] This inscription found at Chaulikeri, Bārkur mentions that Mūruru is situated near Kudukūra.

All the families stated to belong to the category of Aruru *astagṛha* can be seen settled in Kota even today. But strangely these families do not perform *Pūja* at Narasimha temple, Kota.[16] This is performed by śivalli brahmans now. Even today the brahmans of Kota have maintained this tradition.[17] Another important feature of the Kota brahmans is that they consider God Narasimha has their *guru*.[18] They do not accept the hegemony of any mutt, The deity at Sāligrāma itself is called Guru Narasimha.

According to Dr. P. Gururaja Bhat Kota was one of the important brahmanical settlements of South Kanara.[19] Those brahman families who settled in Kota came to be known as Kota brahmans.[20] These brahman families are mentioned in epigraphs starting from 13th c.A.D. They had their own self governing institutions like *Māhajagattu* which was constituted by *Grāmaṇis, Jannis, Madhyasthās* and *Bhattās.*[21]

The main temple of this village is Narasimha temple at Saligrāma. Dr. P. Gururaja Bhat believes that this image may belong to a period as early as C.8th century A.D.[22] Here one can notice a situation where in a Vaisnava deity is worshipped by the people believing in *Smārta* tradition. Perhaps it was a part of *Panchāyatana* tradition expounded by Sankaracharya.[23] In Kota there are nearly twelve Mahalingesvara temples and twenty four Viṣṇu temples. According to Gururaja Bhat the Viṣṇu image at Hande *devalya* belongs to 13th century A.D.[24] The Hande *devasthana is* privately managed by the Hande family of Kota. Kota is also known for *bhūta* worship and the worship of *daivās* There are Bobbarya, Hāyguli, Rakteswari, Katte daiva, Arama devaru and Mani chennakēśava.

Another distinguishing feature claimed by the Kota brahmans is that they believe in *Purva mimamsa* which gives greater importance to study of Vedas and *grahasthasrama* rather than uttara *mimamsa* which believes in *samnyāsaśrama.*[25]

Inscriptional evidence regarding Kota village and its brahman families are available both within Kota and outside it. One inscription dating A.D. 1476 refers to Kota village and families like Hōraḷa (Herala), Hoḷa (Hoḷḷa), Mayya, Henje (Hande) and Bāsiri. This inscription also indicates that these families enjoyed property rights and it refers to Horala gadi.[26] Another inscription found at the Somnath Handeta and also *hande dēvālya*, a temple belonging to the Handes.[27] Another inscription dated A.D. 1477 refers to Urāla.[28] Another inscription dated A.D. 1587 refers to the families like Karanta, Tunga and Alase.[29] The last family is not mentioned in any of versions of *Grāmapaddhati*, although it continues to live in Kota. According to a legend Alase was a branch of one of the main families and once he could not attend the assembly of brahmans called *Kūta mahājagattu* and he was named *ālasya* meaning laziness, a lazy person.[30]

3. Brahmāvara Brahmāvara is in Udupi taluk. Its different names are Brahmavara, Brahmapura, Brahmura, Purahali, Brahmōra *grāma.*[31] According to Dr. P. Gururaja Bhat by 8th and 9th century A.D. this had developed into an important brahmanical centre.[32] D.C. Sircar believes that the very word Brahmapura meant the Brahman settlement.[33] *Grāmapaddhati* also calls it Ajapura.[34]

The brahman families mentioned in GP1 as belonging to this village are Ulluru, Ungarapalli, Vāramballi, Kairamballi, Alupyā Astāmūrthy, Hebbāra and Samblāja.[35] GP2 mentions Ugrampaḷḷi and Vārambaḷḷi as Bhattās, Aluppa as grāmani, Uḷḷurāya and Derampaḷḷitāya as *Jannis*, Mukkarditāya, Apruchala and Astamarthy as adhvāsis.[36] GP3 mentions the families mentioned by GP1.[37]

The different *adhivāsas* of Brahmavara are Cānturu, Matapapdi, Hēlūru, Baikādi, Vāramballi, Hāradi, Handādi and Kumragodu. The *agrahāras* are situated in Cantāru and Hērūru. In the early times Brahmavara was divided into western and eastern parts. The western Brahmavara was under the control of the Vārambaḷḷi family and eastern Brahmavara was under Ugrampalli family.[38]

The main temple of this area is Mahālingeśwara temple. Near this temple we find Uḷḷūreśwara temple. At Nāgaliṅga *agrahāra* there is a Nāgaliṅgēśwara image. The same place has a Viṣṇumūrthy temple. At Handādi we find two Viṣṇumurthy temples. At agrahāra, Janārdhana images belonging to 9th-10th C.A.D.[39] and 14th century are found.[40]

The Vārambaḷḷis were a prominent brahman family of Brahmavara. An inscription found at Vārambaḷḷi dated Saka 1339 refers to Nāraṇa Aubhala dēva Orambaḷḷi of Brahmūra making land grants for the worship of the deity installed in the Arasana Kere matha near the donor's house.[41] An Aḷupa inscription dating, Saka 1267 records the gift of some land by the King Kulasekhara deva Aḷupēndradeva to Aṇṇa Orambaḷi of Brahmavara for a *matha*. Thus we have enough evidence to prove the important position acquired by the Vārambaḷḷis from very early times.

The Vārambaḷḷis are considered to be the gurus of the Nairi community of Brahmavara.[43] The *garadis* used by the Nairis for gymnastic training and as a storehouse of weapons are looked after by the Vārambaḷḷis who worship the deity in the *garadi*. It is also said that Vārambaḷḷis have connections with Kerala.[44] Here we may note that there is a place called Vāramballi *bāyalu* near Kasargod.

There is also a tradition according to which the Bārakūru kings gave ūrambal; land grants, to a brahman family and they later became Vārambali. The place where they settled came to be called by the same name.[45]

The Unguarapali family too figures in inscriptions. An inscription at Matapādi dated Saka 1336 records the appointment by the King and Ūravar of the villages, of a certain Alugātu-Ungurapaḷḷi as the tenant of some land in the village.[46] These inscriptional references show that these two brahman families enjoyed a position of authority in Brahmavara.[47]

Another family mentioned in *Grāmapaddhati* is Uḷḷūru or Uḷḷurāya. This family too figures in the inscriptions. An inscription in the sankaranārāyana temple, Brahmavara, dated A.D. 1403 mentions the family or Ullura as living in "Brahmūra grāma".[48] A few inscriptions speak about the Hebbāra families, but there is also possibility of their being sthānikas.[49] An inscription at Chaulikeri, Bārakūr mentions "A[ḷupe].[50] But it is not possible to clearly identify Aḷupe with Aḷupyā mentioned in GP1. An inscription found at Vaderhobḷi, Kundapur, dated Saka 1328 refers to Sabhāyita.[51] It is possible that Sabhāyita got transformed into Sabyāja. The remaining families Apruchala and Astāmūrthi are not mentioned in inscriptions. The local population is not aware of the existence of such families in the past either.

4. **Varkādi.** This village is situated four kilometres away from Sunkadakatte, Kasargod Taluk, Kerala State. It is on the banks of the tributary of Bangra Majeshwara river.

GP1 mentions Tāletāya, Avyapaināya, Nāralattāya. Nētrattāya, Arināya, Kidikidenāya, Suṇṇoditāya, Kunjitturāya.[52] GP2 mentions Perruvannāya and Vāyappināya as *Bhattās*, Nētrattāya as *Tantri*, *Tālattāya as Grāmani* Kidikerunāya, Sanna Sakattāya, Arrināya and Kojitturāya as *Jannis* and Kārāya and Vārkadināya as *adhivāshis*.[53] GP3 mentions Tālettāya as *grāmani' Nētrattāya* as *Smritikarta*, Aryapaināya as *Bhatta* and other families are Netrattāya, Arrimanettāya and Sunnodittāya.[54]

In Varkādi one can find Kāvu Subrahmanyeswara temple. The original temple is nearby at another place which is called *ādisthana*, and the local people believe that since there was very little space it was found necessary to shift it to present spot which has by its side Kava *tārtha*.

The antiquity of this area may go back to several hundreds of years. Near the temple at an upper region there is a cave-like structure where some big earthenware pots were found. They are, in all probability, megalithic and therefore, may belong to early iron age, roughly corresponding to the turn of the Christian era.[55] This shows the antiquity of the human settlement there, although the brahman settlement there need not be linked with it.

It is difficult to precisely establish the date of construction of this temple. It is considered as one of the sixteen *Māgane* temples[56] which can be found in the region between Brahmavara and River Chandragiri. The sixteen stone pillars in the *mukhamantapa* allegedly represents sixteen *magane* temples. Here the representatives of sixteen temples were expected to assemble and dispense of justice.[57] In the well near the temple some old statues and Śivalingās were found. The temple has

Melushānti, *Kiḷushānti* and *Patāḷi* who are considered as the servants of the temple.

There is a popular legend that the temples which were around here were destroyed by a *daiva* called Mittamagerāya to take revenge against a *tantri*, a brahman, who had arrested it by his Tantric abilities using copper. This process of destruction was stopped by Kūtadwaje and Kanantura *bhūtas* which were even more powerful. These two *bhūtas* are given a place of importance inside the temple. Even today at the place of Mittamagerāya both copper and the descendents of Tantri's farnily are denied admission.

Inside the prākara of the temple two inscriptions are found. According to Y. Umanath Shenoy one is in Kannada script and the other is in Tulu Script. These were inscriptions issued by Kings of Vittla and they contain details of land grants to this temple.[58]

The temple is surrounded by mostly śivaḷḷi brahman families. Some of the families mentioned in *Grāmapadhati* can be identified here. Tālettāya is among the more prominent of them. Perruvaṇṇāya are at present the *pavitrapāṇi* of the temple, who possess the right to manage its affairs. The Nētrattāya family has become extinct. But before that it adopted three more families with the same family deity. These were settled in three villages, Varkadi, Kemminje and Kudupu.[59] Vāyappināya, Kidikerunāya, Sannasakattāya and Vārkādināya do not live in Varkādi any more; at least Saṇṇasakattāya can be believed to have migrated. The others appear to have become extinct. At present the Arināyas live in a nearby place called Arribailu where we see a *Naga brahmana Sthāna* worshipped by a brahman. Here the cultivation do not take place and the land is kept for the *Kambala* sport.[60] The family of Kojitturāya is now extinct, but Kārāyas are still around. There were kinship ties between the brahmaṇ families of Kemminje and Varkādi.[61]

5. **Karavūr.** In different versions of Grāmapaddhati it is variously referred as Karavūr, Tārevūru and Kārūru. At present in South Kanara there is no village by name Karavūr. On the basis of the details of families mentioned in *Grāmapaddhati* (GP2)[62] one can come to the conclusion that Karavar covered the areas like Manjanadi, Ucchila, Talapādi, Madyār and Munnūru.[63] At present we do not find a place called Karavūr or Tarevūru in this area.

GP1 mentions Pāturāya, Pākurāya, Kudurettāya and Poyvattāya.[64] GP2 mentions Munnurāya as *Bhatta*, Ichalantāya as Tantri, Talepaditāya and Manjanaditāya as *Ballāḷas*. Madyārāya as *Grāmaṇi*, Kāturāya and Panambeletāya as *Janni* and Kalashankantāya as *adhivās*.[65] GP3 mentions all the families mentioned in GP1 except Pākurāya. Instead it mentions Kārurāya.[66]

There is a reference to Kāruru in the Sanskrit work *Bhāvaprakaśika* which is dated circa 14th century A.D. and it was written by Nārāyana Panditāchārya. This work refers to Vāsudeva (the earlier name of Madhwacharya) crossing the Netravati river and coming to Kutyādi mutt in Kārevūru *grāma*. It states *grāma* varasya Kāryuru[67]. This shows that the region around Kutyadi mutt was the Karavuru *grāma*.[68]

In Mañjanādi there was the family of Mañjanādittāya which is now extinct. But they had adopted Munnurāya who sēttled in the present Mañjanādi village. This family was also given the designation of the Ballāḷa. Another Ballāḷa family Talepādittāya is now extinct. The family of Ichalantāya at Ucchila now have the designation Tantri.[69] These details prove that the traditions of the Brahman families have continued to exist even today. In Mañjanādi we find a Viṣṇumūrthi Janārdhana temple. Important *daivās* here are Mugera daiva and Malarāya. In Talapādi we have a Durga temple.

6. Pādi. Pādi is in Kasargod taluk, Kerala State. GP1 calls it Pādimogara. It mentions the Brahman families like Amettāya, Sambarattāya, Induvalittāya and Koyakudalāya.[70] GP2 metions *Bālkādināya* as *agnihotri*, Kamatatāya as *Bhatta*, Mannipaittāya as grāmani. The *Jannis* are Anjanantodittāya, Uruḷantoditāya, Tatkālapāditāya, Kakkillāya, Pāramparditāya, Akrapokkināya, Yarapāditāya, Murudompārdināya, Kurukapardināya, Chāpardināya, Taudupārdināya, Mundalampārditya, Kadalampārditāya and Uralampārditāya.[71] GP3 metions all the families mentioned in GP1.[72]

Some of these families had settled in places like Bārikkādi, Chāpadi, Taudupādi, Mullampādi and Kakkola. Some of the families mentioned in GP2 have migrated to Kerala. Two such settlements can be seen in Pattilla and Pullur. Pattilla means ten houses and here ten Brahman families have settled. The families like Yarapārditāya. Uralangoditāya and Kakkotāya have now settled in Nileśvara. Kāmatatāya are now called Kāmada and they have settled in Bārikkādi.[73]

In a document of Edaneer mutt dated A.D. 1850 we find reference to some of the families mentioned in *Grāmapaddhati*,[74] It refers to Kāmada of Bārikkadi, Kuṇikuḷḷāya, Kakkilaya and Baḷḷuḷḷāya.

In *Madhva Vijaya*, written by Narāyana Panditacharya, supposed to belong to 14th-15th century A.D., we find Pādi being sanskritised as Vāta.[75] The Padi village consists of *adhivāsas* like Muttutodi, Pādi and Chēngala. It is also called Pādipadippare which means the place where justice is given. It was under the control of the Māyipādi kings who had their place at Mogrāl. The women of the Māyippadi household were married to the male of any one of the following eight śivaḷḷi Brahman families. These are 1. Imirāya 2. Kakkillāya 3. Kuṇīkuḷḷāya 4. Kote kuñjattāya 5. Tambalantodittāya 6. Baipādittāya 7. Pijiettāya and 8. Ballulāya.[76] This shows the matrimonial alliance between those who claim Kṣatriya caste status and the above Brahman families in the *Sambandham* style typical of Kerala. The house of Māyippadi follows the matrilineal system of inheritance. The male members generally marry into the Nāyar community.[77] The Kāmatatāya Brahman family is given the position of father or *pitṛ* of the Mayippadi Kings.

The two important temples of Pādi are Beluru Māhavisnu temple and śiva temple. The daivas here are Viṣṇumūrthi, Rakteśwari and Dhumāvati. It is also said that in this region there were thirty-nine bhūtas.

7. Mogrāl. It is situated five kilometres away from Kumbale, Kasargod taluk. GP1 does not mention Mogral. Instead it mentions Mogebailu.[78] GP2 mentions Innurāya as *Smārtāgnihōtri* and *bhattās*, Ijalampadittāya as *grāmani*, Mogarālaya, Kaṇṇavurāya and Mākurāya as *Jannis*. The *adhvāsis* are Ijarāya, Māpaditāya, Kanevurāya, Putrattāya, Uḷḷavurāya, Kānatāya. Gulitāya, Kidevurāya, Kidekāntāya and Karekontāya.[79] GP3 mentions Moganādu *grāma*. This village was inhabited by Brahman families like Pijettāya, Pilitkarettāya, Tambalantodittāya and Mudentāya.[80]

Anantpur Tuḷu inscription, which can be dated about 15th century A.D., is concerned with land granted to the temple. It mentions the village of Mogrāl as *Mugaraira grāma*.[81]

Some of the families mentioned above lived in Mogrāl. Kotekunjattāya lived in Mogrāl. The family of Ijalampādittāya has its branches in Bēḷa, Arikkādi, Mantappādi and Kidūru. This family even today has connections with the Mahalingeśwara temple, Nāyikkapu. In Mogrāl we find Śankaranārāyaṇa temple.

8. Kūdalu. It is situated near Mogral, Kasargod taluk. GP1 mentions Kannaraṇṇāya, Kambaraṇṇāya, Irvatturāya and Mittadkatāya.[82] GP2 mentions Kottakunjittāya as Smārta, Dekuṇjittāya, Paravaṇṇaya and Nityavannāya as *Bhattas*. Pijattāya as *Pandita*, Deranjattāya as grāmani, Pilitkerettāya and Pudunkolattāya as *Jannis*.[83] GP3 mentions all the families mentioned in GP1.[84]

Kottakunjittāya had connections with Māyippadi royal family. Dekunjittāya family is still living in Kasargod. Dēranjattāyas are in

Kanhangad, Kerala State. Pudunkolattāya are in Nileśvara. Pijettāyas are still living in Kūdalu and they have maintained the earlier tradition. The Pijettāyas are now called Kāvu Patteri which means Pandita.

In *Madhwa Vijāya* Kūdalu is referred as Kude, Kudelu and Kudil (Amaralāya).[85] In Kūdalu Madhwacharya defeated Trivikrama Panditāchārya who accepted the Madhwa philosophy. In *Madhwa Vijāya* are referred as Likunjanvayodbhava. Trivikrama Panditacharya belonged to this family.[86] Trivikrama Panditāchārya's son Narāyana Panditacharya is the author of *Madhavavijya.* The house of Pijettāya enshrines an image of Lakshmi Nārāyana which is supposed to have been given by Madhwacharya to this family.[87] This family has continued the earlier traditions with sacrifice being performed everyday and it also has a perpetual lamp. The Pijettāya the family has connections with Kavu mutt.

The temple in Kūdalu are, Bārikkādi Viṣṇumūrthi temple, Ajjāvara Mahiśa Mardhini temple, Bārikkādu Sastāvu, Aanampādi Viṣṇu temple and śiva temple. The *Daivās* here are Iriyakōte, Hosamane Viṣṇumūrthi and Raktēśwari.

9. Mittanādu. The present name of Mittanādu is Ubrangaḷa which is situated in Kasargod taluk.

According, to GP1 Mittanādu consisted of Kundagolattāya, Nūjittāya, Gangettāya, and Saralattāya.[88] GP2 mentions Pāvurāya and Puṇyakalattāya as bhattas, Mattipuñjittāya as *grāmani*, Uppangaḷattāya, Uurangaḷatāya, Mūdavādittāya, Dēvādittāya and Bīdi Aadināya as *Jannis.* The adhivāsis are Mittanadittāya, Munivurāya, Kandankodittāya, Narulittāya, Balekaḷattāya, Kanankordittāya, Kodamettāya, Nellittāya, Balillāya. Morrittāya, Mavurāya and Kaḷḷikalattāya.[89]

Most of the families mentioned above have either migrated or have become extinct. Nūjittāyas live in Rāmakuñja, while Saralattāya, obviously Saralāyas live in Udupi. It is possible to identify the places like Nelli, Bāḷla, Uppangala, Ūūrangala, Pāvuru, Kannankordi, Kodyame and Māvuru. These places are found in the present Kasargod district.

The temple in Mittanādu are Parvati Iśwara temple, Durga Parameśwari temple, Mahiśa Mardhini temple and Viṣṇumūrthi temple.

10. Tenakala. Tenakaḷa is also referred as Kenakaḷa and Kelakaḷa. In Kasargod taluk there is a place called Teḷakaḷa and it is found near Manjeshwara.

GP1 mentions Mogerāya, Mittantāya, Madumannāya, Vailāya or Kanchittāya, Vokudināya, Ulirāya, Malenjināya and Kabekodināya.[90]

GP2 mentions Mittantāya as agnihōtri, Mugerāya and Vailāya as *bhattas*, Madavannāya and Vakkunāya as Aṇṇagrāmaṇis, Kachintāya and Maleñjināya as *Jannis*, Uḷirāya. Muddaṇṇāya and Keḷakaḷattāya as adhivāsis.[91] GP3 mentions all the families mentioned in GP1.[92]

According to the local people here in the past there existed a family of Mittantāya, but now they live elsewhere. The only brahman family existing here is permudannāya and they too had migrated from permuda near Katil.

This village shows signs of importance since it has yielded two inscriptions, which according to the local people are unnoticed and unpublished.[93] Of them, one is found in the Gopalakrishna temple and the other inscription is found in a nearby field.

11. Simanturu. Simanturu is situated near Mūlki, Mangalore taluk. GP1 mentions Sīmanturāya, Śibarurāya, Mannurāya, Ipprantāy, Mukhyantāya, Mudikudalāya, Sidikalatāya, Ādaraya, Barvanāya.[94] GP2 mentions Simantūrāya as *Smārtagnihotri*, Muchyantāya and Madikulatāya as *bhattas*, and Tokurāya as *Janni*, Kallakkaratāya and Ayakalattāya as *adhivāsis*.[95] GP3 śibarurāya, Sīmanturāya, Mannurāya, Machhatāya, Madikulatāya and Sidikulatāya.[96]

Sīmanturāyas are still living in Simantāru. Muchyantāyas live in Punarur, a nearly place Śibarurāyas are now living in Katil. One important aspect is that all these families belong to Kāśyapa Gotra and that all those brahman families belonging to Kāśyapa gotra in South Kanara trace their origin to Śimantūru. Hence the brahmans of this village have maintained their earlier traditions and remember their previous connections with this village. According to Dr. K.G. Vasanthamadhava, the brahmans in this region by thirteenth century had occupied a dominant position in the society and they became the landlords. They were patronised by the local rulers.[97]

The main temple of this region is Adi Janārdhana temple, the earlier image of which is supposed to have been erected by Paraśurāma himself. Adi Janārdhana deity is considered as the main God of Duggṇṇa Sāvanta of Padupanamburu. This temple has authority over five villages namely, Sīmanturu, Eltūru, Punarūru, Mānampadi and Kilpādi. In Sīmanturu Janārdhana temple we find an inscription dated 1411 A.D. From this inscription we come to know that Janārdhana temple was regarded as a place where disputes would be settled.[98]

There are more than hundred *nāgasthānas* in this region. There is an important brahmasthāna also. In Kilpādi we find Jārandala daiva while in Mānampadi there is Kāḷikāmba and Iśwara temple. Now this area consists of nearly ten houses belonging to śivalli brahmans. It is said the *daivas*, Kāntabare and Būdabāre were born in this region.

12. Marane. It is not possible to clearly identify this village. There are two Maranes, one in Udupi taluk and another in Karkala taluk.

GP1 mentions Badekedenāya and śulyaṇṇāya. In GP2 the families mentioned are Pāturāya, Poyyāttāya, Pijakkalattāya, Kudrittāy, Anaḷattāya and Mālattāya.[100] GP3 mentions the same families mentioned in GP1.[101] In Karkala taluk we find one Marane near Ajekāru. GP2 refers to Māḷattaya i.e., one who belonged to Māḷa, which is near Karkala. But in neither do we find evidence of the above families having lived here. Hence the identification of this village will have to be left open.

At present Poyyattāya family is found in Kanantūru. From generations they have been worshipping a *bhūta* called Todakukkinār or Vaidyanātha swami.[102] Another family Kudrittāyas are in Belthangadi taluk.

13. Kolavinadu. It is found near Manchi, Bantwal taluk. GP1 mentions Talepāditāya and Mānjanāditāya.[103] GP3 mentions the same families but refers to them as Ballalas."[104] GP2 mentions Nadikaḷatāya as *agnihotri*, Salaiturāya and Manchittāya as *bhattas*, Śullyaṇṇāya and Padakaṇṇāya as Aṇṇa grāmaṇis, Marḷyattāya and Mankudettāya as *Jannis* and Naralattāya as *adhivasi*.[105]

The above brahman families were living in places like Saletore, Sullya, Manchi and Mankude. In Koḷavinādu there is a *Bhūta* called Nāraḷattāya and it is associated with Sode mutt.[106] This *bhūta sthana* now found near Katathila. The Gopalakrishna temple in Manchi consists of sixteen pillars.

This temple has connections with Kavu Subrahmaṇyeśwara temple, Varkādi, which is considered as *sīme* temple for this area. The Mahādeva temple is owned by Sullyaṇṇāyas. The other temples of this region are Mankude Viśṇumūrthi temple and Katathila mutt.

14. Nīlāvara. Nīlāvara, which is also called Niruvāra is in Udupi taluk.

GP1 mentions Nārittāya, Yedabettanāya, Kallurāya, Tumbikallāya, Nūjinnāya, Makkitaya and Pādittaya. It also states that all the above families belonged to the same gotra.[107] GP2 mentions Nāritāya as *smārta*, Kallurāya, Nakśatri and Madhyastha as *bhattas*, Yedabettanāya as *grāmani*, Hebbāra and Makkitāya as *Jannis*, Tumibikallāya and Pādettāya as adhivasis.[108] GP3 mentions Nāriśya, Yedabettanāya, Kallurāya, Tumbikallāya, Hebbāra, Nuritāya, Karapādi and Mukkittāya.[110]

We find traditional account of Nīlvāra and brahman settlements in it in *Nīlavāra Ksetra Mahātme*, which is considered as a part of *Skanda Purana.*[110] It mentions Kallurāya as *agnihotri*. It also mentions other brahman families like Edabettutāya, Makkitāya. Padetāya, Tumbikallāya. Kakratāya and Hebbaratya. This work states that nobody in this *grāma* goes against the wishes of these eight families. It also mentions that the family of Madyastha had come from outside and that he was originally an Udupa. Since he interfered in the quarrel among the eight families regarding the ownership of the temple, he was named Madyastha and was made to settle in Nīruvāra. However, from the Tamil documents in the Cola country, the impression that we get is that the Madyastha was not an arbitrator, an adjutant but that he was a secretary to the *sabha.*[110] It is possible that in the context of the Tulu country, too, this was the case.

Inscriptional evidence is also available regarding the village Nīruvāra and some of the brahman families mentioned in different versions of *Grāmapaddhati*. An inscription dated A.D. 1464 refers to Yedevettu.[112] Yedabettutāya might have stayed in this place. An inscription belonging to A.D. 1259 refers to the village Nīruvāra.[113] The fact that Nīruvāra was an important brahman settlement is proved by the reference to three hundred *Mahājanas* of Nīruvara in the above inscription. The Mahiśamardhini temple at Nīruvara has yielded six inscriptions. One of them refers to the village assembly called *Jagattu Munnūru.*[114] Another inscription belonging to A.D. 1451 refers to Kalukūra (Kallurāya) in Nīruvara *grāma.*[115] The above references show that Nīruvara was inhabited by several brahman families. At present there are nearly one hundred houses belonging to brahmanas. In Nīruvara there is a place called Bhattra bettu.

The main temple in this area is the Mahiśa Mardhini temple and the deity as known in the inscription is Bhagavati. According to Dr. P. Gururaja Bhat, the image in this temple belongs to circa 10th- 11th century A.D.[116]

15. Sivalli. Known differently as Śivahaḷḷi, Śivaḷḷi, Rajatapīthapura, it is situated in Udupi taluk. This village has a number of archaelogical relies proving the antiquity of human settlement there[117] Śivaḷḷi, which means the village of Siva is regarded as the earliest brahmanical centre in South Kanara.[118] In inscriptions from 7th-8th century onwards we find reference to Śivaḷḷi as an important place of brahmans equivalent to Kasi.[119] The brahmans in this area were patronised by dynasties like the Aḷupas, the Vijayanagara empire and the local Chieftains, the Ballalas and Heggades. It is said that those brahmans who came from Ahicchatra first settled in Śivaḷḷi and they were named Śivaḷḷi Brahmans and after that they migrated and settled in other villages.[120] In ancient times Śivaḷḷi included Sagri, Indrāḷi, Gundibāyalu, Putturu, Perampaḷḷi, Nidumpaḷḷi, Nāyampaḷḷi, Kidiyuru, Paduva Mannūru, Kodavūru, Udyāvara, Korangrapādi, Chittupādi, Bāyalūru and Paniyādi.[121]

GP1 mentions several Brahman families in different localities of śivaḷḷi like Alevoor and Sagri. It also mentions three grades of Brahmans viz.

(i) Brahmans of the highest grade.
(ii) Brahmans of middle grade and
(iii) Brahmans of low grade (they are Brahmans only in name).

The following list of Brahmans can be prepared from GP1.[122]

Highest Grade	Middle Grade	Low Grade
20 houses	36 houses	69 houses
	They have the privilege of only bhojana, i.e. feast and not matrimonial alliances with other families.	They are brahmanas only in name.
Alevooru		
1. Alevoorāya	1. Kramādaritāya	1. Tagināya
2. Kodencha	2. Tenkodināya	2. Mitilāya
3. Manjitāya	3. Katarantāya	3. Kutilāya
4. Saralāya	4. Sitirāya	4. Panañji
5. Kadambalitāya	5. Arolitāya	5. Suṇatāya
6. Madipaḷitāya	6. Kuramballitāya	6. Kalambi
Sagri		
7. Saguriraya	7. Badikillāya	7. Uḷitāya
8. Tenkilāya	8. Kalyanantāya	8. Niñjurāya
9. Kunjittāya	9. Nujitāya	9. Nellitāya
10. Naduvantillāya	10. Koḍabaḷitāya	10. Malyantāya
Other families		
11. Putrāya	11. Poḷitāya	11. Hebbāpa
12. Bāyaritāya	12. Nakarantāya	12. Belapati
13. Kekudenāya	13. Vatināya	13. Belāyarāya
14. Kedilāya	14. Śibarantāya	14. Koṇi

(younger brother of Alevoorāya)		
15. Kodachāya (younger brother of Kodacha)	15. Padillāya	15. Karkāvitāya
16. Kornāya	16. Nedilāya	16. Nalitāya
17. Banninjatāya	17. Kannapināya	17. Durge
18. Maraditāya	18. Mankitāya	18. Vadetāya
19. Śivatāya	19. Kottaladināya	19. Vadi
20. Kunjirāya	20. Kodalāya	20. Ubali
Their duties *(Satkarma)*		
	21. Parkaḷatāya	21. Chakkerāya
	22. Arimettāya	22. Mangalattāya
(i) Yajña	23. Koḷaketāya	23. Voritāya
(ii) Yajana	24. Kokādināya	24. Mandabettāya
(iii) Adhyayana	25. Koḷatenāya	25. Adukattāya
(iv) Adhyapana	26. Manikaḷatāya	26. Kodilāya
(v) Dāna	27. Ankilāya	27. Elekodittāya
(vi) Pratigraha	28. Mūdittāya	28. Kulilāya
They are called	29. Pādittāya	29. Aṇṇappi
śatkarmis.	30. Kotantilāya	30. Gude
	31. Kunhimārgentāya	31. Deyigināya
	32. Kannurāya	32. Kodilāya
	33. Keḷatrāya	33. Kūdantāya
	34. Maṇṇaṇitāya	34. Kūdukarāya
	35. Neyampaḷḷitāya	35. Areye
	36. Pudināya	36. Kudināya
	They are Trikarmis	37. Suriye
	The land given by Lokaditya was not privately was not privately owned by them and had to give tax on the basis of produce of the land.	38. Nūji
		39. Kodañji
		40. Kannapaḷḷi
		41. Dōni

42. Mundādi
43. Mundumale
44. Vutiye
45. Ujire
46. Kokkādi
47. Hebbāra
48. Nakkatte
49. Aane
50. Kaḷali
51. Agaḷi

2. Muke

53. Mijikosi
54. Irutturāya
55. Avuje
56. Maipādi
57. Bēvināya
58. Kōvināya
59. Melādi
60. Kudurāya
61. Kolañji
62. Kalāya
63. Majalāya
64. Todināya
65. Irettāya
66. Peralāya
67. Kabetodi
68. Bēye
69. Mañjittāya family is referred as avantara gratia

GP1 also says that the families mentioned under the category of low grade brahmans are brahmans only in name who are not eligible for even bhojāna, i.e., commensality. Their brahmanhood is limited to the thread they wear. These brahmans were given the lands for cultivation and for maintenance of arecanut plantations and they were expected to pay rent to the king. GP1 gives an explanation regarding these brahmans.[123] Some of them had joined fallen brahmans, some others were brahmans converted from moger caste by Paraśurāma and later they were cursed to become Sudras. These brahmans were not even eligible to eat with other brahmans. They were given lands to conduct agricultural activities.

GP2 gives a long list of brahman families in this *grāma* and their designation.[124]

Agnihotris	**Bhatta**	**Gramani**	**Smartagnihotris**
Alevoorāya	Kārantāya	Nadantillāya	Madhāritāya
Kedilāya	Kojankallāya	sivabeḷḷitāya	Banniratāya
Kalatāya	Korenāya	Ubbeḷḷitāya	Sabhāritāya
(The above three belonged to the same family)	Mardittāya	Kadambaḷitāya	Indrāḷitāya
Nāyabaḷitāya	Kēdebaḷitāya	Koḷakaḷatāya	
Madilakulatāya	Karambaḷitāya	Mankitāya	
Mañjittāya	Perambḷitāya		
Saralāya	Karambaḷḷitāya		
Karambaḷitāya	Bunnārāya		
Sagarritāya			
Tenkillāya			
Kuñjittāya			
Nadyantillāya			
Kekkuṇṇāya			
Bāyarittāya			
Putturāya			
Śivatāya			
Maraditāya			
Koradināya			
Banniñjatāya			
Kunjūrāya			

Other Designations

Janni Tantri	Astanaga brahma Puja Janni	Adhivāsi		Samidā-dhivāsi	Pakśanāthas
Chittilāya	Mundārdīnāya	Poḷināya	Golināya	Mudillāya	Putturāya
Mittilāya	Bandardīnāya	Mūdettāya	Attināya	Nidamburāya	
Nadillāya	Nelārdināya		Arivalitāya		Jalasaritaya
Muditāya	Dandārdināya		Karalattāya		Kadarrinaya

Tenkillāya
Paddillāya
Balikillāya
Kordiyillāya
Kadeyillāya
Yatekillāya
Muchumōdināya
Akkikodināya
Airkordināya
Kabekordināya
Mudukodināya
Tenkodināya
Badakordināya
Padukordināya
Nijakordināya
Mungordināya
Yeakodināya

Kanarādināya
Kadalārdināya
Kekkilārdināya
Koppalārdināya

Kannarapaḷḷitāya
Beḷḷarapādittāya
Kalañjināya
Kodañjiṇāya
Kalyānantāya
Mangalantāya
Nerekarettāya
Kāyaventāya
Achakkenāya
Mandanithāya
Kālayimbittāya
Tonithāya
Maṇoḷittāya
Karkalattāya
Bāṇāsi
Modukottāya
Elekordināya
Hūdukārdināya
Upparāya
Ubarāya
Nitturāya
Kayelkarāya
Bhūjirāya
Kudhurāya
Kūnjurāya
Akkaḷarāya
Arigaḷarāya
Jarkaḷattāya
Maṇbaḷatāya
Sambaratāya
Akkodi Hebbāra
Sūjittāya
Punachalattāya
Kadambettāya
Koḷambkallāya

Amritabalitaya
Arkanaya
Dovettaya
Kkirgalanaya

GP2 aslo mentions some other families without designation. They are Śartikalatāya, Vaidantāya, Agnittāya Melarrittāya Kūdantāya, Darbettāya, Gangettāya, Vadanttāya, Madyattāya,Samidhattāya and Aśwarittāya.

GP3 mention that there were nearly three thousand brahmans in Śivabelli or Rajatapīthapura. The families mentioned are Kodencha,

Madapuli, Mañjita, Saralāya, Kadamba, Kunjattāya, Tenkillāya, Alevūrāya, Naduvantillāya, Nūjittāya, Kramdārittāya, Chittillāya, Karambali, Kalyānantāya, Kornāya, Nekkāra, Padillāya, Nadvillāya, Makkitāya, Śivatāya, Sa Kallembi, Padetāya, Kudalatāya, Ucchittāya, Malādi, Koḷambe kallāya and Uppūra Kodināya.

We have inscriptional reference to some of the brahman families mentioned in *Grāmapadddhati.* As inscription dated a 1437A.D.[125] refers to Śivaḷḷi *grāma. Saguriya adhivāsa* and a brahman called Vaikadimbanhi Nodiya Rama Kuñjatava. It also mentions *Mūdila Nidamburavara grāma.* This shows that during that time Sagri was a part of śivaḷḷi. Mudillāya and Nidamburāya were prominent families in the village. Another inscription dated Śaka year 1356 refers to Banninja adhivāsa.[126] An undated inscription found at Krishna Matha, Udi, refers to brahman families like Kramadārekkaḷa and Śattiakkala. It also mentions Naduvantillāya.[127] Another inscription dated 1395 A.D refers to Śankarānārayana Naduvantila, Kedila, Kannarādita, Kaṇṇara Bāyariñjatava.[128] Anundated inscripton mentions *Nadavantillāya*, Kramadāreyakkaḷa, Kudukārakkaḷa.[129] An inscription found in Sambukallu Bhairava temple, Udyāvara refers to brahman families like Bāhiri, Marināya and Mattināya.[130] Another inscription dated A.D.1402 found in Janārdana temple, Yermal, mentions Nellitāya family.[131] Another inscription dated A.D. 1519 mentions Melādi and Mittānt.[133] Another inscription belonging to A.D.1525 mentions Kodaja and Kodacha.[134] Another inscripton dated A.D. 1436 refers to Kalambe Kunhina and Mittanta. Another inscription dated 1393 A.D. mentions Madikudala and Kalukura.[136] Another inscription found at Maṇipura (Udupi taluk), dated A.D.1407 mentions Mūdila.[137]

Chittupādi during the historical times was an important centre of brahminical activies. An inscription dated A.D. 1486 discovered in Chittupādi bīdu mentions that there lived Mūdila in that house and that they gaue grants to a matha at Chittupādi.[138] Inscriptions found at Mangodu Subrāya temple, Kuttupādi, refers to Pādirāya brahman family and Śivaḷḷi 3000.[139] Another inscriptional evidences prove that Śivaḷḷi consisted of several important brahman families. Among them the Mūdilas of Chittupādi and Nidambūru family at Ambalapādi were the most important.

Not only inscription but also literary texts like *Madhwa Vijaya* refers to different brahman families.[141] Madhwacharya's father was Naduvantillāya or Madhyagehabhatta.[142] It also mentions the places like Neyampaḷḷi or Ghritavaḷḷi, Karevooru *grāma*, Kūdalu, Pādi (Vata),

Kudel, Kodipādi, Idetude (Saridantara), Kokkada, Ujīrya or Ucchabhūti. It nentions the brahman families like Madināya, Ideppādittāya, Udupa or Odipe Parpadāne Kabekode, Mudiltāya, Tōtantillāya, Pejattāya or Likujanvayodbhava, Mudampādittāya, Kudupustūrāya and Moradittāya.

Śivaḷḷi boasted several temples and *nāgabanas*. In Mudu Alevooru we find a Viṣṇumūrthi temple. In this area there lived the families like Alevoorāya, Kedilāya, Mañjittāya, Saraḷāya, Kadambaḷittāya, Punichitāya. Also there were temple servants like Mittillāya, Chittillāya and Yichalattāya.[143] In this temple,we find an inscription which is in a bad state of preservation. On the stone are carved a *linga*, two animals and two *dandadhāris*. Now this temple as managed by Madipalittāya family.[144] In Perampaḷḷi, a part of the present śivaḷḷi village, there existed families like Puḷināya, Nekkāra, Sivattāya. Even today there is a family called Perampaḷḷi Nekkāra. In Keppodu near Śivaḷḷi there is a Subrahmaṇya temple, now in ruin. In Śivaḷḷi we have one Mahalingeśwara temple which consist of *bhattranāga* and devaranāga. In Śivaḷḷi there existed four Durgālayās at Kadiyāli Kannarapādi, Bailūru and Puttūru. There are also four Nagalāyas in Tāṇgodu, Māngodu Aritk Ōudu and Muchilk Ō du or Kappettu.[145]

In Ambalapādi there is the Nidamburāya family who are given the designation *Ballāḷas*. They are also *Pakśanāthas* i.e., those who dispensed of justice for the surrounding villages. There is a tradition that these people were originally Udupas and that they came from Kandāvara and while migratring they brought a Janārdana image which is now found in the Kāli - Janārdana temple at Ambalapādi. The Janārdana temple was built by śrīdhara Nidamburāya in c. 1571 A.D.[146] His name is mentioned in the inscriptions found in the temple. Diwan Pūrnaiah of Mysore in a latter recognised the designation of Nidambūru Ballālas and their function as Pakśanātha for thirty-two agrahāras of South Kanara.[147] There is also a tradition that this *bīdu* belonged to the Jains who gave it to the Udupas who became the Ballālas and since they stayed in Nidambūru they became Nidamburāya. This house enshrines of an image of Bhu Varāha supposed to be given by Vādiraja Swāmi himself.[148]

According to a tradition the Mudilāya family originally came from Nīlāvara from where they came and settled in Herga and from Herga they were invited by the Jaina rulers of Chittupādi called Ballāls who died without inheriters and this brahman family became *Ballālas* and occupied the powers of the earlier rulers. This house is also connected the powers of the earlier rulers. This house is also connected with Madhwachara who is said to have visited this house and the milk to Madhwacharya was sent from this house.[149] On the area of six acres around Chittupādi bīdu we find signs of fortification.[150] On other side of fortification we find a bhūtasthana of Rakteswari. In an inscription found in this place we find the representation of Mahavira. it indicates that the inscription may belong to Jaina chieftains. It is posible to infer that the Chittupādi *bīdu* was initially under the Jainas and later it was transferred to the brahman control.[151] In Udupi there is a family of Amritāya.[152] There is a Maraditāva family in Udupi.[153] In a place called Saraḷabettu there lived Saraḷāyas.

Here we can give a list of some temples found in Śivaḷḷi.

1. Anatheśwara—8th century A.D.[154]
2. Chandramouliśwara—10th century A.D.[155]
3. Kriśṇa temple.
4. Asta muttas (i) Pejavar (ii) Palimar (iii) Sode (iv) Kaniyur (v) Puttige (vi) Adamar (vi) Krisnapur (vii) Sirur.
5. Kāli - Janārdana- Ambalapādi.
6. Mūdu Alevooru Visnūmurthi temple.
7. Mahalingesvara temple, Śivaḷḷi.
8. Puttur Durga Paramśwari temple.
9. Kemthur Viśnumūrthi temple.
10. Kakkuñje Janārdana temple.

According to Dr. P. Gururaja Bhat, "The image of Janārdana from the Vishnumūrti temple, Kakkunje, Śivaḷḷi may be regarded as one of the earliest of its kind in Karnataka. The presence of this icon in Śivaḷḷi could suggest the first settlement of Brahmins in this area.[156] There existed brahman settlements around the temples and the temples constituted an important part of *agrahāras*. Even today we notice the existence of brahman population around Kāḷi- Janārdana temple. Ambalapādi, Udupi.

16. **Nīrumārga**: Nīrumārga is in Mangalore taluk. According to Ganapati Rao Aigal, there were Ballals in Nīrumārga and the Nīrumārga Subrava temple was a *sīme* temple.[157]

GP1 mentions that Nīrumārga village counsisted of Icaluttāya, Anantōdittāya, Aalampādittāya, Taraḷāya, Māvarāya, Kumāranttāya.[158]

GP2 mentions Indravaḷittāya as *agnihøtri*, Aasurāya as smārtāgnihørti Kambaraṇṇāya and Kannaraṇṇāya as *bhattas*, Toyakodanāya as grāmani, Irvatturāya and Kaṇṇarāya as *Jannis*, Ametturditāya and Karnamangilattāya as *adhivāsis*.[159] GP3 mentions Jaruyippalattāya. Anantødittāya, Nurittāya, Pāditāya, Kallurāya, Mādarāya and Kumattāya.[160]

Nirumarga Subrāya temple was a *sīme* temple which means it was an important temple for the surrounding villages. At present this temple is in a condition of ruins. It is said that around the temple there are *nāgabanas* indicating that it was an area of antiquity.

In Nīrumarāga we find even today the existence of brahman families like Kamtaraṇṇāya and Kaṇṇaraṇṇāya which are mentioned in GP2. The place where the Kambaraṇṇāya family is living is called *Bhattarakødi* which indicates that this area during the earlier times was inhabited by brahmans. The house of Kaṇṇaraṇṇāya familiy is known as Bolamāgattu where we find the existences of Jārantāya daiva. There is a tradition that this house originally belonged to the Jains and these Jains suffered from leprosy disease which was cured by the brahmans who were rewarded with this house. The Kaṇṇaraṇṇāyas are expected to perform the ritual relating to Jārantaya daiva. The Jārantaya paddana mentions Nīrumarga.[161]

Thus we find the existence of two important brahman families in Nīrumārga. The Iravatturāyas claim origin from Nīrumārga village.[162] Indravaḷittāya might have come from Indrāḷi, a place in Udupi. This place also received royal patronage, this is proved by the existence of two inscriptions in Subrāya temple.

Eastern gramas

1. Sripadi

Sripadi is in Bantwal taluk. Now it is know as Ajjibettu. During historical times it included Ajjibettu and Punjalkatte. Sripadi is in between Veṇur and Kāriñja, where we find the Mahallingeśvare temple respectively.

GP1 mentions Kunhyamaṇṇāya, Vaipāddittāya, Atrādittāya and Putraṇṇāya.[163] GP2 mentions Baipadittāya as *bhatta*, Pāngāṇṇāya as Tantri, Kunhimaṇṇāya and Kavudampādittāya as *Ballāḷas*, Atrādittāya as *grāmani* and śripādittāya as *Janni.*[164] GP3 mentions all the families mentioned in GP2.[165]

Manchi Narāyana Acharya has published a book, *Baipādittāya* in 1964. He has identified all the brahman families mentioned in GP2.[166] There is a tradition that Kavudampādittāya became *Ballalas* after they received land from Jains. Kunhimaṇṇāyas are now known as Kunhaṇṇāya and they are the Pavitrapāṇi for all the temples in śripādi, Regarding the Pāngāṇṇāya there is a tradition that they came from Pāngāḷa near Udupi. In a document dated C. 1800 A.D.[167] We find reference to Pāngaṇṇāya in śripādi•. The Pāngaṇṇāyas are attached to Nadvantādi *matha*. They are expected to give one *mude* rice to Sode mutt to meet the expenses. In the earlier time Atradittāya lived in śripādi.

Now this family is extinct. It is also said that Atradittāya went to Badakkila and they became Badekellāya.[168] Each of these five brahman families own viṣṇumūrthi temple. Pūnja temple belong to the village. There is a belief that this temple was built by Kadamba Mayuravama himself. This temple has authority oṇ villages like Ajjibettu, Iravathur, Mūdupadukodi, Chenāyitōdi, Piliomagru and pilathalabettu. This temple has sixteen pillars. The *bhūta* worshipped here is Kodamaṇittāya.

2. Vodila

Vodila is in Belthanagadi taluk. According to Ganapathi Rao Aigal Vodila was under the rule of Kaḷiya Ballāḷa.[169] There is a *bhūta* connected with this village namely, Vodiḷtāya.[170] GP1 mentions Aḷumaṇṇāya as *bhatta*, Kadamaṇṇāya as *grāmani*. Punachādittāya as *Janni* and Vardimādināya as *adhivāsi*.[172] GP3 mentions Thimpodittāya and Ambalaṇṇāya.

At present we see two families here (i) Kermuṇṇāya (ii). Ammuṇṇāya. The Kermuṇṇāyas own a temple at Padangadi called Vodil temple with its deity Iśvara, This family subscribes to Subrahmanya mutt. The *bhūta* worshipped here is Maddadka *daiva*. At Rama Kermuṇṇāyas house as inscription is seen which is in old Kannada script. On the two side of the inscription we find the figures of Ivara *linga*.[174] It is believed that nearly four hundred years earlier Ammuṇṇāyas were engaged in *narabali* (human sacrifice) which was stopped by Kermuṇṇāyas and they gave land to Ammuṇṇāya as compensation. At Vodil if the Ammuṇṇāyas committed any mistake, they can be questioned only by brahmans of śripādi and not others. At Vodil Yelchilatāya was *grāmani*.[175] Ammuṇṇāyas belong to Sode mutt. In reality have has no right to wear *mudra* (a Madhwa symbol) and this they have accumulated by pauing money to the mutts. In olden time there existed connections among Vodila Nāḷa, Melantabettu and Kárandurāu.

3. Nāla

This village is in Belthangadi taluk. In historical times it was under the control of Kaḷiya Ballālas.[176]

GP1 mentions Madipaditāya and Parvantāya.[177] GP2 mentions Padanttāya as *bhatta*, Mālepāditāya as *grāmani* and Nālatāya as *Janni*.[178] GP3 mentions Vadakilāya family only.[179]

The main temple here is dedicated to Durga Parameśwari. Within the temple we find a Nāgāyaksi image, with seven arms. Outside the temple there is a tree which, according to the local people, produces flower in all 365 days of the year. The temple has connections with Baḷḷamañma. Out-side the temple we see a liṅga. In this village we find a *bhūtasthāna* in Sampigetāya house. The Sampagettāyas originally belonged to Kārnduru. Here we find another family of Bānginnāyas who came from Subrahmaṇya. Earlier Sampigetāyas were looking after administrations of Durga Parameśwari temple and later on it was transferred to Baṅginnāyas. The Padaṅtāya family mentioned in GP2 have settled in Sambaḷe a nearby place. The *bhūta sthāna* here is Pilichāmundi.

4. Kareya

Now known as Karāya it is situated in Belthangadi taluk, three kilo metres away from Uppinaṅgadi. Kareya was under the rule of Bandādi ballāḷas.[180]

GP1 does not mention Kareya. GP2 mentions Puttannāya as agnihotri, Pāvināya and Vaṅgangināya as *bhattas*, Ambalavāya and Kuppaṇṇāya as *Aṇṇagrāmaṇi*, Kareyatāya and Alamunditāya as *Jannis* and Kuḷitāya as *adhivāsi.*[181] GP3 does not mention Kareya.

It is believed that in the earlier times the area around Guruvāyanakere was known for Virasaiva settlement.[182] There is a Virasaiva temple at a nearby place celled Girigudde. The name Karāya is supposed to be derived from Kharāsura. The main temple here is Mahālingeśvara temple. The temple is on the Netrāvati. The *bhūtas* within the area of the temple are Raktēśvari, Kallurti, Kalkuda and Cāmundi. The temple is surrounded by the houses of Śivaḷḷi brahman families like Kuddaṇṇāya, Vailāya, Kedilaya and Nurittāya. None of these corresponds to the list given in GP2. This is significant. GP1 and GP3 does not mention this as one of the thirty-two settlements. It is GP2 which does it, and the details given there are not borne out by the survivals.

The main goddess of the Vailāyas is Durga Parameswari. It is said that this image of Durga Parameśwari they brought from Kollur and since it is representation of Koḷḷuru Mukambika they are not allowed to go to Koḷḷuru.[183]

In this area there are totally three Viṣṇumurthi temples. They are at Pacchangri, Kolepādi and Kudlamāpadi. The temple at Pacchangri is in ruins and is now surrounded by bushes and trees. Only the face of Viṣṇumurthi is seen, other parts of it being lost. The base of the temple is intact and it gives evidence of the structure and plan of the temple.

Here we find the brahman families like Paduvaṇṇāya Pāngaṇṇāya Kuddaṇṇāya, Kedilāya, Vailāya, Nūritāya and Kaḷḷurāya, Kuddaṇṇāyas were the hereditary Patels of the village and it is claimed that they were living in this village at least from 16th-17th century.[184] In this region we also find Vāngināya and Ambaṇṇāya. In historical times this must have been a flourishing brahman settlement.

5. Ujire

This village is in Belthangadi taluk. In *Madhwa Vijaya*, Ujire is refered as Ujirya.[185] In the inscription dated 1469 A.D. it is mentioned as Ujire.[186]

GP1 mentions Aramanettāya, Vappantāya, Kokraḷittāya. Aripādittāya, Mundapādittāya, Kemmundāya, Arbatāya and Bellaṇṇāya.[187] GP2 mentions Mudampāditāya as smārtāgnihōtri, Kokranāya and Bellaṇṇāya as bhattas, Vappantāya as Pandita, Arimanettāya as grāmani, Aripādittāya and Kemmuṅdetāya as *Jannis*, Ujirenāya and Arbitāya as adhivāsis Mundapāditaya and Tudenāya as adivamsis.[188] GP3 mentions Vappaṅtāya, Araḷittāya, Aripādittāya, Medambalittāya Mudampādittāya Kemmundāya, Arbitāya and Bellaṇṇāya.[189]

The original place of Kakrannāya may be Kakke. They came and settled in Kuduma and they became Kudumattāya, At present we see Karraṇṇāyas in Bandāru near Karāya.[190] The Aramanettāya family had the right to worship in Anathaśayanā. Trivandrum. In Ujire at present we find Bolamiṇṇāya, Aripādittāya and Kemmundetāya. There are two families called Mudaṇṇāya and Paduvannāya and these two families are considered as branches of Aramanettāya.[191] There is a family of Arimanettāya in Punjalakatte, Bantwal taluk. Ujire is very near to Dharmashthala, a place of religious significance. The Kaifiyats, the record of village kept by the Sanbhogs of the villages, give a list of traditional lagends regarding Kuduma.[192] At present there are several Śivaḷḷi brahman families in Dharmasthala.

6. Karanduru

It is in Belthangadi taluk. It is approximately eight kilometres away from Guruvāyanakere.

GP1 mentions Sampagetāya and Yadakelatāya.[193] GP2 mentions Sampagetāya as bhatta and Ponnetāya as grāmani.[194] GP3 mentions Sampigetāya.[195]

The deity here is Annapūrneśwari which has connections with the family of Sampagetāya. Another temple is Viṣṇumūrthi temple which belongs to Sampigetāya who have connections with Kāraṅduru Nāga brahma temple which is managed by Muchchinnāyas. The *bhūtas* worshipped here are Mujinnāya and Kodamaṇittāya. At Kandige Janārdana temple Nūrittāyas perform pūja. The central shrine of Kāranduru Viṣṇumurthi temple is circular which is not very usual regarding the temples of South Kanara. This may suggest its antiquity.

Near the Viṣṇumūrthi temple inscriptions are found which was noticed recently by Archaeological Survey of India, Mysore and they have taken the copies of the inscription. Its detail reveal that this area was under the control of Ajilas.[196] It is said that Sampagetāya family was protected by Mucchinnāyas.[197]

7. Kāvaḷa

It is near present Kāriñja, Bantwal taluk. According to Ganapati Rao Aigal, Kavala was under the rule of Ijjetottu Ballāḷa.[198]

GP1 does not mention Kāvaḷa village. GP2 mentions Narisyanāya as Smārtāgnihōtri, Peradatāya as bhatta, Ichalatāya as grāmani, Yerachalatāya and Kumārantāya as *Jannis* and Kunhimagalintāya and Kāriñjatāya as adhivāsis.[199] GP3 does not mention Kāvala.

At Kārinjeśvara temple Peradatāyas are Pavitrapāṇi and they manage the affairs of the temple. The places in Kāvaḷa are Kāvaḷa Mūduru, Kāvaḷa, Padūru, Dēvasya Mūduru and Dēvasya Padūru. There is a tradition that in earlier period there was a Iśvara temple here and later Madhwacharya came and established Mahiśasura Mardhini temple. The Kārinjeśvara temple is mentioned in the inscriptions and they refer to the land grants to Kārinjeśvara.[200] This temple has also the structure of a fort and there is the possibility that it was used as a hiding place for the local chieftains against their enemies. It is said there is a description of Kārinjeśvara temple in Skands Purāna. In the earlier times there were two thirty-two villages, mentioned in GP1 and GP3 Kāvaḷa does not figure. Only GP2 mentions this village and here we find the family of Peradatāya who have continued the traditions.

Earlier there existed the family of Alampurittāya, who are now extinct, the families like Peradatāya, Muchchinnāya and Yelachittāya were considered as *grāmaṇis.* They still live in Kāvala. The families which migrated to this village are Śibarūrāya, Kekuṇṇāya, Baipādittāya, Nadvantillāya, Latturāya and Kermunnāya. The *bhūta* worshipped here is Kodamaṇittāya Rājandaiva.

8. Kunhimarga

At present in South Kanara there is no village called Kunhimārga. It is possible that it has changed its name beyond recognition in the course of time due to various reasons. We can, however, suppose that there existed a village called Kunhimārga because *Grāmapaddhati* mentions Kunhimārgantāya and it is known to us that some of the Śivaḷḷi brahman family names represent the places, e.g.

Alevoorāya = one who belonged to Aḷevooru.

Madyarāya = one who belonged to Madyar.

GP2 mentions Kakraṇṇāya and Koraṅgināya in Kunhimarga. These two families are found settled in a village called Kurāya -Bandāru which is very near to Karāya. GP1 and GP3 does not mention Kareya and only GP2 mentions Kareya. It is possible that during the time of composition of GP2 Kareya and Kunhimārga were two separate villages since both are mentioned there. Since the families mentioned in GP2 as living in Kunhimarga still live in Kurāya-Bandaru and during the period of GP1 and GP3 only Kunhimārga was known, it may be that Kunhimārga as a village is extinct and that those who belonged to it live in Kurāya - Bandāru today.[201]

Thus it may be suggested that the earlier Kunhimārga was Bandāru and that during that time Kāvaḷa, Kārandūru, Śripādi, Kareya, Kunhimārga, Vodila, Nāla and Ujire constituted a group of villages where the brahmans settled. These villages maintained mutual connections.

GP1 mentions Peralattāya and Kunhimargeṅtāya which are stated as doubtful. Other families mentioned are Peraditāya, Uparaṇṇāya. Ichalattāya, Itantāya Madavināya, Kaduṇṇāya, Putayattāya, Kodangināya and Kakaraṇṇāya.[202] GP2 mentions Koraṅgināya as *bhatta* and Kakraṇṇāya as *grāmani.*[203] GP3 mentions all the families mentioned in GP1.[204] In Kurāya-Bandāru, Belthangadi taluk we find only Korangināya and Kakraṇṇāya. The Bandāru Viṣṇumūrthi temple is under the control of Kakraṇṇāyas. Koraṇginnāyas they have the designation patela. This shows that they were handmen of village. The Kuddaṇṇāya family is in Karāya.

9. Kokkada

Kokkada is near Uppinangadi. The name of the village is rendered in Sanskrit Kukkutapura.[205] Since it is situated on an elevated area it was called Kokkada. It is said that Madhwacharya visited this place.[206] In the earlier times Kokkada was ruled by Bailangadi Mūlas.[207]

GP1 mentions Todilāya, Śabarāya, Yadapādittāya and Uparannāya.[208] GP2 mentions Uparannāya *smārtagnihōtri* Bāḷetilāya and Toditilāya as *bhatta*, śabarāya as *sabhāpati* Yedepādittāya as *grāmani*, Bānillāya, Pānillāya and Uriyāḷitāya as *Jannis* and Kokkadināya as addhivamśi.[209] GP3 mentions Kakkakōdillāya, Śabarāya, Yedepādittāya and Uparaṇṇa.

This village consists of Viṣṇumurthi temple, Vaidyanatha temple and Nīlakantha temple. Vaidyanātha temple is dated as belonging to 10th century A.D.[211] It is said that before the arrival of Madhwacharya there existed Divakara *muni* who later became famous as Lilasuka. He went to Anantapur temple, Trivandrum and after his death his descendents, Tulu brahmans from Kokkada, were requested to come to Trivandrum for worship.[212] Even today we find several śivaṇṇi brahman families in Anantaśāyna temple Trivandrum, Keralạ state.

The Bānillāyas are now called Bāltillāyas and now they live in Uppāru and Koṅdadka. The Yedapādittāya family still lives in kokkada. The śabarāya family is in Nelyādi a place near Kokkada, Uparaṇṇa are in Aaladka. Toditillāya are in Belaḷu. Some of these brahman families have migrated to Trivandrum.

We find Uparaṇṇa family in Anantaśayana temple, Trivandrum. They have their properties in Kokkada. At present there is also the family of Punchittāya in Kokkada. We also find the existence of other families like Jogittāya, Parvattāya, Kedilāya, Yedapāditāya in villages in the neighbourhood of Kokkada. These details show that Kokkada was an important brahman settlement and that it had connections with Kerala. These was also a practice of Śivaḷḷi brahmans going to Kerala seeking emploment as priests in temples. They were know as *Pottis* of *Embrantiris*. Some would return after some time. But some of them have adopted Kerala as their permanent place. Thus there was the migration of the brahmans both within South Kanara and also outside South Kanara.

10. Rāmañjūra

Rāmañjūra or Ramiñja is presently known as Ramakuñja and it is situated near Uppinangadi. It is said that the place where Rama worshipped came to be called Rāmakuñja. Rāmakuñja was under the rule of Neranki Chāvadi Heggade.[213]

GP1 mentions Nūjittāya, Matatāya and Munonurāya.[214] GP2 mentions Nūritāya as *agnihōtri*, Peralatāya as smartagnihōtri, Paddalatāya as *bhatta*, Teṅgināya as *grāmaṇi* Ambaṇṇāya and Samparaṇṇāya.

The Nūrittāya family is still living in a place called Neranki. In Neranki we find a mutt which is supposed to have been visited by Madhwacharya. During that time it was known a Saridantara *Kṣetra*. Now there is a family by name Paddillāya in Rāmakunja.[217] This area has an Iśvara temple. Near Neranki mutt thirty-four *nāga* images were found buried in the earth. There is a Kesava Lakśmi image cast in an alloy of five metals. Even now this area is known for the brahman settlements.

11. Pude

It is in Sullya taluk: GP1 mentions Pudenāya.[218] GP2 mentions Mattitillāya as agnihōtri, Kanerāditāya as *smarta*: Kannaṅgaḷatāya as *bhatta*, Nidvannāya and Mūduvaṇṇāya as *Aṇṇagrāmaṇis*, *Pudenaya* and Pudikaḷatāya as *Sāha-Jannis* and Kajenāya as *Janni.*[219] GP3 mentions

Anantōditāya, Peraḷatāya, Pudenāya and yilladitāya.[220]

The one family mentioned commonly in all the above versions, Pudenāya is still living in Pude, which is now a part of Muruḷya village, Suḷḷya taluk. We find that Mudavaṇṇāyas are living in Ujire. In a place called Poliṅkaje there existed the family of Pudenāyas. The Pudenāyas of Pude own a small temple which has a *Nāga bana*, a *nāga Kannike* and bhūtas like Camuṅdi and śirādi. There is also a piecs of land for *bhūta* called *bhūtabana*.

In a nearby place called Pirlampādi there exists the family of Nidvaṇṇāya. The other families found in the surrounding areas are Murdittāya and Muchintāya. Near Murulayā there existed a *matha*. It is also said that the Pude temple, Kerpata Durga parameśvari temple and Edamangala temple were managed by Pudenāyas. There is a place called Pudennāya *Katte*. All these details show that Pudennāyas played an important role in Pude and also the surrounding Villages.

12. Baḷapa

Also known as Beḷapadi, Baḷapa is in Suḷḷya taluk. According to Ganapati Rao Aigal, in the earlier times Baḷapa was under the rule of Mardāḷa Ballāla.[221] We also find the evidences of the rule of Hoysala, Vijāyanagara and Ikkeri kingdoms.

GP1 mentions Bāritāya, Ummaraṇṇāya and Ammani. The last one is stated as doubtful.[222] GP2 mentions Bāritāya as agnihōtri, Timbraṇṇāya and Mittāditāya as *Jannis*, Yibbāditāya and Balapatāya as *adhivāsis*.[223] GP3 also mentions Ammanatāya as doubtful. It mentions Bāyaritāya and Ummaṇitāya.

In Balpa we find three important temples.

(i) Śulini Durga Parameśvari temple.
(ii) Vanadurge temple.
(iii) Viṣṇumūrthi temple.

The first one is a very old structure and it is built wholly of granite. Stangely here the well is in front of the entrance. This temple, is regarded as *grāma devashtāna* and it may belong to the Hoysala period.[225] It consists of different sculptures. One of them can be identified as of a Muslim, Perhaps a Turk.[226] Close to it we find the renovations which took place under the Vijāyanagara rulers and this structure contains no sculpture. It is said that at the inner portion previously there existed a well. But a *Sumangali* (a lady whose husband is alive) was killed and thrown to that well. which was closed and a new well was dug at the outer portion. There is also a story of a brahman being killed who became *Brahmarāksasa*.[227]

In this area two inscriptions have been found, one at Vanadurga temple and the other in a field which is the property of Bidigudde Doddamane Dasappa.[228] They seem to belong to Vijāyanagar and Keladi period.

An inscription dated A.D. 1562 found in a place called Arigudi near Balpa, registers the gift of village Balpa by Sadasivarāya Nāyaka of Kaladi for offerings and lamp in the temple of Subrahamaṇyadeva at Kukke.[229] Buring that time Kukke was under the authorities in Kukke might have sent the Sthanika brahmanas to Balpa to manage the affairs there. The Sulini temple is now under the management of Sthanikas. Here is Balpa we find the Sthānika Moraja family.

The Śivaḷḷi brahman families found here are Ammṇṇāya Kaḷḷurāya and Yādapādittāya. Here we also find Yajña Mūrthy mutt which has Yajñanarasimha image. Originally this mutt belonged to Yedepādittāya. The family deity of Ammaṇṇāyas is Sulini.Kunjattāyas were at a place called Kuñjattādi. At present Bāritāyas are in Karāya.

13. Idekidu

At present it is called Idkidu and it is situated in Bantwal taluk.

GP1 mentions Manikaḷattāya and Śadagattāya.[231] GP2 mentions Śadaṅga as *smārtaganihōtri*, Keletāya and Devaṅgināya as bhattas, Anantōdināya as *grāmani*. Berkaḷatāya and Puṇyakaḷatāya as *Jannis*, Barikaḷatāya and Yidekedanāya as *adhivāsi*.[232] GP3 mentions only Maṇikaḷattāya.[233]

At present this village is known for Havyak brahman settlements. According to local people nearly hundred years earlier there existed Śivaḷḷi brahman families like śadaṅga[234] and Keḷetāya. The *grāma devasthāna* here is sanmukha temple.

14. Parinja

The different versions of *Grāmapaddhati* have called it differently as Pāuinja Pādinja and Pāliñja. Now this place is known a Aṅgiñje and it is situated in Putturu taluk.

GP1 mentions Edabettunāya.[235] GP2 mentions Yirekadatāya as smārtagnihōtri, Madukatatāya as *bhatta*, Kūdantāya as *grāmani*, Pannipettāya as *Janni*, śiriyādittāya and Pariñjanāya as adhivāsis. GP3 mention Yedebettunāya.[237]

Most of these families are not to be seen in Pālinja. Perhaps they have migrated. But there we find other Śivaḷḷi familles like Aṅgintāya, Nakṣatrintāya Madikullāya Sagrittāya Putturāya and Kaṇṇarāya. Now this village is a part of Kuriya *grāma*. In a title deed which dates back atleast fifty years it is referred to as Pāviñja. Here we find a Vishumūrthi temple.

15. Kemmiñje

Kemmiñje is in Putturu taluk.

GP1 mentions Bajatāya.[239] GP2 mentions Bajatāya and Sevyakalatāya.[240] GP3 mentions Bajetāya.[241]

The main temple here is the śaṇmukha temple. Earlier there existed the Viṣṇumūrthi image under Pejettāya and when their family got destroyed the temple came under the control of Madamabaḷḷitāyas whose family deity was Subrahmanya and it replaced Viṣṇumūrthi.

The families seen here are Pejettāya, Modambaḷḷitāya and the Kemminje Tantri family. When Netrattāyas of Varkādi has no inheritors they adopted Perruvaṇṇāyas who settled in Kemmiñje. They are also known as Uppaḷa Tantris. The antiquity of this family is supported by the possession of a copy of *Grāmapaddhiti* by this family. The *bhūtas* here worshipped are Siradi and Raktesvari.

16. Ayirnādu

Now it is called Aivarnādu and it is situated in Suḷḷya taluk.

GP1 calls it Irnādu and mentions Takarannāya Mundapadittāya, śabarāya and Uḷapādittāya.[243] GP2 mentions Suryappināya as *srouta*, Modillāya as *paksanatha* Yillarditāya as *bhatta*, Manikalattāya as *grāmani*, Punnārāya as *janni* and Panditakuṇṇāya as adivāsi.243 GP3 mentions all the families mentioned in GP1.[245]

The Modillāya family found in GP1 is now found in Chittupādi, Udupi, This shows that a branch of Mudilāyas had Migrated and settled in Aivarnādu. Here we find Panchalingeśvara temple. There is a story that it was built by the Pandavas. It is believed that it got the name Aivarnādu, the land of five people, since the Pandavas stayed here. Attached to the temple there is a *Nāgābana*. However, in this village we do not find any of the brahman families mentioned in *Grāmapaddhati*.

Identification of Villages

On the basis of continuing place names and living tradition	On the basis of the identity of brahman houses mentioned and their local exitence	the basis of presence in Epigraphy
Ayirnādu	Kunnhimārga	Śivaḷḷi
Vodila	Karavooru	(SII,VII, No. 284)
Kereya		Brahmāvara

Kāranduru	SII,VII. No. 385
Pude	Nīruvāra (*ibid)*
Kokkada	Kota (*ibid*)
kāvaḷa	Kandāvara
Rāmañjūra	(Inscription
Idekkidu	discovered in the
	place, unpublished)
Pāliñja	Ujire (*ARSIE*
	No. 482)
Kemmiñje	
Varkādi	Baḷapa
	(*ARSIE*, 1930-31
	No. 348)
Kolavinādy	Mogarālu
	(K.V. Ramesh in
	Tuluva, 1980)
Pādi	
Mittanādu	śimantūru
	(K.G. Vasantha
	Madhava)
Tenakala	
Kudalu	
Nīrumārga	
Śripadi	

The above exercise, undertaken with a view to establishing the identity of the village, shows the antiquity of their historical tradition. In these villages we find two strong traditions. One is the Paraśurāma tradition and the other is the Madhva tradition. During the thirteenth century we find the emergence of Madhwacharya. Narāyana Panditacharya's Sumadhwa *Vijāya*[246] speaks about the intllectual campaigns by Madhwacharya. Most of the people who came into contact with him were won over. The details in *Sumadhwa Vijāya* makes it clear that the Śivaḷḷi brahmans had settled not only in Śivaḷḷi but also in a far away place like Kudalu, now in Kerala state. *Sumadhwa Vijāya* speaks about the arrival of Madhwacharya in places like Kokkada, Rāmakuñja, Padi, Kūdalu, Ujire and Kodipādi. There was extension of brahmana settlement along with despried of Madhwa Philosophy. We also find that during the Madhwa and post Madhava period Śivaḷḷi, Kota, Brahmāvara, Nīruvāra and Kandāvara emerged as the most prominent brahman settlements. It is in these places that we find maximum inscriptional evidence regarding patronage by Vijāyanagara kings to the brahmanas on the west coast. It was also during this time that we find the standardisation of the text of *Grāmapaddhati* because the earliest date that can be given to *grāmapaddhati* is later half of 14th century A.D.[247] Thus there was the philosophical movement on the one hand and political patronage on the other which gave an opportunity for the brahmans to consolidate their position in the society by way of preserving the records of brahman families in the form of a literary text. *Grāmanpaddhati* was also used to record the migration of the brahman families which is clear from an analysis of different versions of *Grāmapaddhati*.

Another story popular among the brahmans is to claim that the temples were built by Kadamba Mayūra Varma. It is very significant that the Alupas who ruled in this area for nearly fourteen centuries are not remembered and that instead we find the connections with the Kadambas. We find inscriptional references to Kadambas. An inscription belonging to A.D. 1390[248] found in Tiruvailu, Mangalore taluk, records the *sarvamanya* gift of land by Padmaladevi, daughter of Kamadevarasa of the Mukkaṇṇa Kadamba vamsa. The management of the gift was left in hereditary charge of three members of Bhattittila family. This inscripton belongs to the Vijāyanagara period.

The Paraśurāma tradition is also popular in South Kanara. In Sīmanturu the Aadijanārdana image is believed to be installed by Paraśurāma himself. In Pavinje, Mangalore taluk there is a cave like structure which is claimed to be a place where Bhargava used to meditate. But according to Dr. B. Vasanth Shetty this is a megalithic. In these rural area even the non-brahman community is aware of Prarāsurām *Kestra* which is found even in the Paddanas.

In fact the tradition of Parasurama creating land and donating it to brahmans is not found exclusively in South Kanara. It is seen in Gujarat, Maharatra, Goa, North Kanara, South Kanara and Kerala. In other words, this is a tradition which is common to the entire western coast of the peninsula. The historicity of the tradition which dates from different periods in different regions, lies in the fact that it links all those regions in the matter of brahmanical migrations and settlement. Therefore the participation by South Kanara in this tradition would mean that South Kanara too formed a part of long chain of migration where the migration of a legend suggests the posibility of physsical migration of groups who cherished that legend, viz. brahmanical groups. The function of the Mayura Varma tradition is similar, too with the only difference that the area gets limited to the coastal districts of Karnataka.[250]

Table - I

Identification of Villages and their Continuing Traditions

Details of grāma in Grāmapaddhati	*Location of villages*	*Temples*	*Inscriptions*	*Survivals*	*Remarks*
(1)	*(2)*	*(3)*	*(4)*	*(5)*	*(6)*
A. Western Grāmas:					
1. Kandāvara GP1-Kundapura GP2-Kandapura GP3-Skandapura	Kundapura taluk	Uḷḷūru Sbrahmaṇyeśwara; Janārdana	Six unpublished inscriptions discovered	Brahman families of Udupas and Hebbāras, Place of Kandavara brahmans	Still a flourishing brahman settlement.
2. Kōta GP1-Kōta GP2-Gajatti grama GP3-Kōta	Udupi taluk	Narasimha: Hande *dēvalya;* Viṣṇumurthi; Siva temples.	Published inscriptions in Vol VII and Vol. IX, Pt.II.	All the families mentioned still continue tradition, Place of Kōta brahmanas.	Still a flourishing brahman settlement.
3. Brahmāvara GP1-Brahmapura GP2-Brahmavara GP3-Brahmapura	Udupi taluk	Mahaliṅgeśvara; Agrahāra temple	Published inscriptions, B. Vasanth Shetty *Brahmāvarada Itihāsa.*	Varamballi family still exists.	Brahmapura means brahman settlement. It is a flourishing brahman settlement.
4. Varkādi GP1-Varkāḍi GP2-Varkāḍi GP3-Varkāḍi	Kasargod taluk	Kavu Subrahmanyeswara temple	Two inscriptions discovered	Families like Taletāya, Arināya, Peruvannaya, Kārāya.	It has very fertile landscape.

Contd.

Contd.

	(1)	(2)	(3)	(4)	(5)	(6)......
5.	Karavūr GP1-Karavūr GP2-Karavūr GP3-Karavūr	Mangalore taluk	Mañjanādi Viṣṇumūrthi; Janārdana temples, Talapādi Durga Parameśvari temple.	-	Ucchiltāya, Munnurāya continues tradition	At present this village does not exist.
6.	Pādi GP1-Padi Mogara GP2-Padi GP3-Padi	Kasaragod taluk	Mahāviṣṇu; Siva temples	-	Kamatātāya family in Bārikkādi	-
7.	Mogrāl GP1-Mogebaila GP2-Mogrāla GP3-Moganadu	Kasaragod taluk	Śankara Nara- -yana temple	-	Families do not continue today but found elsewhere.	Brahman settlement extinct.
8.	Kūdalu GP1-Kūdalu GP2-Kūdalu GP3-Kudila	Kasaragod taluk	Viṣṇumūrthi; Mahiṣa Mardini; Siva temples	-	Pejattāyas, perpetual lamp	Continuation of tradition.
9.	Mittanādu GP1-Mittanādu GP2-Mittanadi GP3-Mittanādu	Kasaragod taluk	Pārvati Īśvara; Durga Paramēśvari; Mahiṣa Mardini: Visnumūrthi	-	No survivals of families	Brahman settlem- become extinct.

Contd.

Contd.

	(1)	(2)	(3)	(4)	(5)	(6)
10.	Tenakaḷa GP1-Tenakaḷa GP2-Kenakala GP3-Kenakala	Talekaḷa, Kasaragod taluk	Gopala Krişṇa temple	Two unpublished inscriptions discovered	No survivals of families	Settlement inhabited by other families.
11.	Simantūru GP1-Simantūru GP2-Simantūru GP3-Simantūru	Mangalore taluk	Janārdana	Two inscriptions (K.G. Vasantha Madhava)	Existence of Simantūrāya, Śabarāya	Continuing tradition
12.	Maraṇe GP1-Maraṇe GP2-Maraṇe GP3-Maraṇe	-	Unidentified	-	-	-
13.	Koḷavinādu GP1-Kolyanadu GP2-Koḷavinādu GP3-Koḷavinādu	Bantwal taluk	Gopala Krişṇa; Vişṇumūrthi	-	Continuation of Placenames connected with brahman family names.	Migration of brahmans.
14.	Nilāvara GP1-Nirvara GP2-Nilāvara GP3-Nilāvara	Udupi taluk	Mahiṣa Mardini temple	Six published inscriptions in the temple	earlier tradition Bhattara bettu	Settlement Survives.
15.	Śivaḷḷi GP1-Śivabeḷḷi Rajatapitha GP2-Śivaḷḷi	Udupi taluk	Anantēśvara; Chandramaul Iśvara; Krişṇa; Janārdana;	Many inscriptions (SII, VII, IX, pt. II).	Some families identified and still maintain tradition	A flourishing brahman settlement.

Contd.

Contd.

(1)	(2)	(3)	(4)	(5)	(6)
Rajatapītàh GP3-Śivabeḷḷi Rajatapitha		Mahalingelśvara: Viṣṇumūrthi.			
16. Nirumārga GP1- GP2- GP3-	Mangalore taluk	Subrāya temple	Two inscriptions	Existence of families Kumbaraṇṇāya Kaṇṇaraṇṇāya	Settlement survives
B. Eastern Gramas					
1. śripādi GP1-sripadi GP2-sripadi GP3-sirripadi	Ajjibettu, Bantwal taluk	Viṣṇumūrthi temple	-	Five families identified Baipadittāyas survive.	Settlement continues
2. Vodila GP1-Odilu GP2-vodila GP3-vodilu	Belthangadi taluk	Durga Paramēśvari	One unpublished inscription	Survivals of Ammn-Uṇṇāyas and Kermuṇṇāyas	Settlement exists.
3. Nala GP1-Nala GP2-Nala GP3-Nala	Belthangadi taluk	Durga Parameśvari	-	Temple with other brahman families	*Grāma* survives.
4. Kareya GP1-Not	Belthangadi taluk	Mahalingelśvara	-	Temple with families like Kudannāyas	Settlement exists Indicates migra-

Contd.

Contd.

(1)	(2)	(3)	(4)	(5)	(6)
mentioned GP2-Kareya GP3-Not mentioned					tion of brahman families.
5. Ujire GP1-Ujire GP2-Ujire GP3-Ujire	Belthangadi taluk	Manjunatha temple, Dharmasthala	Two inscriptions	Family of Aramanettāya	Settlement survives.
6. Kāranduru GP1-Karandura GP2-Kāranduru GP3-Karandura	Belthangadi taluk	Aṇṇapurnēśvari; Viṣṇmūrthi	One inscription	Sampagettāya	Settlement exists.
7. Kāvala GP1-Not mentioned GP2-Kāvala GP3-Not mentioned	Bantwal taluk taluk	Kariñjelśvara	Two inscriptions	Peradattāya	Settlement survives.
8. Kunhimarga GP1-Kunyamārga GP2-Kunyamārga GP3-Kunhimarga	Belthangadi taluk	Viṣṇumūrthi temple	-	Families, Korangināya: Kakraṇṇāya	*Grāma* extinct

Contd.

Contd.

(1)	(2)	(3)	(4)	(5)	(6)
9. Kokkada GP1-Kokkada GP2-Kokkada GP3-Kokkada	Belthangadi taluk	Vaidyanatha; Nilakantha temples	-	Families like Uparaṇa. Yedāpāditāya survive	*Grāma* and Settlement survives.
10. Ramakunja GP1-Raminja GP2-Ramanjura GP3-	Puttur taluk	IIśvara temple	-	Nūrittāya; Place name Neranki	*Grāma* and Settlement survives.
11. Pude GP1-Pude GP2-Pude GP3-Pude	Suḷḷya taluk	Viṣṇumūrthi	-	Pudenāya family with temple	*Grāma* survives. migration of some families.
12. Balapa GP1-Belapadi GP2-Balapa GP3-Balpa	Suḷḷya taluk	Śūlini Durga Parameśvari temple	three inscriptions	Temple with other brahman family	*Grāma* survives Settlement extinct.
13. Idekidu GP1-Idakedu GP2-Idakkedu GP3-Idakedu	Bantwal taluk	Śanmukha temple	-	Temple with other brahman families	*Grāma* survives Settlement extinct.
14. Pāliñja GP1-Padinja GP2-Palinje GP3-Paminja	Puttur taluk, Now also called Anginje	Viṣṇumūrthi	-	Other brahman families	*Grāma* survives Settlement extinct.

Contd..

Contd.

	(1)	(2)	(3)	(4)	(5)	(6)
15.	Kemmiñja GP1-Kemmiñja GP2-Kemminje GP3-Kemmiñja	Puttur taluk	Śanmukha temple	-	Family of Bajetāya survives.	*Grāma* and Settlement exist.
16.	Aivarnādu GP1-Irnadu GP2-Ayirnada GP3-Airnadu	Suḷḷya taluk	Panchalingeśvara temple	-	Temple exists, but no brahman families.	*Grāma* survives Settlement extinct.

Table - II
Survivals of Traditions in Brahman Settlements

	Gramas		*Families as in GP*	*Families as in Inscription*	*At present*
	(1)		*(2)*	*(3)*	*(4)*
A. Western Gramas					
1.	Kandavara	GP1	Udupa Hebbāra	Udupa Hebbaruva Aṇṇa Udupa (Unpublished incriptions found in Kandavara)	Udupa Hebbāra
		GP2	Udupa Hebbāra Aṇṇa Udupa Aṇṇa Hebbāra Uppūru Udupa Kandāvara Udupa		
2.	Kōta	GP1	Hande. Bāsari. Tuṅga. Nāvada. Hoḷḷa. Mayya. Hebbāra. Kāryavanta	Heṇje (SII. VII. 346) Haṅde (SII. VII. 359) Ṭuṅga (SII. VII. 331)	All these families live in Kōta.

Contd.

Contd.

(1)	(2)		(3)	(4)
			Navada (SII, VII. 356) Hoḷa (SII, VII, 345) Mayya (SII, VII. 346) Hebbāra (SII. VII, 372) Kāranta (SII, VII, 390) Alase (SII, VII, 356)	
	GP2	Tuṅga Holla Kāranta Hērala Haṅde Bāsari Hebbāra Haṅde Mayya Uurala	Kārantadi (ARSIE 1929-30, 556) Hērala (SII, VII, 390) Bayiri (SII, VII. 346) Uurala (SII, VII, 372)	All these families live in Kōta
		ādināya Mādināya Alsattāya Dotsattāya Ammanittāya Manikattāya Koṇakattāya Rudguṇattāya		Ādināya etc., do not live in Kōta.
3. Brahmavara	GP1	Uḷḷūru Ungarapaḷḷi Vārambaḷḷi Kairambaḷḷi Aḷupya Aḷtāmūrthy Hebāra		

Contd.

Contd.

(1)	*(2)*	*(3)*	*(4)*
	Samblaja	Allupe Hebara (SII, VII, 343) Hebbāra (SII, VII, 465) Sabhāyita (SII, IX, Pt. II, 430)	
	GP2 Ugrampaḷḷi	Ungurapaḷi (ARSIE, 604) Orambali (ARSIE, 1929-30, 603), Varambaḷḷi exists Uḷḷuru (B, Vasanth Shetty, *Brahmāvarada Itihāsa*) Kaṇmaṃpali (SII, VII, 334)	Varambaḷḷi exists
	Varambaḷḷi		
	Aḷuppa		
	Allurāya		
	Derampallitāya		
	Mukkarditāya		
	Apruchala		
	Astāmūrthi		
4. Varkadi	GP1 Tāletāya		Tālettāya
	Ayyapaināya		
	Nāraḷattāya		
	Netrattāya		
	Arināya		Arināya
	Kidekidenāya		
	śuṇṇodittāya		
	GP2 Perruvaṇṇāya		Peruvaṇṇāya
	Vāyappināya		
	Netrattāya		
	Taḷattāya		
	Kidekerunaya		
	Saṇṇasakattāya		
	Arrināya		
	Kojitturāya		

Contd.

Contd.

(1)	(2)		(3)	(4)
		Kārāya		Kārāya
		Varkādināya.		
	GP3	Taḷettāya		
		Netrattāya		
		āryapaināya		
		Nāraḷattāya		
5. Karvor	GP1	Pāturāya		
		Pākurāya		
		Kūdureṭtāya		
		Poyyaṭtāya		Poyyatāya.
	GP2	Munnurāya		Munnurāya
		Ichalantāya		Ichalantāya
		Talepāditāya		
		Mañjanāditāya		
		Madyarāya		
		Paṅambeletāya		
		Kalaśankantāya.		
	GP3	Kārurāya		
6. Padi	GP1	Amettāya		
		Śambarattāya		

Contd.

Contd.

(1)	(2)		(3)	(4)
		Induvaḷittāya		
		Koyakudalāya		
	GP2	Bālkādināya		
		Kamatātāya		Kāmada
		Mannipaittāya		
		Anjanantōdittāya		
		Urulantordittāya		
		Tatkalāparditāya		
		Kakkillāya		Kakkillāya
		Pāramparditāya		
		Akrapokkināya		
		Yarapārditāya		
		Murudompārdināya		
		Kurukapārdināya		
		Chāpārdināya		
		Taudupādināya		
		Mundalampārditāya		
		Kadalampārditāya		
		Urulampārditāya.		
7. Mogrāl	GP2	Innurāya		Innurāya
		Karekunjattāya		
		Tambalantōditāya		
		Inṇurāya		
		Ijalampādittāya		
		Mogarālāya		

Contd.

Contd.

(1)	*(2)*	*(3)*	*(4)*
	Kaṇṇavurāyạ		
	Mākurāya		
	Ujarāya		
	Māpāditāya		
	Kaṇevurāya		
	Putrattāya		
	Uḷḷavurāya		
	Kanatāya		
	Guḷitāya		
	Kidekāntāya		
	Karekontāya		
8. Kūdalu	GP1 Kaṇṇaraṇṇāya		
	Kambaraṇṇāya		
	Iravatturāya		
	Mittadkattāya		
	GP2 Kottakunjittāya		
	Para-vaṇṇāya		
	Nityavaṇṇāya		
	Pijattāya		Pijettāya (Reference in *Modhwa Vijaya*)
	Deranjattāya		
	Pilitkeretāya		
	Pudaṅkoḷatāya		
9. Mittanādu	GP1 Kundagolattāya		
	Nujittāya		

Contd.

Contd.

(1)	(2)	(3)	(4)
	Gangettāya		
	Saraḷattāya		
	GP2 Pavurāya		
	Puṇyakalattāya		
	Mattipunjittāya		
	Uuppangaḷattāya		
	Urangaḷattāya		
	Mudavādittāya		
	Dēvādittāya		
	Bidiādināya		
	Mittanādittāya		
	Mākurāya		
	Baralāya		
	Mukkālattāya		
	Kaḷakaḷattāya		
	Munivūrāya		
	Kōdittāya		
	Naruḷittāya		
	Bālekaḷattāya		
	Kanankordittāya		
	Kodamettāya		
	Neḷḷittāya	Nelli (SII, VII, No. 270)	Nellitāya family exists.
	Balillāya		
	Morritāya		

Contd.

Contd.

(1)	(2)	(3)	(4)
	Kaḷḷikaḷatāya.		
10. Tenakaḷa	GP1 Mogerāya Mittantāya Vailāya (Kanchittāya) Vokudināya Ulirāya Maleñjināya Kabekodināya.		
	GP2 Mittantāya Mogerāya Vailāya Madavaṇṇāya Vakkuṇṇāya Kachint-āya Malenjināya Ulirāya Muddaṇṇāya Keḷakaḷattāya.	Mittantakala (SII, VII, 620) Mogara (SII, IX, PII, 446)	
11. Simanturu	śimantūrāya śibarūrāya Mannūrāya Iprantāya Mukyantāya		Simantūrāya śibarūrāya

Contd.

Contd.

(1)	*(2)*		*(3)*	*(4)*
		Madikudalāya	Madikudala (SII. VII, 344)	
		Śidikalatāya		
		Ādarāya		
		Barvanāya.		
	GP2	Śimantūrāya		
		Muchyantāya		Muchyantāya
		Madikulatāya		
		Śibarūrāya		
		Śartikaḷatalya	Shattiakkaḷa (SII. VII, 298)	
		Adarāya		
		Tōkurāya		
		Kallakkaratāya		
		Ayakaḷattāya		
	GP3	Śibarūrāya		
		Śimantūrāya		
		Maṇṇurāya		
		Macchantāya		
		Madikuḷatāya		
		Sidikuḷatāya		
12. Maraṇe	GP1	Badekedenāya		
		Śulyannāya		
	GP2	Pāturāya		
		Poyyattāya		

Contd.

Contd.

(1)		(2)	(3)	(4)
		Pijakkalattāya Kudrittāya Anaḷattāya Māḷattāya		Place name Máḷa. Karkala taluk.
	GP3	Same as GP1		
13. Koḷavinādu	GP1	Talepāditāya Mañjanāditāya		
	GP2	Nadikalatāya Salaiturāya Manchittāya Śulyannāya Padakaṇṇāya Marḷyattāya Mankudettāya Naraḷattāya.		Place name Manchi. Bantwal taluk. Place name Mankude, Bantwal taluk.
	GP3	Same as GP1		
14. Nilāvara	GP1	Nārittāya Yedabettanāya Kallurāya Tumbikallāya	Nārata (494 of 1929) Yedevettina (SII. VII. 373) Kalukūra (494 of 1929) Tumbikala (191 of 1929)	Yedabettunāya. Kallurāya.

Contd.

Contd.

(1)	(2)	(3)	(4)
	Nujinṇāya		
	Makkitāya		
	Pādittāya		
	GP2 Nāritāya		
	Kalluray		
	Nakṣḷatri		
	Madhyastha	Madyastha (SII, VII. 296) Madyastha.	
	Yedabettināya		
	Hebbāra	Hebbāra (SII, VII, 343) Hebbāra	
	Makkilāya		
	Tumbikallāya		
	Padettāya		
	GP3 Nariśya		
	Yedabettināya		
	Kallurāya		
	Tumbikallāya		
	Hebbāra		
	Nuritāya		
	Karapadi		
	Makkitāya		
15. Śivaḷḷi	GP1 Alevōrāya		Alevōrāya
	Kodencha	Kodacha (SII. IX, PII. 517)	Kodencha
	Maṇjittaya	Mañjata (SII, VII. 334)	Mañjitāya
	Saralāya		Saraḷāya

Contd.

Contd.

(1)	(2)	(3)	(4)
	Kadambalittāya		
	Madipalittāya		
	Sagurirāya		Saguritāya
	Tenkiḷāya		
	Kunjittāya	Kunjatava (SII. VII. 296)	
	Naduvantillāya	Naduvantila (SII. VII. 299)	Naduvantillāya,
	Putrāya		
	Bāyaritāya	Bāhiri (SII. VII. 344)	
	Kekuḍenāya	Kekude (487 of 1929)	Kekuṇāya,
	Kedilāya	Kedila (VII. VII. 344)	Kedilāya
	Kodachāya	Kodaja (SII. IX II. 517)	
	Kornāya		Kornāya now in Belthangadi taluk.
	Maraditāya		
	Śivatāya		śivatāya.
	Kunjirāya		
	Kramadaritāya	Kramadareyakkala (SII. VII. 303)	
	Tenkodināya		
	Kataranāya		
	Śitirāya		
	Arolitāya		
	Kurambaḷḷitāya		
	Badikiḷḷava		
	Kalyaṇantāya	Kalyānata (ARIE 1964. No. 2)	
	Nūjitāya		
	Kadambalitāya		
	Politāya		

Contd.

Contd.

(1)	(2)	(3)	(4)
	Nakarantāya		
	Vatināya		
	Śibarantāya		
	Paddilāya		Paddillāya
	Nedilāya		
	Kaṇṇapināya		
	Mankitāya		
	Kottalādināya		
	Kodalāya		
	Parkaḷatāya		
	Arimettāya		
	Koḷaketāya		
	Maṇikalatāya		
	Ankitāya		
	Mudittāya		
	Padettāya		
	Kōtantiltāya		Totantillāya (mentioned in *Madhwa Vijaya*)
	Kunhimargentāya		
	Kannurāya		
	Kelatrāya		
	Maṇṇaṇitāya		
	Neyampaḷḷitāya		
	Pudināya		
	Tagināya		
	Mitilāya		

Contd.

Contd.

(1)	*(2)*	*(3)*	*(4)*
	Kutitāya		
	Panañji		
	Sunatāya		
	Kalambi	Kalambi (SII, IX, pt. II, 446)	
	Ulitāya		
	Niñjūrāya		
	Nellitāya	Nelli (SII, VII, 270)	
	Malyantāya		
	Hebbāpa		
	Beḷapati		
	Beḷyarāya		
	Kōni		
	Karkāvitāya		
	Nāḷitāya		
	Durge		
	Vadetāya		
	Vadi		
	Ubali		
	Chakkerāya		
	Mangalattāya		
	Voritāya		
	Mandabettāya		
	Adukattāya		
	Kodiāāya		
	Elekodittāya		
	Kuḷitāya		

Contd.

Contd.

(1)	(2)	(3)	(4)
	Aṇṇappi		
	Gūde		
	Deyiginãya		
	Kudantāya		
	Kudakarāya	Kudukārakkala	
	Aruye	(SII, VII, 303)	
	Kundināya		
	Suriye		
	Nūji		
	Kodañji		
	Kaṇṇapalli	Kaṇṇampaḷi (SII, VII, 334)	
	Dōni		
	Mundādi		
	Mūdumale		
	Vutiye Ujire		
	Kokkādi		
	Hebbāra		
	Nakkātte		
	Āne Kalaḷi		
	Agaḷi		
	Muke		
	Mijikośi		
	Irutturāya		
	Avuje		
	Maipādi		
	Bēvināya		

Contd.

Contd.

(1)	(2)	(3)	(4)
	Kōvināya		
	Melādi	Melādi	
	Kudurāya	(SII, IX, P II. 511, 540)	
	Kalañji		
	Kalāya		
	Majalāya	Majalāya (Unpublished Kinnigoli inscription, noticed by P. Srinivas Bhat, Katēl)	
	Todināya		
	Irettāya		
	Peralāya	Pērala Sabhya	
	Kabetōdi	(SII, IX, Pt. II, 430)	
	Bēye		
	Manjittāya		
	GP2 Alevōrāya		
	Kedilāya		
	Kaḷatāya		
	Madilakuḷatāya		
	Manjittāya		
	Saraḷāya		
	Karambaḷitāya		
	Sagarritāya		
	Tenkillāya		
	Kunjittāya		
	Nadyantillāya		

Contd.

Contd.

(1)	*(2)*	*(3)*	*(4)*
	Kekkuṇṇāya		
	Bāyarittāya		
	Putturāya		
	Śivatāya		
	Maraditāya		
	Koradināya		
	Banninjatāya	Bāyarinjatava (SII, VII, 299)	
	Kunjurāya		
	Karantāya	Kāranta (SII, IX, Pt. II, 452)	
	Kojankellāya		
	Korenāya		
	Murdittāya		
	Nāyambaḷitāya		
	Karambalitāya		
	Perambaḷitāya		
	Bunnārāya		
	Nadantillāya		
	Śivabellitaya		
	Ubbeḷḷitāya		
	Kadambaḷitāya		
	Kadebalitāya		
	Mankitāya		
	Madharitāya		
	Banniritāya		
	Sabharitāya		
	Indraáitāya		

Contd.

Contd.

(1)	*(2)*	*(3)*	*(4)*
	Koḷakaḷatāya		
	Murdiḷḷāya	Mūdila (SII, VII, 350)	
	Nidamburāya	Nidambūra (SII, VII, 299)	
	Putturāya		
	Chittillāya		Chittillāya
	Mittillāya		Mittillāya
	Nadillāya		Nadillāya
	Mudittāya		Mudittāya
	Tenkiḷḷāya		
	Paddillāya		Paddillāya
	Balikillāya		
	Kordiyillāya		
	Kadeyillāya		
	Yatekillāya		
	Muchumodināya		
	Akkikodināya		
	Arikordināya		
	Kadekodināya		
	Mudukodināya		
	Tenkodināya		
	Badakordināya		
	Padukordināya		
	Nijakordināya		
	Mungordināya		
	Yeakodināya		
	Mundārdināya		

Contd.

Contd.

(1)	(2)	(3)	(4)
	Bandāradināya		
	Nelārdināya		
	Dandārdināya		
	Kanarārdināya		
	Kadalārdināya		
	Kukkilārdināya		
	Koppalārdināya		
	Golināya Attināya		
	Jālaśarittāya		
	Kadarināya		
	Amritabaḷittāya		
	Arkanāya		
	Dōvettāya		
	Kkirgālanāya		
	Vaddantāya		
	Agnittāya		
	Melarittāya		
	Kudantāya		
	Darbettāya		
	Gangettāya		
	Vādantāya		
	Madyattāya		
	Samidhattāya		
	Aśwarittāya		
	Polināya		
	Mūdettāya		

Contd.

Contd.

(1)	(2)	(3)	(4)
	Areveḷittāya		
	Karalattāya		
	Kaṇṇarapallittāya		
	Beḷḷārapādittāya		
	Kalañjināya		
	Mangalantāya		
	Nekerettāya		
	Kāyaventāya		
	Achakkenāya		
	Mandaṇittāya		
	Kalayimbittāya		
	Tōnittāya		
	Maṇoḷittāya		
	Karkalattāya		
	Banasi		
	Modukottāya		
	Elekordināya		
	Hudukordināya		
	Uprāya		
	Ubarāya		
	Nittunāya		
	Kayelkarāya		
	Bhujirāya		
	Kūdhurāya		
	Kuñjūrāya		
	Akkalarāya		

Contd.

Contd.

(1)	*(2)*	*(3)*	*(4)*
	Arigoḷarāya		
	Jarkaḷatāya		
	Mambalatāya	Mumbala (SII, IX, Pt. II, 446)	
	Śambarattāya		
	Akkodi Hebbāra		
	Sūjittāya		
	Punchalattāya		
	Kadambettāya		
	Koḷambekallāya		
16. Nirumārga	GP1 Lichaluttāya		Ichalatāya (in Ucchila)
	Anantōdittāya		
	Alampadittāya		
	Taralāya		
	Māvarāya		
	Kumārantāya		
	GP2 Indravalittāya		
	Āssurāya		
	Kaṇṇaraṇṇāya		Kambaraṇṇāya
	Toyakodināya		Kaṇṇaraṇṇāya
	Iravatturāya		
	Kaṇṇarāya	KAṇṇara (SII, VII, 299)	
	Ametturditāya		
	Karnamangilattāya		
	GP3 Jāruyippalattāya		
	Anaṇtodittāya		

Contd.

Contd.

(1)	(2)	(3)	(4)
	Nurittāya		
	Pāditāya		
	Kallurāya		
	Mādarāya		
	Kumattāya.		
B. Eastern Grāmas:			
1. Śripādi	GP1 Kunhyamaṇṇāya		Kunhaṇṇāya
	Vaipāditāya		
	Atrādittāya		
	Putraṇṇāya		
	GP2 Pangaṇṇāya		Pangaṇṇāya
	Baipādittāya		Baipadittāya
	Kunhimaṇṇāya		
	Kavudampadittāya		Kavudampādittāya
	Atradittāya		
	Śripadittāya		
	GP3 Same as GP1		
2. Vodila	GP1 Alumaṇṇāya		Ammuṇṇāya
	Uḷipādittāya		
	GP2 Alumaṇṇāya		
	Kadamaṇṇāya		
	Punchādittāya		
	Vardimādināya		

Contd.

Contd.

(1)		(2)		(3)	(4)
		GP3	Thimpodittāya		
			Ambalaṇṇāya		
3.	Nala	GP1	Madipādităya		
			Parvantāya		
		GP2	Padantāya		Padantāya
			Mālepādităya		
			Nālatāya		
		GP3	Yadakilāya		
4.	Kareya	GP2	Puttaṇṇāya		
			Pāvināya		
			Vangangināya		
			Ambalavāya		
			Kuppaṇṇāya		Kuddaṇṇāya
			Kareyatāya		
			Alamundităya		
			Kuḷitāya		
5.	Ujire	GP1	Aramanettāya		Aramanettāya
			Vappantāya		
			Kokralitāya		
			Aripādittāya		
			Mundapadi		
			Kemmundāya		Kemmundāya
			Arbatāya		
			Bellaṇṇāya		

Contd.

Contd.

(1)		(2)		(3)	(4)
		GP2	Mudampādittāya		
			Kakraṇṇāya		Kakraṇṇāya
			Bellaṇṇāya		
			Vappantāya		
			Arimanettāya		
			Aripādittāya		
			Kemmundetāya	Kemude (P. Gururaja Bhat,	Kermuṇṇāya
			Ujirenāya	*Udupina Itihasa*)	
			Arbitāya		
			Mundapāditāya		
			Tudenāya		
		GP3	Vappantāya Arbittāya		
			Arripādittāya		
			Modambādittāya		
			Mudampādittāya		
			Kemmundāya		
			Arbitāya Bellaṇṇāya		
6.	Karandura	GP1	Sampagetāya		
			Yadakelatāya		
		GP2	Sampagettāya		Sampagettāya
			Ponnetāya		

Contd.

Contd.

(1)	*(2)*	*(3)*	*(4)*
	GP3 Sampigetāya		
7. Kāvala	GP2 Nariśyānaya		
	Peradatāya		Peraditāya
	Ichalatāya		Ichalatāya
	Yerachalatāya		
	Kumarantāya		
	Kunhimagaḷintāya		
	Karinjatāya		
8. Kunhimarga	GP1 Peraḷattāya		
	Kunhimārgentāya		
	Peradittāya		Perdattāya
	Upparaṇṇāya		
	Ichalattāya		
	Itantāya		
	Madavināya		
	Kuduṇāya		Kuddaṇṇāya
	Putāyattāya		
	Kodanginaya		Koranginaya
	Kakraṇṇāya		KakrAṇṇaāya
	GP2 Koranginṇāya		
	Kakraṇṇāya		
	GP3 Same as in GP1		
9. Kokkada	GP1 Todilāya		
	Śabarāya		

Contd.

Contd.

(1)	*(2)*	*(3)*	*(4)*
	Yadapādittāya		Uparaṇṇṁya
	Uparaṇṇāya		
	GP2 Uparaṇṇāya		
	Baḷetilāya		
	Toditilāya		
	Śabarāya		śabarāya
	Yedepādittāya		Ycdapadittāya
	Banillāya		Baḷetilāya
	Panillāya		
	Kokkādināya		
	Uriyaḷittāya		
	GP3 Kakkakōdillāya		
10. Ramanjura	GP1 Nūjitāya		
	Matatāya		
	Munnūrāya		Munnūrāya
	GP2 Nūritāya		
	Peraḷatāya		
	Paddalatāya		
	Tengināya		
	Ambaṇṇāya		
	Sambaraṇṇāya		
	Kangināya	Kanginatava	
	Nerankināya	(P. Gururaj Bhat.	

Contd.

Contd.

(1)	(2)		(3)	(4)
			Udupina Itihāsa)	
	GP3	Same as GP1		
11. Pude	GP1	Pudenāya		
	GP2			
		Mattittillaya Kanerāditāya Kaṇṇangalatāya Niduvaṇṇāya Muduvaṇṇāya Pudeṇāya Pudikaḷatāya Kajenāya		
KAṇṇaradika (SII. VII, 299)				
	GP3	Ametōditāya Peraḷatāya Pudenāya Yillāditāya		Pudenāya
12. Balapa	GP1	Bāritāya Ummaraṇṇāya Ammani		
	GP2	Bāritāya Umaraṇṇāya		

Contd.

(1)	(2)	(3)	(4)
	Baḷumatāya		
	Ambraṇṇāya		
	Timbraṇṇāya		Ammaṇṇāya
	Mittāditāya		
	Yibbāditāya		
	Balapatāya		
	GP3 Ammanatāya		
	Bāyaritāya		
	Ummaṇitāya		
13. Idekidu	GP1 Maṇikaḷattāya		
	Śadangattāya		
	GP2 Śadanga		
	Kelatāya		
	Dēvangināya		
	Anantōdittāya		
	Bērkalatāya		
	Puṇyakalatāya		
	Bārikaḷatāya		
	Yidekedanāya		
	GP3 Maṇikaḷattāya		
14. Parinja	GP1 Edabettunāya		

Contd.

Contd.

(1)	*(2)*		*(3)*	*(4)*
	GP2	Yirekadattāya		Erkaditāya
		Madukatāya		
		Kudantāya		
		Punnipettāya		
		Siriyādittāya		
		Parinjanāya		
	GP3	as in GP1		
15. Kemminje	GP1	Bajatāya		Pejittāya
	GP2	Bajatāya		
		Sevyakalatāya		
	GP3	Same as GP1		
16. Ayirnadu	GP1	Takaraṇṇāya		
		Mundapādittāya		Śabarāya
		Śabarāya		
		Ulapadittāya		
	GP2	Sūryappināya		
		Modillāya		
		Yillārditāya		
		Maṇikalattāya		
		PAṇṇarāya		
		Panditakaṇṇāya		
	GP3	Same as GP1		

1. Out of the several families mentioned above, sixty-one families figure in inscription.
2. Out of the thirty-two villages, in nineteen villages GP1 and GP3 agree regarding the list of families given.

Table III
Variations in the Ocation of Brahman Families

Family	Village in GP1	Village in GP2	Village in GP3
(1)	(2)	(3)	(4)
1. Hebbāra	Kandāvara Kōta Brahmavara śivalli	Kandāvara Kōta Nilāvara	Niḷāvara
2. Kāranta	Kōta	Kōta Śivaḷḷi	Kōta
3. Kairambaḷḷi	Brahmāvara	Śivaḷḷi	
4. Nāraḷatāya	Varkādi	Koḷavinādu	Varkādi
5. Pāturāya	Karavōr	Maraṇe	
6. Poyyatāya	Karavōr	Maraṇe	
7. Kudurettāya	Karavōr	Maraṇe	
8. Mannurāya	Rāmakuñja	Karavor	Rāmakuñja
9. Ichalantāya	Nirumārga	Karavor	Kāvala
10. Talepāditāya	Koḷavinādu	Karavōr	Koḷavinādu
11. Mañjanāditāya	Koḷavinādu	Śivaḷḷi	
12. Induvaáittāya	Pādi	Nīrumārga	
13. Kaṇṇaraṇṇāya	Kūdalu	Nīrmarga	
14. Kambaraṇṇāya	Kūdalu	Nīrumārga	
15. Iravattūrāya	Kūdalu	Śivaḷḷi	
16. Pijatāya	Kūdalu Kemminje	Kemmiñje	Kemmiñje
17. Mapaditāya	Śivaḷḷi	Mogrāl	
18. Nellittāya	Śivaḷḷi	Mittanādu	
19. Śabarāya	Śimantūru Kokkada	Śimantūru Kokkada	Simantūru Kokkada
Ayirnādu			
	Ayirnādu		

Contd.

(1)		(2)	(3)	(4)
20.	Madikudalāya	śimantūru	Simantūru śivaḷḷi	śimantūru
21.	Padakaṇṇāya	Maraṇe	Koḷavinādu	Maraṇe
22.	Sulyaṇṇāya	Marane	Koḷavinādu	Maraṇe
23.	Nariṇṇāya	Nīlāvara	Nīlāvara Kāvala	Nīlāvara
24.	Kallurāya	Nīlāvara	Nīlāvara	Nīlāvara . Nirumārga
25.	Yedabettunāya	Nilāvara Parinja śripādi	Nilāvara śripādi Kāvala	Nilāvara Parinja śripādi Kunhimārga
26.	Kunhimaṇṇāya	Kunhimārga		
27.	Peraḷaṇṇāya	Kunhimārga	Kunhimārga Ramakunja	Kunhimārga
28.	Kuddaṇṇāya	Kunhimārga	Kareya	Kunhimārga
29.	Uparaṇṇāya	Kunhimarga Kokkada	Kokkada	Kunhimārga Kokkada

Table IV

List of Personal Names and Family Names of Brahmans Figuring in Inscriptions

No.	*Source*	*Date (A.D.)*	*Name of the grama*	*Name of the family*	*Name of the person*	*Remarks*
(1)	*(2)*	*(3)*	*(4)*	*(5)*	*(6)*	*(7)*
1.	Bailur: ARSIE, 29-30 No. 583	1335	Bailur	Mūdila	Vasudeva	This family is mentioned in *Grāmapaddhati* (GP)
2.	Vāramballi; ARSIE, No. 603	1345	Vāramba i	Oorambaḷi	Aṇṇa	This family is mentioned in GP.

Contd.

Contd.

(1)	(2)	(3)	(4)	(5)	(6)	(7)
3.	Vārambaḷḷi; ARSIE, No. 602	Undated	Brahmavara	Vārambaḷḷi	Viḷhṇu	This family is mentioned in GP.
4.	Bainduru; ARSIE, No. 535	1364	Bainduru	Hebāruva	Vithala	This family is mentioned in GP. This village is not mentioned in GP.
5.	KoteIśvara; SII, Vol, IX pt, II	1365	KoteIśvara	Batta	Hangara	
				Hatvārayya	-	These two families and the village are not mentioned in GP.
6.	Bārkūru; SII, VII 319	1371	Bārkūru	Mandacha	Keva	This family and village are not mentioned in GP.
7.	Kodavūru 186 of 1972	1379	Kodavūru	Nidambura	Aṇṇa	This family is mentioned in GP, but not the village.
8.	Bārkur; SII, VII, 362	1389	Bārakūru	Bhatta	Bhāvana	The family and the village are not mentioned in GP.
9.	Tiruvailu; ARSIE, 465	1390	ōmañjuru	Bhattittila	-	The family and the village are not mentioned in GP.

Contd.

Contd.

(1)	(2)	(3)	(4)	(5)	(6)	(7)
10.	Bārakūru; SII, VII 344	1393	Bārakūru	Madikudala Kedila Bāhiri Upādhya	Keesāva Keesāva Kuduga Nārana	Except Upādhya all the families are mentioned in GP.
11.	Barakuru; SII, VII, 356	1394	Bārakūru	Ṇāvada Kāranta Alase	Vishnu Gōvinda Vāsūdeva	Except Alase, all the families are mentioned in GP.
12.	Udupi; SII, VII, 299		1395	śivaḷḷi Naduvantila	Bhatasōmiya narāyana Govinda	Shankara- Except Bhata somajya all the families and the village are mentioned in Govinda GP.
13.	Yermal; SII, VII, 270	1402	Yermal	Nelli Pande	Narana Harihara	The Nelli family is mentioned in GP but not Pande and the village.
14.	Vaderahōbli; SII, IX, II. 340	1406	Kundapur	Vayidya Sabhya Sabhayita Kāranta	Vasteva Peerala Narana Vishnu	Kāranta family is mentioned in GP. The village is not mentioned
15.	Kandāvara: un-	1409	Kandavara	Udupa	Aṇṇa	The Udupa and Hebbāra

Contd.

Contd.

(1)	(2)	(3)	(4)	(5)	(6)	(7)
	published. with Dr. P.N. Narasimhamurthy			Kodagi Hebbāruva Odeya	Aṇṇamale Vishnu Aṇṇa	family and the village in mentioned in GP.
16.	Matapādi: ARSIE. 604	1414	-	Ungurapali	Alugātu	This family is mentioned in GP.
17.	Bārakūru: SII, VII, 307	1416rf	Bārakūru	Māsuravali	-	This family is not mentioned in GP.
18.	Pāvañja; SII, VII, 261	1418	Pāvañja	Sanatana	-	This family and village are not mentioned in GP.
19.	Bārakūru; SII, VII, 365	1420	Bārakūru	Heerala oja Kāranta	Śankara Aṇṇa	The Ooja family is not mentioned in GP.
20.	Kadekaru ARSIE. 571	1426	Kadekar	Nidambūru	Aṇṇa	The family is mentioned in GP, but not the village.
21.	Udyāvara Chambukallu inscription: P. Gururaja Bhat, Udupina Itihasa	1429	Udyavara	Baheri Bahiri Marināya Mattināya	Kesa Naraṇṇa Badhya Krishna	All these family are mentioned in GP.
22.	Bhārakūr: SII. VII. 311	1431	Bārakūru	Bhatta	Śankara	This family is mentioned in GP.

Contd.

Contd.

(1)	*(2)*	*(3)*	*(4)*	*(5)*	*(6)*	*(7)*
23.	Bārakūr: SII, VII. 378	1432	Brahmūra	Bhatta	Rangaṇṇa	This family is not mentioned in GP.
24.	Kandāvara: unpublished inscription see, above	1433	Kandavara	Udupa Hebbaruva Upadhya Udiya	Aṇṇa Nachyuta Vasteva Aṇṇa	Upadhya and Udiya are not mentioned in GP.
25.	Bārakūr; SII, VII. 382	1434	Bārakūru	Upadhya	Māyaṇṇa	This family is not mentioned in GP.
26.	Basrur; SII. IX II 446	1436	Basaruru	Mumbatta Ulura	Bachaṇṇa Madanna Kalambe	Mumbatta and the village are not mentioned in GP. Kuyina Mumbala Krishna Ungurapali Rama Mogara Vishnu Śiva Manjara Mittanta
27.	Bārakūru; SII. VII. 372	1437	Manavūru	Mayya Bāhiri	Vasteya	The Village is not mentioned in GP.
28.	Udupi Krishna matha: SII. VII. 296	1437	śivaḷḷi	Kunjata Madyasta	Rama	The village and the family are not mentioned in GP.

Contd.

Contd.

(1)	(2)	(3)	(4)	(5)	(6)	(7)
29.	Bārakūru; SII. VII. 313	1440	Bārakūru	Ayya	Chikkaṇṇa	This family and the village are not mentioned in GP.
30.	Bārakūru; SII. IX II 452	1450	Basrūr	Hebara Sabhāyita Mittānta Kāranta	Nārana Narana	All the families are mentioned in GP, but not mentioned in village.
31.	Kundesvara insc-ription; SII, IX, pt. 455	1451	Kundapura	Joyisa	Hariyappa	The village and the family are not mentioned in GP.
32.	Kandāvara; unpub-lished, see above	1456	Kandavara	Udupa Kalukura	Aṇṇa Kunyaṇṇa	The village and the family are not mentioned in GP.
33.	Bārakūru; SII. VII. 376	1459	Rajādi Kanyanā	Pandita	-	The village and the family are in GP.
34.	Bārakūru; SII. VII. 373	1464	Bārakūru	Yedevettu	-	The family are mentioned in GP but not the village.
35.	Bārakūru; SII. VII. 334	1469	Brahmavāra Kaṇṇampali Manjata	Heerala Ungurapali Rama	Sreedhara Mahādeva	The village and the family are men-tioned in Gp.

Contd.

Contd.

(1)	(2)	(3)	(4)	(5)	(6)	(7)
36.	Basrur: SII. IX Pt. 465	1472	Basarur	Kāranta Hebara	Nandi Narāyana	The families are mintion-ed in GP.
37.	Bārakūru; SII, VII, 346	1476	Mānavūru	Hōrala Mayya Bhatta Mayya	- - -	The families except Bhata are mentioned in GP.
38.	Bārakūru; SII, VII, 360	1477	Bārakūru	Haṅde Sabhyita Heerala Urāḷa	Aksara - Aṇṇa	The families are mentioned in GP. -
39.	Udupi Badaga-bettu inscription; ARSIE, 582	1486	Chittapadi	Mudila	Laxminṁ-rāyaṇa	The family is mentioned in GP.
40.	Giliyāra: SII, VII, 511	1498	Kōta	-	Narasaṇṇa	The village is mentioned in GP. but, not mentioned in family.
41.	Bārakūru: SII. VII. 345	1503	Bārakūru	Bahiri Madhyasta Hoḷa	Vishnu -	The families are mentioned in GP. Narana
42.	Basrur: SII. IX Pt. II 511	1519.	Basrur Meladi Bahiri			Śankara The families are mentioned in GP. IIśvara
43.	Basrur:	1525	Kandāvara	Udupa	Vasudeva	The families

Contd.

Contd.

(1)	(2)	(3)	(4)	(5)	(6)	(7)
	SII, IX, Pt II, 517		Kodaja Kodacha Gujadi			except Gujadi are mentioned in GP.
44.	Nilavar; 494 of 1929	1529	Nilāvara	Kalukūra	Śiva	The village and the family are mentioned GP.
45.	Basrūr; SII, IX Pt II, 540	1531	Basrūr	Melādi Udupa	Śankara Aṇṇa	The families are mentioned in GP.
46.	Handadi; ARSIE, 597	1543	Brahmura	Haduvala	Aṇṇa	This family is not mentioned in GP.
47.	Basrūr; SII, IX Pt. II, 655	1554	Kandavara	Udupa	Aṇṇa	The village and the family are mentioned in GP.
48.	Koteśvar temple 1562 inscription; SII, IX, Pt. II, 673	1562	KoteIśvara	Asaraṇa Māsaraṇa Sabhāyata Bhatta Dhanya Karta Yedehala	Vishṇu Krishna Nārana Śankara Narana-Nārāyana	The village and the family are not mentioned in GP.
49.	Shankaranārāyana	1562	Shankara-nārāyana			The village and the family are not mentioned in GP.
50.	Kumbhakāśi; SII, IX Pt. II, 673	1562	Kumbhakaśi	Upādhya Hebāra Mudya	Krishna Aṇṇa	Except Hebāra, the family and also village are note mentioned in GP.
51.	Bārakūru; SII, VII, 366	1564	Brahmāvara	Oorambaḷi Hebbāra	Aṇṇa Śankara	The village and the family are mentioned in GP.

Contd.

Contd.

(1)	(2)	(3)	(4)	(5)	(6)	(7)
52.	Bārakūru; SII, VII, 389	1569	Bārakūru	Heerala Muḷadi	Aṇṇa Aru-vaḷa	The families are mentioned in GP.
53.	Ambalapādi; ARSIE 574	1571	Ambalapadi	Nidamura	Sridhara	The family is mentioned in GP.
54.	Bārakūru SII, VII, 375	1581	Bārakūru	Adigaḷu Hatvāra	-	The families are in GP.
55.	Bārakūru; SII, VII, 331	1586	Bārakūru	Tuṅga Heerala Basuri	Keśava Śankara Krishṇa	The families are mentioned in GP.
56.	Udupi P. Gururaja Bhat, *Udupina Itihāsa*	1614	Huvinakere	Kemude Krama-dāre Kramadāre	-	The families are mentio-ned in GP but not the village.
57.	Kattupādi; ARSIE, 570	Undated	Kattupadi	Pādirāya	Nārāyana	The family is not mentioned in GP.
58.	Paduva Paṇamburu; SII, VII, 264	Undated	Ucchila	Bayiri	-	The family is mentioned in GP.
59.	Uppunda; ARSIE, 556	Undated	Uppunda	Kārantadi	Nārana	The family is mentioned in GP.
60.	Udupi; SII, VII, 298	Undated	Śivaḷḷi	Karamadārekkaḷa Shattiakkaḷa Kunjata Naduvanti	- - - -	The village and the family are mentioned in GP.

References

1. GP2, *op. cit.,* 10 p. 2.
2. P.Gururaja Bhat, *Studies in Tuluva History and culture,* (Kallianpur,1975), p. 349.
3. *Ibid.*, Plate 295 A (b).
4. *Naagamandala*-A ritual in the form of *naaga* dance by *naaga patri* (Priest).cf., P. Gururaja Bhat, *op. cit.,* p. xxix.
5. This detail was given to me by Subrāya Udupa, trustee of Ulluru Subrahmany a temple. This probably shows that Kandavara was not unsettled on the eve of Brahman settlement.
6. *Naagabanas* are kept reserved for the worship of *naaga* stones.
7. Baalekudru mutt follows the *Smaarta* tradition and according to its authorities, this mutt existed prior to the establishment of *asta mattas* in Udupi which follow Madhwa tradition.
8. Decipherment of the inscriptions was done by Dr. P.N. Narasimha Murthy, Karkala. The author likes to thank him for providing the copies of the inscriptions. These inscription are still unpublished.
9. This line mentions Naaraāyana dévaru Subrahmanya dévaru, *Subrahmanya.*
10. P. Gururaja Bhat, *Tulunaadu,* Udupi,1963, p.145.
11. GP1, *op. cit.,* p. 28.
12. GP2, *op. cit.,* p.12.
13. Cf, .Ko. Sa. Karanta, *Kūuta Mahā Jagattu,* (Saligrāma,1958), pp.15-19.
14. GP2, *op. cit.,* p.12.
15. SII, Vol. VII, No. 348.
16. Kota Sankaranarāyana Karanta believes that this is because the Kota Brahmans considered that those who perform puja at temple are not high grade brahmans. Cf., ko. Karanta, *op. cit.* p. 35.
17. This detail was given to me by KeSava Karanth, Manipal.
18. Ko, Sa, Karanta, *op. cit.,* p. 38.
19. P. Gururaja Bhat, *Antiquities of South Kanara,* (Kallianpur,1969), p. 9.
20. We find that even some of the Sivalli Brahman families like Kodanchas, who settled in *Kota, have become Brahmans.*
21. P. Gururaja Bhat, *Antiquties of South Kanara, op. cit.,* p. 9.
22. P. Gururaja Bhat, *Studies in Tuluva History and Culture, op. cit.,* Plate 210 (a).
23. Ko. Sa. Karanta, *op. cit.,* p. 38.
24. P. Gururaja Bhat, *Studies in Tuluva History and Culture, op. cit.,*

Plate 201(b).

25. This detail was given to me by Nitilapura Krishna Murthy, Manipal.
26. *SII* Vol.VII, No. 346.
27. *Ibid.*, I. No. 359.
28. *Ibid.*, No. 360.
29. *Ibid.*, No. 331.
30. Ko.Sa. Karanta, *op. cit.*, p. 37.
31. B. Vasanth Shetty, *Brahmaavarada Itihaasa* (Brahmavara,1988) p. 3ff.
32. P. Gururaja Bhat, Antiquities of South Kanara, *op. cit.*, p. 3f.
33. D.C.Sircar, *Indian Epigraphical Glossary*, (Delhi,1966) p. 62
34. Also cf. Baikadi Venkata Krishna Rāya, *Namma Ajapura*, (Brahmavara, 1961).
35. GP1, *op. cit.*, p. 28.
36. GP2, *op. cit.*, p. 12.
37. GP3, *op. cit.*, p. 16.
38. This detail was given to me by Dr. B. Vasanth Shetty, *Brahmavara.*
39. Cf., P. Gururaja Bhat, *Studies in Tuluva History and Culture.* Plate. 178(b).
40. *Ibid.*, Plate. 189 (b).
41. *ARSIE*,1920-30, No. 601.
42. *Ibid.*, No. 603.
43. Alphonsus D'Souza S.J. Economic and Social Conditions of the Nairis of Dakshina Kannada" in *Samaja Shodhana* Vol. 2, No. 2, October,1993.
44. This information was given to me by Nagaraja Varamballi, Muduragadi, Brahmavara.
45. *Ibid.*
46. ARSIE, No. 604.
47. During the earlier times Ōramballis were the *grāmani* of B Vasanth Shetty, *Barahmaavarada Itihaasa*, p.14.
48. B.Vasanth Shetty, *op. cit.*, p. 40.
49. SII.,Vol. IX, Pt. II. No. 465.
50. *Ibid.*, Vol. VI!. No 343.
51. *Ibid.*, Vol. IX Pt II. No.430.
52. GP1, op. cit., p. 29.
53. GP2, *op. cit.*, p. 7.
54. GP3, *op. cit.*, p. 14. III. 1.
55. Regarding the megalithics is South India, cf., A. Sundara. *The Early Chamber Tombs of South India*, (Delhi,1975) B.K. Gururaja Rao,

The Megalithic Culture in South India. (Mysore, 1972).

56. *Maāgane* is a unit of administration in South Kanara cf, P. Gururajá Bhat, *Studies in Tuluva History and culture, op, cit.*, p.148
57. This detail was given to me by Dinesh Krishna Tantri, Varkadi.
58. This detail was given to me by Y. Umanath Shenoy Ujire.
59. At present these three families have the title Tantri.
60. *Kambaḷa* is buffalo race sport popular in South Kanara.
61. This detail was given to me by Krishna Tantri Kemminje.
62. GP2, *op. cit.*, pp. 6-7.
63. It is possible to identify some of the places, where the brahmans settled, on the basis of their family names, *Kulanāamas.*
64. GP1. *op. cit.*, p. 29.
65. GP2, *op.cit.*
66. GP3, *op. cit.*, p.14. III.1.
67. Dr. Uppangala Rama Bhatta *Maanasa*, (Udupi,1990), p.10.
68. But unfortunately this author could not trace the Kutyadi mutt in South Kanara.
69. These details were given to me by Rama Ballal, Majanadi, who belongs to the Munnuaāya family adopted by Mañjanaadittaāya before becoming extinct.
70. GP1, *op. cit.*, p. 30
71. GP2, *op. cit., p.* 8
72. GP3, *op. cit.*, p.14, III.4.
73. This detail was given to me by Ratan Kumar, Baarikkadi.
74. This document is published by Rama Bhatta in his, *Gadinādu Kāasaragoodu*, (Udupi,1994), pp.128-130.
75. Dr. Uppangala Rama Bhatta, *Mānasa, op. cit.*, p. 30.
76. Cf., Padmanabha Kekunnāya *Śivaḷḷi Brāhmanara Kulanāmagalu Ondu Adhyāyana*, Unpublished dissertation submitted to university of Madras,1982, p.43, Also cf. H.Vishnumurthy Rao (ed). Brahmavāni (Kasargod,1993), p. 56.
77. The above details were given to me by Ratan Kumar Kaamada. Barikkadi.
78. GP1,*op. cit.*, p. 30.
79. GP2,*op. cit.*, p. 8.
80. GP3,*op.cit.*, p.14. III. 5.
81. Dr. K.V. Ramesh in *Tuluva, Sanchike*, 4, (Udupi,1980), p. 36.
82. GP1,*op, cit*, p. 30
83. GP2,*op. cit.*, p. 7.
84. GP3, *op. cit.*, p.14. III. 4.

85. Dr. Uppangala Rama Bhatta, *Mānasa op. cit.*, p. 30.
86. *Ibid.*, p. 15.
87. This detail was given to me by Vasudeva Kavu Patteri Kuudalu.
88. GP1, *op. cit.* p. 30.
89. GP2, *op. cit.*, p. 8.
90. GP1, *op. cit.*, p. 31.
91. GP2, *op. cit.*, p. 9.
92. GP3, *op. cit.*, p.14. III. 10.
93. This detail was given to me by Sudhama Kalkura, Talekaḷa.
94. GP1, *op. cit.*, p. 31.
95. GP2, *op. cit.*, p. 9.
96. GP3, *op. cit.*, p. 14. III. 8.
97. K.G. Vasanthamadhava, *Muulikeya Itihaasa* (Mulki, 1988), pp. 38-39.
98. I thank Dr. K.G.Vasanthmadhava, Mulki, for providing me a copy of his inscription. The text of this inscription is in Epigraphy Department, Mysore.
99. GP1, *op. cit.*, p. 29.
100. GP2, *op. cit.*, p. 7.
101. GP3, *op. cit.*, p. 14. III. 3.
102. Cf., Rasika Puttige, *Kanandūru Dharma Arasu Śri Todakukkinar Daivasthāna Paricāya* (Kananduru, 1967).
103. GP1, *op. cit.*, p. 30. GP2 mentions these families as living Karavoor., Cf. GP2, p. 6-7.
104. GP3, *op. cit.*, p. 14. III. 2.
105. GP2, *op. cit.*, p. 7. In this list there is no duplication of names from Karavoor.
106. This detail was given to me by Narāyana Acharya, Munchi.
107. GP1, *op. cit.*, p. 29.
108. GP2, *op. cit.*, p. 12.
109. GP3, *op. cit.*, p.16. III. 38.
110. Venkatakrishna Adiga (ed) *Nītavara Mahiśa Mardhini Suprabhāta Muttu śri Kṣetra Mahaatme*, (Nīruvāra, 1992 Second edition).
111. K.A Nilakanta Sastri, The Cōḷas, (Madras. 1984), p. 510.
112. *SII*, Vol VII No. 373.
113. *ARSIE*, 1920-30. No. 490.
114. *Ibid.*, No. 498. Regarding such assemblies and Brahman families like Munnuraāya. cf., Kesavan Veluthat, "The Nature of Agrarian Corporations in South Canara under The Aḷupas and Hoysalas" in *Proceedings of the Indian History Congress*, (Delhi, 1992), p. 111.

115. *ARIE* 1929, No. 494.
116. P. Gururaja Bhat, *Studies in Tuluva History and Culture, op. cit.*, Plate,125 (c).
117. *Ibid.*, p. IX.
118. Dr. Uppangala Rama Bhatta "Śiva Mereda śivaḷḷi" in his *Maanasa*, p. 3 ff.
119. P. Gururaja Bhat, *Aaḷuparasaru*, (Bangalore,1976) pp. 33-34.
120. In most of the villages discussed here, the brahmanas attached to them still claim that they are Śivaḷḷi brahmanas.
121. P.Gururaja Bhat, Antiquities of South Kanara, p. 21ff.
122. GP1, *op. cit.*, pp. 32-36.
123. GP1, *op. cit.*, p. 36.
124. GP2, *op. cit.*, pp. 9-12.
125. SII,Vol. VII No. 296.
126. *Ibid.*, No. 297.
127. *Ibid.*, No. 298.
128. *Ibid.*, No. 299.
129. *Ibid.*, No. 303.
130. *Ibid.*, No. 288.
131. *Ibid.*, No. 270.
132. *Ibid.*, Vol. IX Pt. II, No. 452.
133. *Ibid.*, No. 511.
134. *Ibid.*, No. 517.
135. *Ibid.*, No. 446.
136. *Ibid.*, Vol. VII No. 344.
137. B.R. Gupta (ed). *Vijāyanagara Inscription* Vol. II. (Mysore, 1986), KN 1189.
138. *ARSIE*, No. 581.
139. *Ibid.*, No. 570.
140. SII, Vol. VII, No. 319.
141. Narāyana Panditacharya (translated into Kannada by Vyasanakere Prabhanjanacharya), *Sumadhwa Vijāya*, (Bangalore, 1988).
142. Dr. Uppangala Rama Bhatta, *Manasa*, p. 8.
143. This detail was given to me by Mohana Tantri, Muddu Alevooru, Udapi.
144. This detail was given to me by Ananta Padmanabha Upadhya, Mudu, Alevooru.
145. This detail was given to me by P. Anantarama Bhat, Sivalli.
146. ARSIE, No. S 74.
147. This letter is now in the custody of the Nidambuuru family,

Ambalapaadi, Udupi.

148. This detail was given to me by N. Sreesa Ballal, Ambalapadi, Udupi.
149. This detail was given to me by Rāya Ballal, Chitpadi, Udupi.
150. I thank Dr. Gopala Ḳrishna Ballal, Chitpadi, Udupi for allowing me to personally examine the place.
151. Most of the Ballaaḷ families give the same explanation regarding the designation Ballāḷas. However Rama Bhatta says that Ballaaḷas designation might have come from Hoysala ballaaḷas who were Jains. cf. Dr. Uppaṇgala Rama Bhatta, *Gadinādu Kāsaragodu* (Udupi, 1994), p. 8.
152. This detail was given to me by Śripati Tantri, Udupi.
153. There is a place called Maradi lane in Udupi.
154. P. Gururaja Bhat, *Udupi Tradition, Antiquity, History and Culture, in Vivekananda Kendra Patrika - Pilgrimage centres of India,* February 1974, p. 91.
155. *Ibid.*, p. 92.
156. P. Gururaja Bhat, *Studies in Tuḷuva History and Culture*, p. 315
157. Ganapati Rao Aigal, Dakṣina Kannada Jilleya Prāchina ltihāsa (Mangalore, 1923), p. 391.
158. GP1, *op. cit.*, p. 30.
159. GP2, *op. cit.*, p. 9.
160. GP3, *op., cit.*, p. 14. III. 7.
161. Dr. B.A Viṿek Rai, *Tuḷu Janajpada Saahitya* (Bangalore, 1985), p. 146.
162. This detail was given by Harikrishna Tantri, Udupi.
163. GP1. *op. cit.*, p. 37.
164. GP2. *op. cit.*, p. 3.
165. GP3. *op. cit.*, p. 17. III. 43.
166. This book was published by Manchi Narāyana Acharāya for private circulation.
167. This document is with Śaśidhara Paanganna, Sripadi.
168. This detail was given to me by Ganapati Sastri, Punjalkatte.
169. Ganapati Rao Aigal, *op, cit.*, p. 413.
170. Dr. B.A. Vivek Rai, *op. cit.*, p. 35.
171. GP1. *op. cit.*, p. 37.
172. GP2. *op. cit.*, p. 3,
173. GP3. *op. cit.*, p. 17. III. 43.
174. I was able to examine this unpublished, un noticed inscription by the kind courtest of Sri Rama Kermunnāya, Vodila.
175. This detail was given to me by Rama Kermunnāya, Vodila.

176. Ganapati Rao Aigal, *op. cit.*, p. 413.
177. GP1. *op. cit.*, p. 37.
178. GP2. *op. cit.*, pp. 3-4.
179. GP3. *op. cit.*, p. 17. III. 44.
180. Ganapaati Rao Aigal, *op. cit.*, p. 412.
181. GP2. *op. cit.*, p. 4.
182. This detail was given to me by Sitarama Bhat Uppinangadi.
183. This information was given to me by Gopala Krishna Vailāya, Karāya.
184. This detail was given to me by Viśṇumuurthi Kuddaṇṇaāya, Karāya.
185. Dr. Upanagala Rama Bhatta Mānasa, *op. cit.*, p. 13.
186. *ARSIE*, No. 482.
187. GP1. *op. cit.*, p. 37.
188. GP2. *op. cit.*, p. 4.
189. GP3. *op. cit.*,17. III. 45.
190. This detail was given to me by B. Sripati Rao,Puttur, who belongs to Kudumattāya family.
191. This detail was given to me by Ramakrishna Mudannāya, Ujire.
192. K. Kushalappa Gowada, K. Chinnappa Gowda (ed), *Dakshina Kannada Jalleya Kaifiyattugalu*, (Ujire, 1983), p. 23.
193. GP1. *op. cit.*, p. 37.
194. GP2. *op. cit.*, p. 4.
195. GP3. *op. cit.*, p. 17. III. 45.
196. Dr. P. N. Narasimha Murthi, Karkala, has the details of inscription.
197. This detail was given to me by Vishnu Sampagetaya, Karanduru.
198. Ganapati Rao Aigal, *op. cit.*, p. 396.
199. GP2.*op. cit.*, p. 4.
200. This temple has yielded two inscriptions.
201. In GP1 Kudunnaāya family is menttined in Kunhimaarga while in GP2 this family is mentioned in Kareya and not in Kunhimaarga.
202. GP1. *op. cit.*, p. 37.
203. GP3. *op. cit.*, p. 5.
204. GP3. *op. cit.*, p. 17. III. 47.
205. Y. Umanath Shenoy (ed)., *Śri. Vaidyanātha*, (Kokkada, 1987), p. X.
206. *Ibid.*, P.X1.
207. Ganapati Rao Aigal, *op. cit.*, p. 35 f.
208. GP1. *op. cit.*, p.38.
209. GP2. *op. cit.*, p.5.
210. GP3. *op. cit.*, p.17. III. 49.
211. Y. Umanath Shenoy (ed)., *op. cit.*, p. X.

212. *Ibid.*, p. xiv.
213. Ganapati Rao Aigal, *op. cit.*, p. 411.
214. GP1. *op. cit.*, p. 38.
215. GP2.*op. cit.*, p. 5.
216. GP3. *op. cit.*, p.17. III. 50.
217. It is said that since this family settled on the western side (*Pudu*) to the temple they came to be called Paddillaāyas.
218. GP1.*op. cit.*, p. 38.
219. GP2.*op. cit.*, p. 5.
220. GP3. *op. cit.*, p. III. 51.
221. Ganapati Rao Aigal, *op. cit.*, p. 405.
222. GP1. *op. cit.*, p. 38.
223. GP2. *op. cit.*, p. 5.
224. GP3. *op. cit.*,17. III. 51.
225. This detail was given to me by Dr. K.G. Vasanthamadhava, Mulki.

5

The Sahyādri Khānda

The *Sahyādri Khānda* which claims to be a part of Skānda Purana is intimately connected with *Grāmapaddhati*. In *Sahyādri Khānda*, which is written in Sanskrit, one can find direct connections with purānas and here we find representation of puranic personages like Śhatanika, Śaunaka, the Skānda and Vyāsa and here we find inevitable puranic claim. There is an elaborate description of the creation of *Parāśurāma kṣētra*. In one place, the land is stated to have been created by shooting an arrow[1] while in another place the land is created by throwing an axe.[2] In the earlier situation, the land is called merely *Rāma* kṣētra, while in the later situation it is referred to as *Parāśurāma ksētra*.

Grāmapaddhati and *Sahyādri Khānda*

Sahyādri Khānda as a work is lengthier, while *Grāmapaddhati* is a brief work. But the latter consists of more details regarding the brahmana family names and the villages. *Sahyādri Khānda*, on the other hand, gives more importance to mythological narrations and also the stories of different varieties of fallen brahmanas. In *Sahyādri Khānda*, we find the migration of brahmanas from different parts of India and most of these migrated people are described as fallen brahmanas.[3] *Sahyādri Khānda* does not give the *Vamśāvali* of Mayura Varma and his successors, while *Grāmapaddhati* purports to give one. Thus, both *Grāmapaddhati* and *Sahyādri Khānda* make puranic claims, the extent of mythological narration in the two are being different. The *Grāmapaddhati* does not give any narration of how brahmanas in different villages became fallen or degraded. Only GP3 mentions the story of fall of Koteśhwara brahmanas. In *Sahyādri Khānda*, we find that some of the fallen brahmanas are purified by converting them to Vaishnavism. This may point to the post

Madhwacharya dating of this text. In the villages mentioned also there are variations between the names of the villages mentioned in *Sahyādri Khānda* and *Grāmapaddhati*. Even the brahmana family names found in different versions of *Grāmapaddhati* are not to be found in *Sahyādri Khānda*, the purpose of which seems to be different. The purpose of *Grāmapaddhati* is to claim a certain antiquity to the brahmana groups of South Western India and a certain respectability and legitimacy on account of their origins; their settlement in different villages and their internal migration within these villages are also taken up. The purpose of *Sahyādri Khānda* on the other hand seems to be the recording of the migration of the brahmanas from areas other than Ahikshetra as well. The authors of *Sahyādri Khānda* also would like to put their control on these newly migrated groups. Thus, we find certain similarities and dissimilarities between these two texts, *Grāmapaddhati* and *Sahyādri Khānda*.

Kannada Sahyādri Khānda

Apart from the text or texts in Sanskrit, there is a *Sahyādri Khānda* in Kannada language as well.[4] It concentrates on giving list of pilgrimage centres and narrating the Sthalapurànas. According to its editor Y.C. Bhanumati, Kannada *Sahyādri Khānda* has no similarities with Sanskrit *Sahyādri Khānda*.[5] She says that the original version of Kannada *Sahyādri Khānda* must be different work which is not available now.[6] However, this Kannada version of *Sahyādri Khānda* also claims that it is a part of Skānda Purana and here we discern the importance given to the puranic details. There is also reference to the creation of land by Parāśurāma. It does not mention Mayura Varma. But it gives a list of different tīrthas, some of which are also mentioned in Sanskrit *Sahyādri Khānda*.

The Kannada *Sahyādri Khānda* mentions the places like Anga deśa, Arunachala, Avanti, Amalaka, Kakudagiri, Kāśmiri, Kundinipura, Kaivartaka, Kotiśvara, Kodiyaśhrama, Gajakṣetra, Gokarna, Trigarta deśa, Dakshinavarta, Durgeśvara ksētra, Dvāravati, Dhwajapura, Pāndya deśa, Brahmagiri, Brahmapura, Bhāganda ksētra, Madhupura, Maharastra, Rajatagiri, Vasupura, Vateśhwara, Vanāvāsi, Venkatāchala, Velāvana, Sahyādri, Sahyāmalaka, Sālagrama, Sunandakagrāma, Subrahmanya, and *Syānanduru*.

The Kannada *Sahyādri Khānda* also mentions the *tīrthas* like Agastya tīrtha, Angirasa tīrtha, Kanva tîrtha, Karkotaka tîrtha, Kâveri, Kâœmiri, Kutaje, Kubjanadi, Kumudvati, Kotitirtha, Khatwangi, Gālava tīrtha, Godāvari, Chakranadi, Tamraparni, Tungabhadra, Dhāra, Nētravati, Payasvani, Bhrigutirtha, Rāma tīrtha, Vasista tīrtha, Varahi, Vetālavarada,

Śhuktimati, Sīta, Svarnanadi, and Svetavamśa tīrtha.

Thus, here one can find the topographical details in Kannada *Sahyādri Khānda* some of which correspond to the topographical references found in Sanskrit *Sahyādri Khānda*. Thus, the historical tradition of South Western India can be found articulated in the form of literary texts like *Grāmapaddhati*, Kannada *Sahyādri Khānda* and Sanskrit *Sahyādri Khānda*. A look at these texts shows that their authors were brahmanas that they presented only those relevant aspects which they expected would determine their position in the society. These factors were added in these texts with a view to establishing their identity. The search for identity is the principle purpose of these texts; such an identity would be helpful in strengthening the position of the brahmanas in the society.

Sanskrit Sahyādri Khānda

The Sanskrit *Sahyādri Khānda* claims to be a part of Skānda purāna which is considered to be one of the eighteen purānas. There are several versions of *Sahyādri Khānda* and for our analysis we shall take up the printed version edited by Gerson da Cunha in 1877, which as the editors himself says, is based on nearly fourteen manuscripts.[7]

The purānas in general, deal with the evolution of the universe, recreation of the universe from its constituent elements, the genealogies of gods and seers and the history of royal families. We can identify two kinds of purānas: ancient and later. Ramachandra Dikshitar says that the classification of eighteen purānas marks a definite stage in the evolution of puranic literature. To give an air of antiquity so as to be acceptable the redactors of the extant purānas did not disregard ancient materials and tried as far as possible to maintain them as much as suited their purpose.[8] He says that tradition has accepted the existence of eighteen greater purānas and eighteen lesser purānas. The lesser purānas are very later productions, of a sectarian character and purely of local interest[9]. Here we are discussing precisely regarding the lesser purānas, which exhibited the characteristics listed by Dikshitar. The *Sahyādri Khānda* also typically utilizes these puranic materials in the greater purānas and the topographical as well as mythological details are found inserted in *Sahyādri Khānda*. This explains the correspondence between certain of topographical references in *Sahyādri Khānda* with topographical details found in larger purānas like *Brahmanda Purāna, Vāyu Purāna, Mārkandeya Purāna* and *Matsya Purāna.*[10]

An analysis of *Sahyādri Khānda* reveals its function and we shall proceed to give a summary of contents of *Sahyādri Khānda*. The portions which are relevant to the social history of South Western India in *Sahyādri Khānda* consist of following sections:

BK III *Renuka Mahātmyam* which is said to be part of the Skānda Purana.

BK IV Skānda Purana uttarardhasya Chandrachuda Mahātmya.

BK V Nagahvahaya Mahātmyam.

BK VI Varunapura Mahātmyam.

BK VII Kamakoti Mahātmyam.

BK VIII Mangisa Mahātmyam.

Skānda Puranantargatam *Sahyādri Khāndam Uttarārdham*

Chapter 1.

1. Chitpāvana brahmanopattih (the origin of Chitpavana brahmanas).
2. Kārāśtra brahmanotpattih (the origin of Karastra brahmanas).
3. Gomānchala Ksētra Mahātmyam (the glory of Gomānchala ksētra).
4. Vividha brahmanotpattih (the origin of different groups of brahmanas).
5. Brahmana Vichāra (the consideration of brahmanas).
6. Prthvidāna praśamśa (in praise of land grants).
7. Parāśurāma Ksetraotpattih (the origin of Parāśurāma *ksētra*).
8. Grama nirnayah (demarcation of villages).
9. Bhārgāvena Krta stutih (the praise composed by Bhārgava).
10. Pātityagrāma Panchagrāma nirnaya (demarcation of inferior villages).
11. Title not given-related to thirty-two villages.
12. Pātitya grāma kathanam (story of fallen village).
13. Pātitya grāma nirnayam (demarcation of fallen village).
14. Pātitya grāma nirnayam (demarcation of fallen village).
15. Pātitya grāma nirnayam (demarcation of fallen village).
16. Title not given-related to the area of river Sita.
17. Mithunāhara brāhmana kathanam (the story of Mithunāhara brahmanas).
18. Pātitya grāma kathanam (the story of fallen village).
19. Pātitya grāma (fallen village).
20. Ksētra Mahātmya (glory of a *ksētra*).
21. Mahālingeśha Mahimā (glory of Mahalingeśha)
    End of *Sahyādri Khānda* Uttara Khānda.
22. From the above list of contents we shall only take up the chapters from 6 to 21 since it is they that are relevant for our present study and it is in these chapters that we find certain details regarding the brahmanas of South Western India.[11]

The sixth chapter consists of the story of *dāna* (gift) by Bali to Vāmana. Hari (Vishnu) who was in the form of Vāmana gave away the land, which he gained from Bali to Kāśyapa who gave land to Gowda brahmanas and Dravidas living in the region between Himalaya and Vindhya and this region came to be known as Aryavarta. Time passes in this way until the beginning of Tretāyuga. When Kārtāvirya and other strong kings appropriated this land, the brahmans approached God under the leadership of Kasyāpa. The God became son of Jamadagni and Renuke and he came to be known as Bhārgava Rāma who started doing penance. Pleased by his penance Śiva who was in Kailasa gifted his axe to him and told him that he would become famous as Parāśurāma. As ordered by his father he killed his own mother. When his father asked him for any boon in return, Parāśurāma requested him to give life back to his mother. After that Rama went to visit the tīrtha kshētras on the earth during which time Kārtavīrya forcibly took away Kamadhenu. Then Parāśurāma killed kshatriya kings twenty-one times. He gave away the land to Kashyapa, Vasistha and other great sages. He was suggested by Narada to create a piece of land for himself by driving away the sea by using an arrow. He stood on the top of the Sahyādri and asked sea to send all animals to the eastern sea so that their lives would be protected if he uses an arrow to create land out of the sea. On the land created by sending the sea backwards, Bhārgava created two villages. Then Rāma shot an arrow and created five villages. Thus the land created by using arrow came to be known as Ramaksētra and there Parāśurāma started living. This place which is the lower part of Sahyādri consists of several divisions and this place came to be known as Banavalli. Parāśurāma ksetra came to be divided in to Kērala, Tulanga, Saurāshtra, Konkana, Karahata, Karnata and Barbara and these divisions came to be known as Sapta Konkana.

An area of land within three yojana breadth and five yojana length came to be called Gokarna where Shiva started living in the name of Mahabala. In a place ten yojana north of it there is a place Naravẹ where there is Sapta Kotisvara linga where Rama started living and divided the land among the brahmanas and created agraharas for vedic scholars.

The brahmanas like Karnāta, Maharāshtra, Tailanga, Gurjara, Kanyakubja, Chittaputa, Payosniti, who were born in Aryavarta, Kānchi, Kausala, Saurāshtra, Devarashtra, Indukaccha and Madhyama brahmanas on the banks of river Kāveri, also brahmanas of Abhira, Dravida, Dakshinapatha, Avanti, Magadha and brahmanas from Ahikshetra and also brahmanas with the name Chitpavana were given land donations. After telling these brahmanas that they could call him if they faced any trouble, Parāśurāma went to Mahendra hill for the protection of the brahmanas.

The brahmanas decided to test Parāśurāma by calling him who

immediately responded by appearing before them. He became angry after knowing their real intention and cursed them that they should lead a very hard life. Let the śudras give gifts when the brahmanas ask for it, let the ksatriyas consider them as *dutas* or servants. Thus, cursing he went to Mahendra hill and started living in their villages and agraharas.

In the seventh chapter there is re-narration of Parāśurāma creating land by sending the sea backwards; this time not with the help of arrow but by throwing his axe. As he had earlier given away all the land to Kāśhyapa and others they told him that he should not live in their land and that he should go away immediately. So he went to the western direction and came to Sahya hills from where he saw the sea and asked king of sea to give some land to him. The king of sea suggested Parāśurāma to throw his axe. When Parāśurāma threw his axe, the sea went backwards. Parāśurāma got three yojana of land. Since this land consisted of no brahmanas, he converted the fishermen by investing the thread on them. He bade them to live happily and call him whenever they were in danger. Thus saying he went to Gokarna to sea god Mahabala there. The brahmanas wishing to test Paraśurāma called him who came there and realized their motive and cursed them to become equal to śudras and after that he went away to Mahendra hill to do penance there.

After some time Mayura Varma belonging to Surya vamśa became the king of this region. He brought pure brahmanas from his country Ahicchatra and gave them thirty-two villages.

In the eighth chapter we notice that Mayura Varma, the son of Hemanga Rāja gave all respects to the pure brahmanas whom he had brought from Ahikshetra and made them to settle in thirty-two villages. Here we find the details of villages given by Parāśurāma to the brahmanas.

Kadamba kānana	-	3 villages
Gokarna	-	4 villages
On the banks of Śhuktimati	-	2 villages
On the southern bank of Sita Ajapuri	-	4 villages
Near Anantesha	-	10 villages
On the northern bank of Netravati	-	9 villages
Gajapuri- Narasimha	-	Kuta village

To the east of Kota, there is Siddeśhvara, to the west there is sea, to the north there is Kotilingesha and to the south there is Sita river. The nine villages on the northern bank of river Netravati were given by Paraśurāma to brahmana priests called srotris who were engaged in the worship of Śhiva, Vishnu and Ganapati. Mayura Varma was also ruling this region very religiously. After many years due to invasion of Kalki, Mayura Varma kept the administration in the hands of his ministers. The brahmanas went back to Ahicchatra. During this time, the brahmanas who had come from Gorashtra started living in the outskirts of these villages.

Chandrangada, the son of Mayura Varma came to know about the return of the brahmanas to their homeland and he went to Ahicchatra and requested them to come to his country and created villages in two categories: western and eastern villages.

Western Villages

Name of village		*Number of households*
Kāreruru	-	04 households
Varkādi	-	08 households
Marane	-	02 households
Kānavi	-	02 households
Pādigrama	-	04 households
Vodila	-	04 households
Māghava	-	04 households
Mittanādu	-	07 households
Nirumārga	-	07 households
Shīmanturu	-	09 households
Śhivahalli	-	30 households
Ajapuri	-	08 households
Nīlāvara	-	08 households
Skāndapura	-	02 households

Here we have only fourteen villages rather than sixteen found in *Grāmapaddhati*. Kānavi and Māghava are the new villages which are not mentioned in *Grāmapaddhati*. Vodila, which is mentioned in eastern villages section in *Grāmapaddhati*, is put in the western villages section here.

Eastern Villages

Name of village		*Number of households*
Shripādi	-	05 households
Kāundila	-	02 households
Karamuru	-	02 households
Ujjaya	-	16 households
Kattumārga	-	08 households
Chikodi	-	N.A.
Vāmiñjuru	-	02 households

Contd.

Contd.

Name of village		*Number of households*
Puragrāma	-	04 households
Ballamañja	-	03 households
Hainādu	-	04 households
Ichuka	-	06 households
Kemiñje	-	01 households
Pālinje	-	02 households
Saripādi	-	05 households
Kodipādi	-	07 households

Here we notice that villages Kaundila, Kattumārga, Chirkodi, Vāmañjuru, Ballamañja and Hainadu are villages which are not mentioned in *Grāmapaddhati*. This chapter of *Sahyādri Khānda* mentions that the eastern households are, without any doubt, thirty-seven. The western households are 206.

In the ninth chapter there are details about Krodha Muni who worshipped Shankara and Shrisha, created a tīrtha and a grāma by his own name. Parāśurāma on his way to Gokarna saw Mahendra hill and coming he saw Tulu country. Going to the west on the banks of Śhuktimati river he saw nine depressed women who requested him to protect them. They revealed that they were the daughters of śrotris and that they had lost their husbands in an early age. Parāśurāma took them to Kodeśha and told them to stay there for some time and after this he went to Gokarna.

The tenth chapter says that nine women gave birth to sons called Gōlakas or those who are born after the death of their fathers. For livelihood, they depended on agriculture and other activities which were supposed to be done by śudras. They again approached Parāśurāma who assured them his help. A brahmana called Somapithi made them to take bath in Śhuktimati and gave their families different names. They are Gāsila, Kānata, Vaidya, Anichātara, Hēramba, Arayala, Edala, Kōmagihemna and Kalkuru.

In order to settle them he created Paruśhabda grāma which is near Sīta river to the west of Śhuktimati. There we find Gajamukha which is in the form of Vighnaraja. To the north of it there is a Sārangapāni temple which is famous as Karavēla. To its west there is Asurāntaka who is famous as Vamana. In front of Śhuktimati, there is Devi temple. There is also a Mahalinga. These nine families were made to settle in these five villages. Their gotra is Atri. In the Sahyādri valley there is the garden of Golakas whom this chapter calls fallen brahmanas who are not expected to mingle with other pure brahmanas.

The eleventh chapter refers to another fallen village on the banks of Śhuktimati river. This grama was given to the brahmanas by śudras. Earlier there were śudra kings named Madhwa and Kanda, who had respect towards the brahmanas. During this time eight brahmanas came to this area and with the motive of gaining money praised the śudra kings and succeeded in obtaining wealth and live for twelve years. During this time the younger of the two kings wanted to remarry since he had no children from the first wife. In order to go to the wedding he requested the brahmanas to take him in a palanquin which had eight legs. The brahmanas agreed to carry him on the palanquin. In return, they obtained all comforts of life. When they returned to the village they had to confront the anger of the other brahmanas who tried to attack them. They ran away to the śudra king and pleaded for protection and he gave the village and his own wife, whom he had married very recently, to the brahmanas in the Narasimha temple. Since these brahmanas had served the śudras and accepted the materials given by the śudra king, they became fallen brahmanas.

The twenlth chapter narrates the story of another fallen village near Kotilingeshwara and the people of this village speak lies. There was a conflict between the Koteśhvara brahmanas and those who lived on the banks of Śhuktimati regarding the ownership of some land. The king Vasu Chakravarti decided to give impartial judgment. The Koteśhvara brahmanas adopted cunning ṃethods by digging the land and keeping a man there who was expected to tell that land belonged to Koteśhvara brahmanas.[12] However, they failed to convince the king and other brahmanas who cursed them to become fallen brahmanas. They were saved by Madhwa saint who converted them to Vaishnavism and protected them.

The thirteenth chapter refers to the arrival of pregnant women from different countries like Anga, Vanga, Kalinga, Saurāshtra, Gurjara, Andhra, Dravida, Karnāta, Kāśhmira, Karahāta, Maharāshtra, Sindhu, Magadha, Gowda and Gorashtra. They went to Bhārgava who assured them that he would protect them.

In the fifteenth chapter, we find reference to the fallen brahmanas on the banks of Chakra river. Parāśurāma created these. They were ignorant of the vedas and were consuming non-vegetarian food. Mayura Varma kept them in a place called Vallabhi and gave other villages to good brahmanas. When the fallen brahmanas questioned this act of Mayura Varma he gave them four villages, Kudalaka, Padika, Matti and Nāga.

The sixteenth chapter refers to Belanjiti which is situated to the north of Sita river. In Rathnamālinagari there was a brahmana who had two wives Gunavati and Gunamālini. The former had a child. During that time a brahmana from Gorāshtra came and slept there for one night. In the night Gunamālini went and killed the child. The brahmana went to the king who sent for a logician in Jayantika on the banks of western sea. The brahmana began his journey to Vijayapuri.

The logician put a test which was very difficult to perform for a lady with good character. While Gunavati refused to do it, Gunamālini performed the test before the assembly. But the logician decided that Gunamālini was the culprit. This brahmana was given two villages for the right judgment.

However, this brahmana from Gorāshtra became a fallen brahmana since he had killed his wife and her lover. The brahmanas of Gorāshtra went to several tīrtha *ksētras*, holy places. This chapter states that these are the fallen brahmanas and that these were converted to Vaishnavism by a Madhwa saint.

The eighteenth chapter refers to a brahmana of Gorāshtra who possessed magical powers and impressed the king and got eight villages as gift.

The nineteenth chapter continues the narration of earlier brahmana who on his way to his homeland went to Chandika river where he got eight children from a maid servant and gave the eight villages which he had obtained from the king to these eight sons. They were not expected to sit with other pure brahmanas. The *gotra* of these brahmanas is Kasyāpa *gotra*. These sons of maid servant are fallen brahmanas.

In the twentieth chapter, we find reference to rahma-kshtra which meant the combination of brahmanical and ksatriya characters in the same person. There is also description of divergent varieties of brahmanas. There are Aryāvartas and they are named so because they had come from Aryāvarta. There are Prāgjyotisas who are described as Aryas and they predict regarding the future.[13] There are Garadas who are not Aryas, Yamalas who had come from Yamala, those who come from desert region are Konkanas who eat fish; there are also Devarashtriyas and Padikas. There are *sankara jatis* or mixed castes also.

It is possible to identify the point of contact between *Grāmapaddhati* and *Sahyādri Khānda*. An analysis of both the texts reveals the similarities between them. This is particularly visible in the themes and symbolism of the mythological sections. Firstly, both the texts mention the story of Parāśurāma creating the land and donating the land to the brahmanas who were converted community. They lose their caste and status only because of their silliness in attempting to test Parāśurāma himself. Another episode common to both the texts is the bringing of brahmanas from Ahikshetra by Mayura Varma, their re-emigration to their earlier place after abdication of throne by Mayura Varma and the act of Chandrangada bringing the brahmanas again from Ahikshetra and donating land to the brahmanas and the division of households. Thus, there are certain themes common to these texts which would go to strengthen the brahmanical position in the society.

In *Sahyādri Khānda*, it is possible to identify repetitions of some of the episodes with or without slight variations and there is the repetition of the episodes with similar symbols and themes. The sixth chapter mentions the story of Parāśurāma creating land out of the sea by using an arrow while in the next chapter there is a repetition of the same episode. This time Parāśurāma creates land by throwing his axe and this corresponds to the story found in the traditions in the region. There are also episodes with the same theme and symbol; either brahmana is given *dana* of certain number of villages or a group of brahmanas become fallen due to various causes as mentioned in these episodes.

It is also possible to identify variations between *Grāmapaddhati* and *Sahyādri Khānda*. In one of the versions of *Grāmapaddhati* (GP3) there is narration of Kārtavīrya taking away Kāmadhēnu and killing Jamadagni. We find that the same story is mentioned in *Sahyādri Khānda* with minor variations. There are also major variations between these two texts. The story of fight between Hubbasiga and brahmanas which is narrated in so much detail in *Grāmapaddhati* is not mentioned in *Sahyādri Khānda*. The Hubbasiga legend, perhaps was not considered relevant by the authors of *Sahyādri Khānda*. While *Grāmapaddhati* concentrates only on the brahmanas who were brought from Ahikshetra, *Sahyādri Khānda* on the other hand deals with not only brahmanas from Ahikshetra but also the brahmanas of other regions like *Kāśhmira*, *Gorāshtra, Anga, Vanga, Magadha*, etc. We find also totally different situations in these texts which do not correspond to each other. In *Grāmapaddhati*, the Shivalli brahmana families are mentioned and each of these families are associated with a particular village and these details are missing in *Sahyādri Khānda* which gives a list of additional villages which are considered as fallen villages. Another significant feature is that most of the fallen villages mentioned are stated to be on the banks of rivers like Sīta, Śhuktimati, Chakra, etc. In *Sahyādri Khānda*, there is a direct reference to Madhwa saints and their proselytizing activities concerning the fallen brahmanas. This demonstrates the attempt of the Vaishnava mathas to bring different brahmanical groups under its authority. Thus, it is possible to identify the connections between *Grāmapaddhati* and *Sahyādri Khānda*.

When viewed from the angles of modern historical methodology we can find the unusual way of expressing the notices regarding the social changes that were taking place during the contemporary times. The Sanskrit *Sahyādri Khānda* refers to the migration of different groups of brahmanas like from Gowda deśa, Anga, Vanga, Kalinga, Kāśhmira, etc.

It is possible to identify the migration of different brahmanical groups like that of Gowda Saraswats[14], brahmanas from Kāśhmir[15] and brahmanas from Kerala[16] to South Western India. The authors of *Sahyādri Khānda* noticed this migration of different brahmanical groups.

Thus, *Sahyādri Khānda* gives details of the migration of the brahmanas from different parts of the country to South Western India. On the one hand it preserves the memories of these migrated groups regarding their connections with the territory where they lived earlier. On the other it reveals the psyche of the authors of this work, their attitude towards these groups which is one of contempt and jealously and a sense of insecurity. This also shows the tension that prevailed among the different brahmanical groups themselves. Another aspect which we find here is vaishnavization process which became popular particularly after the great tours of Madhwacharya and establishment of eight mathas in Udupi.

In spite of the above corresponding historical references, when *Sahyādri Khānda* is focused in the context of *Skānda Purāna* as one of the eighteen purānas, one can easily identify certain discrepancies. A linguistic study of this shows that most of it are additions, interpolations. It is possible that the different stories regarding the degradation of the brahmana caste groups are added with the purpose of curbing the interest of certain brahmanical communities.[17] Although it contains the features of a puranic text, still it is useful as a source to identify the different migrated groups in South Western India and also to comprehend the attempt of one group to establish the authority over others. Again, in the story of Parāśurāma Ksētrotpatti it is the attempt to validate the brahmanical hold over the tracts of land over which the brahmana communities claimed ownership. This work represents the historical consciousness of Indians and it has recorded only those things that are considered as essential for furtherance of the hold of the caste groups over the society.

References

1. J. Gerson Da Cunha, *Sahyādri Khānda—Skānda Puranantargata*, Bombay, 1877, pp. 325-326, 331.
2. *Ibid.*, Chapter 20, *Ksētra Mahātmya.*
3. *Ibid.*, Chapters, 10, 12, 13, 14, 15, 18, 19.
4. Y.C. Bhanumati (ed.), *Sahyādri Khānda*, Mysore, 1984.

5. *Ibid.*, p. 151.
6. *Ibid.*, p. 152.
7. Kota Shankaranarayana Karanta quotes from Da Cunha and mentions Kota version and Chempi version from South Kanara, see Ko. Sa. Karanta, *Kuta Mahajagattu*, Saligrama, 1958.
8. V.R. Ramachandra Dikshitar, "The Purānas: A Study", Narendra Nath Law (ed.), *The Indian Historical Quarterly*, Volume VII-4, Delhi, Reprint, 1985, p. 751.
9. *Ibid.*, p. 755.
10. D.C. Sircar, "The Text of Puranic list of Rivers", Narendra Nath Law (ed.), *The Indian Historical Quarterly*, Volume XXVII-3, pp. 215-238.
11. J. Gerson Da Cunha, *Sahyādri Khānda Skānda Puranantargata*, pp. 323-387.
12. A variant of this story occurs in GP3.
13. Pragjyotisha here is wrongly understood as prediction of future. Pragjyotisha meant aspects related to the east. See Sir Monier-Williams, *A Sanskrit English Dictionary*, Delhi, Reprint, 1981.
14. A.K. Priolkar, *The Goa Inquisition*, New Delhi, 1961, p. xii.
15. *SII* VII, No. 376; K. G. Vasanthamadhava, "Prachina Karnataka Mattu Kasmira", *Sadhane*, Sanchike – 2, Bangalore, 1974, pp. 107-110. I thank Dr. Vasanthamadhava for drawing my attention to this detail.
16. *SII* VII, No. 190.
17. To give an example, *Sahyādri Khānda* mentions the story of the fallen brahmanas, the Patalis who are also known as Sthanikas. P. Gururaja Bhat has showed that Sthanikas were in reality a part of Shivalli brahmana community. P. Gururaja Bhat, *Tulunādina Itihāsadalli Sthvāikaru*, Udupi, 1966.

6

The Function of Tradition

A tradition can be defined as the passing of opinions, beliefs or stories from one generation to the next. When such types of traditions are put into writing, they become literary traditions. Indian Historical Tradition represented both oral tradition and literate tradition. In most cases there is possibility that literary tradition draws on what is contained in the oral tradition. Our concern here is with what is reduced to writing.

The creation of Purąnas was an evolutionary process. It took several years for the authors of the Puranas to compile the various sections of the puranic literature. A cursory look at the characteristics of various Puranas indicates that all the puranas in India did not exhibit the similar features. It is here that we discern certain differences between the *mahapuranas* and local *puranas*.

Need for Puranas: The Historical Experience

The compilation of puranas represented the standardisation of Sanskritic tradition of post-Gupta period. Most of the eighteen puranas were compiled during the Gupta and post-Gupta period. After seventh century A.D. there was the spread of the greater brahmanical culture of North India to other parts of India, particularly South India. This expansion of brahmanical culture in South India was due to the process of creation of brahman settlements in the context of the emergence of local kingdoms in South India. After seventh century A.D. there was the emergence of many local kingdoms.[1] This process led to the need for legitimacy and integration of the greater brahmanical culture and the original tribal customs of the locality. What was needed was an agency through which a balance could be maintained between the two broad cultures: the brahmanical culture and non-brahmanical culture. It is in this context that we should analyse the creation of certain texts in western India. Broadly, we can classify puranic literature into greater puranas and lesser puranas. The greater puranas were the eighteen mahapuranas like Skanda, Vishnu, Matsya, etc. They were standardised during the early medieval period. The greater puranas incorporated data of certain antiquity. The lesser puranas were the creation of local genius and they tried to claim logical link with the greater puranas by incorporating certain motifs. Now our concern is with the circumstances and people who contributed to the creation of the local puranas.

Purpose and Function of Puranas

What was the function of the creation of puranas? A study of ancient Indian historical tradition indicates that the evolution of puranas represented transfer of authorship from the bards like *sutas* and *magadhas* to the brahman sages like Vasishta and Bharadhwaja.[2] The bards or the wandering poets who were the earlier owners of knowledge were dispossessed of their claim to early Vedic traditions by the brahmans.[3] It was the latter who put into writing what was hitherto an oral tradition. This enabled them to claim ownership over puranic literature. The major function of these puranas was to legitimise the rule of royal families of North India. After the Gupta period there was a phenomenal increase in the number of the land grants to brahmans in the core as well as peripheries.[4] After seventh century A.D. there was the migration of brahmans from North India to South India. Migration was due to the emergence of regional kingdoms like Kadambas on the western coast. Migration was also due the competition among brahman population since there was increase in the population. Decline of certain urban centres like Ahicchatra in U.P. led to further increase in the migration of brahmans from North India to South India. When the brahmans landed in new localities they did not leave completely their heritage. Perhaps they remembered the greater puranic tradition. Now they needed certain instruments of social sanction. They were patronised by the local kings since brahmanas through *yagas* and literature legitimised their rule. Why the local puranas were created? It was to rationalise the ownership of brahmans over land in the locality. Through the creation of *brahmadeyas* the kings allowed the brahmans to become owners of land. These local puranas might not have belonged to early historic period. It is possible that some puranas were composed in early medieval period and some others were written during the medieval and later medieval period.[5]

Indian Attitude Towards Past

Writing on the Indian consciousness of history, few scholars have averred that Indians lacked a sense of history since they did not maintain systematic records as one can find in Europe. However, these scholars did not realise the fact that Indian sense of history was expressed in a rather different way. It was through myths, traditions and chronicles that Indians tried to preserve their history. In the case of ancient India it was the brahmans, the community with the knowledge of reading and writing, who first started preserving historical tradition in written form. Therefore, it was quite natural that European scholars did not find details regarding rise and fall of kingdoms in the Indian historical tradition. Thus, the details found in the Vedic literature, purānas and other regional works, though they mention about dynasties and kings, helps one to reconstruct social history rather than political history.

The traditions in the Indian context were one way of expressing a sense of history. A sense of history, as Romila Thapar says, is "a consciousness of past events, which events are relevant to a particular society, seen in chronological framework and expressed in a form which meets the needs of that society...."[6]

This sense of history is also revealed in the form of a myth, which represents the self-image of a given culture and it expresses its social assumptions.[7] The purānic myths represented the group experience of a given society. The myths were transmitted from generation to generation and they represented the sense of history of pre-modern Indians. Through the myths, it was easy to preserve the historical traditions and it became a part of the literate traditions of upper classes in the society. The significance of studying the historical tradition is to identify the relevance of a particular event mentioned in a tradition. The analysis of the structure of a myth can reveal the structure of society from which it emanates. Thus the traditions had a particular function to perform and close analyses of such traditions reveal their purpose.

Myths were incorporated in certain purānas that were written during the post-Gupta period. Kunal Chakrabarti has analysed that the purānas were an instrument for the propagation of brahmanical ideals of social reconstruction and sectarian interests, a medium for the absorption of local cults and associated practices, and a vehicle for popular instruction on norms governing everyday existence.[8]

This statement indicates that the major function of brahmanical tradition was to establish and legitimise a social order which was well suited to interest of the dominant community. The puranic myths or traditions acted as the vehicle of establishment of brahmanical hegemony in the peripheral regions. A glance at the folk literature of south western India, a region on western coast reveals that there were several Sanskritic elements which had entered into the non-brahmanical sphere. Perhaps this hegemony of brahmanical religion is symbolised by the co-existence of both brahmanical temples and small shrines of *dāivas* and *bhūtas* in a region like South Kanara, a region of western India.

The puranas can be broadly categorised into *mahāpurānas* and *upapurānas*. It was the latter category, due to its flexibility, which can be seen in the peripheral regions where the brahmanas took some time to establish their hegemony. Though the *upapurānas* made tall claims that they were part and parcel of *mahāpurānas*, they were written during comparatively later time when the brahmanas started migrating to peripheral zones.

Traditions as Source for Social History

The more traditional school of thought did not consider the importance the use of the traditions for writing history. However, now traditions are no longer neglected simply because they are the creation of imagination of a particular community in the society; they are looked upon as those unlikely sources from which it is possible to deduce historical phenomena, social changes, cultural divergence and class orientations. Rather than the form of tradition it is its function, which is given, more importance for tradition was one way of expressing historical consciousness among ancient Indians.

All over India, we discern different varieties of myths regarding the origin of a region, an institution or a community in the society. So also in western coast of India certain myths were circulated as to explain certain geographical peculiarities or emergence of a caste. The dominant myth found in Western Coast concerns with the creation of what is called 'Paraśurāma ksetra', the land which was created by none other than Lord Paraśurāma. This myth is mentioned in a *mahāpurāna* like *Skanda Purāna.* The dominant communities of the western coast used this tradition. The tradition stated that land was created by Paraśurāma, who also donated the land to the brahmans. By discussing the Paraśurāma tradition, we do not intend to speak for or against the historical authenticity of the geographical changes in the Western Coast. It becomes problematic to locate the historicity or a historicity of any of the temporal figures like Mayura Varma as mentioned in these traditions. This is because there are limited sources to support the hypothesis that Kadambas ruled south western India as we know that it was the Alupas who ruled the region called South Kanara, a part of western India. In fact, going by the inscriptional data it was during the Vijayanagara period after 14th century that we find the growth of temple complexes, donations to temples and brahmans by kings and elite communities in society. Here use of the name Mayura Varma indicates the symbol of royal patronage rather than a historical reality. The use of myth regarding Mayura Varma is understandable for we know that before establishing the Kadamba kingdom, Mayura Varma himself was a brahmana. The tradition that Mayura Varma was converted from a brahman to a kṛatriya must have been responsible for the brahmans considering Mayura Varma as their patron. In fact the brahmanical tradition of South Kanara, *Grāmapaddhati* claims to give a *vamṛavali* of Kadambas who succeeded Mayura Varma.

There is an explicit attempt made by the brahmanical authors to claim justification, in the larger society, for the ownership of fertile agrarian tracts. This variety of myth can be found in the brahmanical texts, *Grāmapaddhati* and *Sahyādri Khānda.* Here we propose to study the hidden agenda of these brahmanical traditions. These traditions represent historical consciousness of a particular community. For our purpose, it will be significant to analyse these brahmanical texts. They reflected on those events, which their authors thought would be helpful to determine their position in society. The brahmanical traditional chronicle of south western India, *Grāmapaddhati,* claims that after creating the land out of the sea by the use of his axe, Paraśurāma donated the land to a section of brahmans to be enjoyed by them perpetually. It is said that during historical times Mayura Varma donated thirty-two villages to some brahman communities, some of who, however, become fallen due to their silly actions. There are stories of dissent and protest from both brahmanical and non-brahmanical groups. While the protest of brahmans was treated with tact by donating lands to them, the protest of śūdras and untouchables was dealt with firm hand by subjugating and forcing them to work as servants of upper castes in the society. Another brahmanical traditional chronicle, *Sahyādri Khānda*, consists of similar stories regarding occupation of land by brahmans after the donation of land by Paraśurāma. However, this tradition consists of several narratives of fallen brahman *grāmas*, which shows that within the brahmanical groups there were certain sections which tried to become dominant in the overall structure of brahmanical society. This indicates the need to emphasise not simply stratification within the larger society, but also stratification within a single caste.

Literature and Dominant Caste

An analysis of *Grāmapaddhati* and *Sahyādri Khānda* reveals that these were the brahmanical traditions authored by brahmans who reflected on those events which were considered as important for them. These texts consist of many brahmanical details like the brahman family names, their assemblies, their designations and the different activities of the brahmanical society. This shows that their authors were consciously recording such things. The brahmanical claims are sought to be strengthened by such statements as about the creation of the land by Paraśurāma, an *avatāra* of Viṣnu himself and an arch brahmana, his gift of land to brahmans (whatever their origin), the way in which the kings invited and settled brahmans in the land and the other concerns of the text with brahmans.

Thus, here we find the attempt for justification of the position, the social status claimed by the brahmans. There is also an attempt to claim the ownership of large tracts of land on the West Coast. As D.D. Kosambi says that this ownership of land was facilitated by a collaboration with native communities on the West Coast and these native populations were the actual cultivators of land, the produce of which was ultimately appropriated by the brahman landLords.[9]

The statement in the *Grāmapaddhati* that the peasants such as Nādavar or Nāyars were brought from Ahicchatra by Mayura Varma himself acquires better sense in this light. So also, the way in which the fallen brahmans or the defeated chandālas were accommodated as farm peasants or farm labourers as given in the text can be explained in this way. Thus, these traditions represented the expression of the needs of the brahman landLords. The brahmans tried to justify land ownership and dominant social position in the society. Along with the control of the temples and the land owned by those institutions it was possible for at least a section of the brahman community to accumulate properties. Both had to be legitimized. Apart from all that the entire ideology supporting caste and the hegemony of brahmans, in it had achieved, traditions such as those contained in the texts went a long way. The land itself is sacred because Paraśurāma creates it. The brahmans were themselves the creation of Paraśurāma. Mayura Varma, the ruler himself had gone all the way to Ahicchatra to get the brahmans here. His successors had to prevail upon them on more than one occasion to come back. In fact, on the final occasion such an important person as Bhattācharya had to pursuade and accompany them. All this shows the eagerness of brahmans to show that they are so very important.

In South Kanara, there was a position of co-operation between the different sections like and upper class peasants, which constituted the upper classes in the society. *Grāmapaddhati* refers to the lands being given to the Nādavas and Nāyars. According to this tradition the Nāyars were expected to assist the brahmans in all business activities. In *Sahyādri Khānda* there is a direct reference to collaboration between the brahmans and chieftains. Perhaps the brahmans validated the social status of the śūdra kings in the regional society of western coast.

Origin and Growth of Paraśurāma Tradition

The story of the origin of Paraśurāma kśētra must have had, to begin with, an oral origin. It was put into writing to meet the needs of a particular community in the society. It is possible that migration of brahmanical groups might have been responsible for the spread of this tradition throughout western coast.

The studies made by Pargiter showed that Paraśurāma represented *brahma-ksatra,* who combined the characters of both a brahman and a ksatriya.[10] Similarly, we can consider Mayura Varma belonging to the same tradition since initially he was a brahman and later he was converted into a ksatriya. It is possible to identify the Paraśurāma tradition in various regions of South India.

J.S. Rao says that all the regions indicated as inhabited brahmins as a result of exploits by Paraśurāma still abound with adherents belonging to brahmanical castes and sections who owe their allegiance and relate their origin to their settlement through Lord Paraśurāma's exploits in their respective regions.[11]

He also gives the example of the brahman settlements of the *sapta konkana* region in the western coast, Bengal, Assam in the East, Kanauj-Maithila-Vāranasi in the Northern U.P. region, Rajasthan and Vindhya Pradesh in the central region, and Gujarat Kutch in the north-west region which still trace their origin to the exploits of Lord Paraśurāma.[12] There were changes that took place in the Paraśurāma tradition and it did not remain stagnant during the course of time.

Transformation of the Tradition

The above study shows that a tradition popular as oral might have been put into writing and as time passed new additions were made to the story. It also shows the story of Paraśurāma's exploits as popular in Sūrparaka and there might have been a geographical movement of this story to other regions like Konkan coast, regions of coastal Karnataka and Kerala. Along with migration of brahmans there was also migration of brahmanical traditions. The brahman authors of *Grāmapaddhati* claim that they migrated to western coast from Ahicchatra, (Ahikśētra) which can be located in U.P. During the post-Gupta period with the decline of urban centres of North India, it is possible that brahmans migrated to South India. Pressure of population on land must have been the major cause of migration of brahmanical groups. This phenomenon of migration is seen in the Agastya tradition in the Tamil country.[13]

With the migration of brahmans to the south there was sanskritization and brahmanization of a non-brahmanical society. This is reflected in the local Tuḷu dialect which was adopted by the majority of brahman populace of South Kanara. The Tuḷu spoken by brahmans consists of large number of Sanskrit words.

Thus certain of the elements of Paraśurāma tradition which was oral to start with and which was reduced to writing in the document form obtained the accepts by the inscriptions which was one kind of acceptance of the land ownership rights claimed by brahmans. In later years, certain images in the temples came to be believed as installed by Paraśurāma. The authors of different *sthaḷamahātmyas* also used this tradition. The places like Rajatapītha (Udupi), Kumaradri, Kumbhakāśi, Dhwajeshwara, Kródha, Mukāmba and Gōkarna are considered as creations of Paraśurāma. *Kéraḷótpatti,* a traditional chronicle of Kērala, also claims that Kērala was the creation of Paraśurāma.[14]

The above study of depiction of Paraśurāma tradition in literature show that there was certain connection between Paraśurāma, his creation of land and his donations of land to brahmans. The study of geo-morphology and paleo-archaeology of the Western Coast, however, would lead us an altogether different direction of analysis. Nevertheless, since we have not used archaeological data, our present concern is entirely with brahmanical texts and analysis of these texts. The above survey goes to suggest that the story of the origin of Paraśurāma *kśētra* which had a oral origin was put into writing to meet the needs of a particular community in the society. This tradition, when applied by the authors of traditional history of the regions, conveyed the functions of justification of brahman's position in the society of western India. Such functions we can find in the brahmanical texts, *Grāmapaddhati* and *Sahyādri Khānda.*

Content of Traditions

The authors of *Grāmapaddhati* and *Sahyādri Khānda* gave utmost importance to the brahmans. Paraśurāma after creating the land, donates it to the brahmans. These brahmans lose their caste and privileges since they irritated Paraśurāma by trying to test him. Later Mayura Varma and his successors donated villages to brahmans brought from Ahicchatra. There are references to brahmanical assemblies where the brahmans were expected to assemble and discuss issues of *varnāśrama dharma. Grāmapaddhati* also gives a list of brahman families who are supposed to have settled in the thirty-two villages in South Kanara with ownership of land. Such grants of villages gave the brahmans the economic control over the rural areas. *Sahyādri Khānda* gives details about several groups of brahmans who are supposed to have migrated to South Kanara.

This brahmanical tradition also comprises of details regarding non-brahmanical communities. There is reference to the *Mogers* (fisher folk) who were converted as brahmans. They were given all privileges of brahmans. But as they were silly enough to test Paraśurāma, their benefactor, they lost their status, privileges and land.

In all India situation we find that certain of the tribes were incorporated into the caste structure and they were given the status of brahmans, and assigned a *gōtra* but had a low rank within the status group.[15] The Maga brahmans, the Abhira brahmans and the Boya brahmans had low caste status in the North Indian society. In Tuḷunādu, the *Mogers* after being cursed by Paraśurāma, lose their brahman status and they become equal to the śūdras. This forced the king Mayura Varma to bring chaste brahmans from Ahicchatra and these brahmans were assured of all necessary facilities. When Mayura Varma abdicates the throne, the Ahicchatra brahmans returned to their original place as they found this country anarchical. However they were persuaded to come back to Tuḷunādu by Chandrāngada, successor of Mayura Varma, indicating that the brahmans become indispensable for the kings of Tuḷunādu. The protection of life and property of brahmans is also guaranteed. This indicates the expectation of the brahmanical authors regarding their position in the larger society.

Another community represented in *Grāmapaddhati* are Nādavas or Nāyars who were the peasants and considered as śūdras. There one can find co-operation between the śūdra peasants and brahmans.

Not only are the brahmans given villages but they are expected to be assisted by Nādavas in agricultural activities. For this act the Nādavas obtained *nādus* (independent agrarian unit). All business activities were expected to be carried through Nāyars. Thus, with the help of the Sūdras the brahmans were able to exercise control over land. This land ownership was also accompanied by ownership over the tribes who were converted as servile farm labourers who were expected to serve the brahmans without anything more than subsistence wages.

Certain episodes in *Grāmapaddhati* show the protest[16] of those who are described as fallen brahmans against bringing of other brahmans and their establishment. These brahmans questioned the authority of Mayura Varma to do so, who being a kind person satisfied them by giving them some *grāmas*. Another episode of protest we find from the side of the chāndalas (lowest in the caste hierarchy of South Kanara), who are described as being led by a chandāla chief Hubbāsiga. He jeopardised the position of the brahmans and they ran away to their earlier place. However, this protest was put down and after their subjugation, these people were made as holeyas (menial servants) to work as servile farm labourers in the land owned by the brahmans. These details in *Grāmapaddhati* show that it includes not only the details about brahmans, but also details about Nādavas, Nāyars, mogers and holeyas. But these details are presented from the point of view of the brahmanical groups. This indicates the attempt made by the brahmans to claim highest position in the society as a whole.

The *Sahyādri Khānda* also gives the details about conversion of mogers into brahmans. It considers that Ahicchatra brahmans were pure brahmans. Nevertheless, it refers to other types of brahmanical groups as well most of them were fallen brahmans. Some of the fallen brahmans, since they lost their earlier caste status, had to depend on agricultural and horticultural activities. Another important factor we find in *Sahyādri Khānda* is the reference to inter caste marriages. There are situations where a brahman marries a Śūdra girl, but those who are born as a result of such marriage are considered as fallen brahmans. There is also reference to *sankara jātis.* Another important aspect we find in this tradition is the collaboration between the brahmans and śūdras. There is reference to śūdra kings Madhwa and Kanda who gave land donations to the brahmans.

In the above brahmanical texts the authors attempted to claim superior social status for themselves in the larger society. In order to validate the ownership of land by brahmanical groups, which had come from outside, it was found necessary to put these traditions in literate form and present the brahmanical groups as those communities who had every right to own large tracts of land since it was given by Lord Paraśurāma who was not only an *avatāra* of Vishnu but also was responsible for the creation of this land out of the sea.

Conclusion

These works represent the sense of history as reflected in Indian historical tradition, and they recorded those aspects or events, which would strengthen their position in the society. Whatever events they recorded, were those, which they considered as relevant for their existence in the society as a whole.

That, however, does not make these traditions any less valuable. In fact, by preserving the memories of the group experience of these sections, the *Sahyādri Khānda* and *Grāmapaddhati* were indeed preserving a historical tradition in a strong way. These two texts should be seen in the context of the emergence of brahman communities in the western coast and their need to strengthen their respective position in the society. The domination of brahmans is also a sign of the emergence of a feudal society. It was an age when the state was losing its control over administration over peripheries, particularly the village administration. In this sense the brahman villages were emerging self-sufficient and free from the control of the state officials since they were donated by the kings to the brahmans for their enjoyment in perpetuity. The ownership rights over the villages gave rights for the brahmans over the non-brahmanical sections in the villages. Brahman settlements were the surest ways for the state to propagate its ideology. The sacral power was able to dominate the particular psyche of the community as a whole. The brahmanical traditions standardised the hegemony of both the state and the brahmanas.

References

1. B.D. Chattopadhyaya, *The Making of Early Medieval India*, Delhi, 1994, p. 217.
2. Romila Thapar and Sabyasachi Bhattacharya, *Situating Indian History for Sarvepalli Gopal*, 1986, p. 361.
3. *Ibid.*
4. R.S. Sharma, *Indian Feudalism*, Delhi, 1980, pp. 1-56.
5. B.A. Saletore, *Ancient Karnataka Volume I History of Tuluva*, Poona, 1936,

p. 36.

6. Romila Thapar, *Ancient Indian Social History Some Interpretations*, New Delhi, 1978, p. 268.
7. Romila Thapar, *Interpreting Early India*, 1994, p. 140.
8. Kunal Chakrabarti, 'Texts and Traditions: The Making of Bengal *Puranas*', in, Champakalakshmi, R, and S. Gopal, (eds.), *Tradition, Dissent and Ideology Essays in Honour of Romila Thapar*, Delhi, 1996. p. 64.
9. D.D. Kosambi, *An Introduction to the Study of Indian History*, Bombay, Second Edition, 1975, pp. 328-329.
10. F.E. Pargiter, *Ancient Indian Historical Tradition*, Delhi, Reprint, 1997, p. 199.
11. J. S. Rao and P. Gururaja Bhat, *Archaeological Survey and Temple Worship*, Bombay, 1976, p. 17.
12. *Ibid.*
13. Rajagopalan, 'Role of Agastya in Tamil Literature – An Enigma', in, *Indica*, Volume 35, No. 1, March, 1998, pp. 29-30.
14. Kesavan Veluthat, *Brahman Settlements in Kerala Historical Studies*, Calicut, 1978, p. 4.
15. Romila Thapar, *The Past and Prejudice*, Delhi, 1993, p. 28.
16. Regarding episodes of protest in *Grāmapaddhati*, see Kesavan Veluthat, 'Non-Brahmana Protest in Brahmanical literary Expressions: the *Grāmapaddhati* From South Kanara", Unpublished paper presented at a seminar on "Literature and Social Protest: Perceptions on the oppressed groups", University of Hyderabad, March, 1995.

Appendix - I

Grāmapaddhati

Earlier Lord Paraśurāma made the western sea to give land. Since this land did not consist of brahmans Mayura Varma brought brahmans from Ahicchatra on the banks of the river Godavari and he divided this land into Taulava and Kerala and assigned land and the villages to brahmans. Shatkarmis were expected to perform agnihotra panchamahayajna and Trikarmi brahmans were given the land to manage and they were supposed to give tax to the kings. The prose version of these duties of brahmans is known as *Grāmapaddhati.*

On the east of Parasurāma *ksetra* we have Sahya hills, on the south exists Kanyakumari, on the north Nashika and on the west exists salt sea. This land with 300 *yojana* has been divided into 7 divisions: Karata, Varata, Marata, Konkana, Haviga, Toulava and Kerala. This land is known as Parasurâma ksetra and Paraœurâma śristi. Since Ksatriyas tried to kill his father Jamadagni, Paraśurāma decided to destroy the Ksatriyas from earth and 21 times he destroyed the race of Ksatriyas. In order to expiate this sin he gave his land to Kasyapa. Then the brahmans told Parasurâma thus: You have donated land to us. It is not wise to stay in the donated land. Immediately you should leave this place. If you stay in the donated land you will gain *dattapahara dosha.* Earlier Nrigaraya was giving large number of donations of cows to brahmans. One donated cow ran away and joined the group of those cows which were not yet donated. Not realising this Nragaraya gave the same cow to another brahman. This created conflict between the two brahmans. They refused to take the cows since they thought that the donor was creating *dattapahara dosha* for them. Due to this Nrigaraya has been suffering from above cited *dosha.* Brahmans told Parasurâma that if he stays in the donated land then he would gain the same *dosha* and Kasyapa and other sages advised him to vacate as early as possible. Thus Parasurâma decided to create a new land for himself by sending the sea backwards.

Later Lord Parasurâma in order to people the land created by him invited brahmans from northern region. But since they refused to oblige, he put sacred thread (*yajnopavita*) on the local fisher folk called *dasas-Revaras – Kaivartas* who belonged to the Moger caste. He asked them to live like brahmans and made all arrangements for them like the northern country and he assured them his support if they needed.

Parasurâma decided to go to Mahendra hills for penance and he told the brahmans to live happily and to call him whenever they were in any trouble. Brahmans used to live happily. One day the brahmans decided to test the words of Paraœurâma and they called for Lord Paraśurāma. Lord Paraœurâma immediately came to help them. But realising that the brahmans tried to test him, Paraœurâma became angry. He cursed them that they should lose all their privileges given by him and that they should live like Sudras. Now the brahmans started to cultivate the land which was given to them by Paraœurâma.

After Parasurâma went to Mahendra hills, Parvati and Parameśvara descended from Kailasa. They came to Sahya hills. They relaxed on earth and this resulted in the birth of a child. He had three eyes. Since he was born near a Kadamba tree, he was given the name Kadamba. Shiva and Parvati blessed that he may rule the land.

Later Kadamba started administering this land and he followed a benevolent policy towards all living beings. In this family was born Vasu Chakravarti. He ruled the state according to principles of *varnashrama dharma*. Vasu Chakravarti obtained a daughter named Sushile. Impressed by her beauty and qualities Hemanga Raya of Solar race married her. Later he started ruling this state as per the *dauhitra dharma.*[1] He ruled the state according to *varnashrama dharma*. After some time Sushile gave birth to Mayura Varma.

Hemanga Raya's son Mayura Varma was ruling Parasurâma *ksetra* as per the *dauhitra dharma* and *varnashrama dharma*. Sages advised him that since there are no brahmans in this land sages find it very difficult to visit his kingdom and hence they suggested that he should bring highly learned brahmans from Ahicchatra, on the banks of River Godavari. Mayura Varma decided to follow their advice and he went to Ahicchatra and brought agnihotra and other brahmans by offering them land and other donations. Mayura Varma settled brahmans in Haiva, Toulava and Kerala. Haiva is situated between Sahya hills on the east and salt sea on the west. Toulava is situated between River Gangavali on the north, River

Nilishwara on the south, Sahya hill on the east and salt sea on the west. Kerala is situated between River Nileshwara on the north, Sahya hills on the east and sea on the west.

He established 18 brahman villages in Haiva, 32 brahman villages in Toulava and 64 villages in Kerala. He asked them to adjust with the local conditions and customs. He gave them land, wells, and gardens. He also brought Sudras called Nayars and made them to assist brahmans.

Mayura Varma made all arrangements for the brahmans to live without any trouble in the land that was gifted to them. Mayura Varma gave them the direction to live with their children as long as sun and moon exists. Initially Mayura Varma gave 18 village agraharas to Haiva brahmans, who were given Haiva desha including Vanavasi. Secondly, he gave 32 agraharas to Toulava brahmans who consisted of Kota Kandavara and Shivalli. Thirdly, in Kerala *desha*, he gave 64 agraharas to Kerala brahmans.

During this time the earlier brahmans who were cursed by Paraśurāma, now came to Mayura Varma and said that the land was actually given to them by Paraśurāma earlier and they questioned the right of Mayura Varma to donate their land and the right of the other brahmans to stay in their land. These brahmans threatened that they may beat up these new brahman groups. In order to pacify this group of earlier brahmans Mayura Varma devised *sanketa paddhati*. Accordingly he gave separate four villages to these earlier brahmans. These villages are: Naguru, Matti, Kushashthali and Swasthi.[2] He told these people to live in their villages and not to cross their limits and that they should live like Sudras indulging in the profession of the Sudras like agriculture and horticulture. After doing this, Mayura Varma concentrated his attention on the brahmans to whom he had given land in his state and he thought that in order to make them to happily perform agnihotra and yagas they should be provided with all facilities and support. Thus he appointed nadavas as the assistant's of brahmans. He gave nadus to these nadavas. They were called nadu-nadus. These nadus were Kelanadu, Nalvatta Nadu, Halasanadu and Yaradunadu.

In this way Mayura Varma established brahman settlements in Haiva, Toulava and Kerala. The brahmans of these region were performing their duties like Ishwara puja, MahaVishnu puja and Mahaganapati aradhana and various other duties of the Shatkarmi brahmans. The state of Mayura Varma was similar to Krita yuga. Here ends the story of Mayura Varma.

When Mayura Varma was ruling his state he got his son named Chandrangada. When Chandrangada was young Mayura Varma gave the responsibility of administration and welfare of his son to his minister and he went to do penance.

When this was done, the brahmans thought that Mayura Varma has left them to forest and now state and king Chandrangada are under the control of the minister who did not take much interest in their welfare. Thus these brahmans who were brought from Ahicchatra decided to leave to their earlier place due to lack of royal patronage. This made the land as non-brahmanical or abrahmanya. When Chandrangada came to the throne he realised that earlier brahmans who were brought by his father Mayura Varma had left to Ahicchatra and he thought that this would lead to destroy his reputation as a king. Thus he went to Ahicchatra and pleaded with the brahmans and made them to return to his state.

After some time Chandrangada obtained a son called Lokaditya. Since he was born in a *dosha* called *pitrarishta*, after some time Chandrangada passed away. Since Lokaditya was very young, his mother was taking care of administration. Since there was no capable person to maintain administration, one Chandala chief called Hubbasiga with his followers started giving trouble to the royal family and others. The queen unable to tolerate the harassment went to northern country.

Many brahmans who had come from Ahicchatra also fled to their earlier place. But some among these brahmans decided to stay and they agreed to accept the rule of Hubbasiga. Now the earlier brahmans created by Paraśurāma went to Hubbasiga and with his help acquired the property of the brahmans. Meanwhile many nayars also with the help of Hubbasiga acquired the land of earlier brahmans. Thus the Chandala chief Hubbasiga was ruling with brutal force and tortured the population. During this time Chandasena wanted to give his sister Kanakavati in marriage to Lokaditya. With this intention Chandasena came to Gokarna. But realising the power of Hubbasiga, Chandasena thought that he should deal tactfully with Hubbasiga. Thus he hatched a conspiracy along with Lokaditya to kill Hubbasiga and his men. Chandasena assured Hubbasiga that the former would give his sister in marriage to the former with the condition that he and his men should come to the marriage place unarmed. When Hubbasiga and his men came to the marriage place, Lokaditya and his men butchered many of the Chandala army and also their chief Hubbasiga. Now the Chandalas asked for mercy and they requested Lokaditya to protect their life. During this time Kanakavati was given in marriage to Lokaditya.

Many Chandalas fled away from the state. Many other holeya castes like Bakka, Bakuda, Mera, Goddi, Bile, Hasalava and Koragas were made to work as servants of brahmans. Lokaditya made the arrangements for their livelihood by working in the house and field of brahmans and they were not free to pursue their own profession. They were required to live under the control of the brahmans.

After his marriage and after he destroyed Chandala ruler Hubbasiga Lokaditya now turned his attention towards administration of his kingdom. He asked nayars to look after the land which they had occupied from the brahmans. The nayars were required to follow the orders of brahmans and they had to look after the land that was left by holeya castes as well. Since the brahmans had left this place to Ahicchatra, Lokaditya thought that this place has become non-brahmanical (*abrahmanya*). Thus he went to Ahicchatra and pleaded with the brahmans that they should return to his state. But the brahmans refused to oblige since they thought that his state was unsafe. Then he went Bhattacharya and requested him to pursuade the brahmans to come to his state. Now Bhattacharya called all the brahmans and told them that since Lokaditya had come all the way to Ahicchatra they should go with them. But the brahmans again narrated the earlier story that brahmans were taken by Mayura Varma to his state. But after the rule of Mayura Varma they had returned to Ahicchatra. Again they had gone to the state of Chandrangada who assured them all safety. But after the death of Chandrangada, they were looted by Chandala chief Hubbasiga. The brahmans said that already they have suffered a lot and they do not have any idea of returning to that place. Bhattacharya told the brahmans that since Hubbasiga has already been killed and there is no chance of his return and so the brahmans could without any doubt go to the kingdom of Lokaditya. Now the brahmans agreed to leave Ahicchatra to the kingdom of Lokaditya. Lokaditya gave gifts like pyajana, paduka, chatrayana, etc. to brahmans and he brought Bhattacharya and brahmans with much respect and they went to Gokarna *ksetra*.

Lokaditya brought brahmans from Ahicchatra in Yudishtira shaka, sarvajitu samvatsara 1089 and made them to settle in Haiva, Toulava and Kerala. In Gokarna he performed the puja of Mahabaleshwara and gave the right of puja (*tantritva*) to 2 Kota brahmans. In Haiva desha he gave 18 villages to brahmans and in Toulava he gave 32 villages to brahmans. The following is the detail of brahman villages in Toulava.

The western sixteen villages are Tarevuru – Varkadi - Marane – Kolyanadu – Padi – Kudalu – Mogebailu – Mittanadu – Niramarga – Simanturu – Tenekala – Shivabelli – Brahmapura – Nirvara – Kuta – Skandapura.

The eastern sixteen villages are Sripadi – Odilu – Nala – Karanduru – Ujare – Kunyamarga – Kokkada – Raminja – Pudegrama – Belapa – Airnadu – Idakedu – Kemminja – Padinja – Siriyadi – Kudipadi.

1. Skandapura grama – Udupa and Hebbara – two households.
2. Kutagrama – Hande – Basari – Tunga – Navada – Holla – Mayya – Hebbara – Karyavanta – eight households.

3. Brahmapura or Ajapura – Ulluru – Ungarapali – Vorambali – Kairambali– Alapya – Ashtamurthi – Hebbara – Samblaja – eight households.
4. Nirvara grama – Narittaya – Yadabettanaya – Kalluraya – Tumbikalaya – Hebbara – Nujinnaya – Makkitaya – Padittaya – eight households.
5. Karevoora grama – Paturaya – Pakuraya – Kudurettaya – Poyyattaya– four households.
6. Varkadi grama – Taletaya – Ayapainaya – Naralattaya – Netrattaya – Arinaya – Kedekidenaya – Shunnoditaya – Kunjitturaya – eight households.
7. Tritiye Marane grama – Badekedanaya – Shulyannaya – two households.
8. Kolavi grama – Talepadittaya – Manjanodittaya – two households.
9. Padimogara grama – Amettaya – Shambarattaya – Induvalittaya – Koyakodalaya – four households.
10. Kudalu grama – Kannurannaya – Shambarannaya – Irvatturaya – Mittadkattaya – four households.
11. Mogebail grama – Pijittaya – Pilikarittaya – Kabbukodittaya – Mudettaya – four households.
12. Mittanadu grama – Kundagolattaya – Nujittaya – Gangettaya – Sharalattaya – four households.
13. Nirumarga grama – Ichaluttaya – Anantodittaya – Thalam Padittaya– Sharalaya Mavaraya – Kumarantaya – six households.
14. Simantura grama – Simanturaya – Sibaraya – Mannuraya – Ippyantaya – Mukhyantaya – Mudikudalaya – Sidikalataya – Adaraya– Barvanaya – nine households.
15. Tenekala grama – Mogeraya – Mittataya – Madumannaya – Vailaya– This family is also called Kachintaya – Vokudinaya – Uliraya – Mallanjinaya – Kabekodinaya – eight households.
16. Shivabelli grama – First ten – Middle forty – Last twenty – twenty best hoseholds – thirty six out of forty are middle grade – common dining rights only – sixty nine are only name sake brahmans.

    Totally 125 households.

    Alevooraya – Kodencha – Manjitaya – Sharalaya – Kadambalitaya – Madipalitaya – in Alevoor total households are six.

    Sagari grama – Shaguriraya – Tenkilaya – Kunjittaya – Naduvantilaya – four households.

Ten households are best – next forty six are middle grade – next seventy households are low grade brahmans (*adhamas*) – totally 120 households.

120 households are inhabitants of Sivalli grama.

Putraya – Bayiritaya – Kekudenaya – three households – these three households add to the earlier 10 households.

Alevooraya's brother is Kedalaya – Kodacha's brother is Kodajaya – two households – totally five households – totally fifteen households – these fifteen households are best out of forty households – Kornaya – Banninanjittaya – Maradittaya – Shivattaya – these four are best out of forty households.

Out of seventy households Kunjiraya is the best.

Totally twenty best households – They should indulge in shatkarma (six duties) – yajana, yajana, Adhyayana, adhyapaka, dana, pratigraha.

Details of thirty-six Households Out of Forty

1.Kramadaritaya 2. Tenkodinaya 3. Tatarantaya 4. Shitiraya 5. Arolitaya 6. Kurumballitaya 7. Badikillaya 8. Kalyanantaya 9. Nujetaya 10. Kodabalitaya 11. Politaya 12. Nekarantaya 13. Vatinaya 14. Shibarantaya 15. Padillaya 16. Nedilaya 17. Kannapinaya 18. Mankitaya 19. Kottiladinaya 20. Kodalaya 21. Parkalataya 22. Arimettaya 23. Kolaketaya 24. Kokadinaya 25. Kalatenaya 26. Manikalataya 27. Ankilaya 28. Mudittaya 29. Padettaya 30. Kotantillaya 31. Kunnimargentaya 32. Kannuraya 33. Kelatraya 34. Manninitaya 35. Neyampallitaya 36. Pudinaya. These thirty-six households have the right of common dining only and they are trikarmis.

Detail of sixty-nine Households Out of Seventy is as follows

1. Taginaya 2. Mitilaya 3. Kutilaya 4. Pananji 5. Sunataya 6. Kalambi 7. Ulitaya 8. Ninjuraya 9. Nellitaya 10. Malyantaya 11. Hebbapa 12. Belapati 13. Belayaraya 14. Koni 15. Karkavitaya 16. Nalitaya 17. Durge 18. Vadetaya 19. Vadi 20. Ubali 21. Chekkeraya 22. Mangalattaya 23. Voritaya 24. Mandabettaya 25. Adukattaya 26. Kodilaya 27. Elekodittaya 28. Kulilaya 29. Annappi 30. Gude 31. Deyiginaya 32. Kodilaya 33. Kudantaya 34. Kudukaraya 35. Areye 36. Kudinaya 37. Suriye 38. Nuji 39. Kodanji 40. Kannapalli 41. Doni 42. Mundadi 43. Mudumale 44. Vutiye 45. Ujire 46. Kokkadi 47. Hebbara 48. Nekkatte 49. Ane 50. Kalali 51. Agali 52. Muke 53. Mijikoshi 54. Irutturaya 55. Avuje 56. Maipadi 57. Bevinaya 58. Kovinaya 59. Meladi 60. Kuduraye 61. Kolanji 62. Kalaya 63. Majalaya 64. Todinaya 65. Irettaya 66. Peralaya 67. Kabetodi 68. Beye 69. Manjittaya.

These sixty-nine households do not have the right to common dining with higher grade brahmans.

Lokaditya made arrangement for the livelihood of these name sake brahmans by giving them land and garden which could be cultivated by the brahmans.

Explanation for the Statement that These were Name Sake Brahmans

Some of them lived with fallen group of brahmans. Some others had followed the aboriginal non-brahmanical customs. Some others were created by Paraśurāma and later were cursed by Paraśurāma himself. Thus there was a creation of a group of fallen brahmans. Lokaditya gave cultivable land to these brahmans and made arrangements for their day to day existence.

Details of Eastern Villages

1. Sripadi – Kunyamannaya – Vaipadittaya – Atradittaya – Putrannaya – five households.
2. Odila grama – Alumannaya – Ulipoditaya – two households.
3. Nala grama – Madipaditaya – Parvantaya – two households.
4. Karandura grama – Sampagenaya – Yadakelataya – two households.
5. Ujire grama – Aramanettaya – Vappantaya – Kokaralittaya – Aripadittaya – Mundapadittaya – Kemmundaya – Arbataya – Bellannaya – eight households.
6. Kunyamarga grama – Peralattaya – Kunnimargentaya – these two are doubtful. Peradittaya – Upparannaya – Ichalattaya – Itantaya – Madavinaya – Kudunnaya – Putayattaya – Kodanchinaya – Karakannaya – nine households.
7. Kokkada grama – Kodilaya – Shabaraya – Yadapadittaya – Uparannaya – four households.
8. Ramanja grama – Nujitaya – Matattaya – Munnuraya – three households.
9. Pude grama – Pudenaya – one household.
10. Belapadi grama – Baritaya – Umarannaya – Ammani is doubtful – three households.
11. Irnadu – Takarannaya – Mundapadittaya – Shabaraya – Ulapadittaya – four households.
12. Idakedu grama – Manakalattaya – Shadangattaya – two households.
13. Kemminja grama – Bajataya – one household.
14. Palinja grama – Edabettunaya – one household.
15. Siriyadi grama – Kannuraya – one household.
16. Kodipadi grama – Panataya – Irekalattaya – two households.

Lokadityaraya thus constructed agraharas for the brahmans and donated land to them by performing various *pujas* and *yagas*. Regarding the maintenance and cultivation of the land of brahmans it was decided that Sudras should be assigned this duty. Lokaditya made provisions for the list of brahmans living in the thirty-two villages and guaranteed all rights in the land where they lived.

Bhattacharya suggested to Lokaditya that since brahmans were prohibited from working in the agrarian fields, he should give all right of looking after agricultural and other business activities to the nayars under whom the Sudras and other cultivators should work. Brahmans should indulge only in *shadkarmas* like *agnihotra, panchamahayajna,* study of Vedas, etc. Nayars were allowed to enjoy the land on *mulageni.*[3]

The details of the positions of the brahmans of different villages is given below:

Bhattas 40 – Agnihotris 24, Smartas 24, Sabhapatis 2, Panditas 2, Prabhus 4, Tantris 6, Agramanis 24, Mandi adhivasis 21, Mandi pakshanathas 2, Jannis 8.

1. Sabhapatis: - Shabaraya, Tiburaya – totally two.
2. Panditas – Kalluraya, Uparannaya – totally two.
3. Tantris – Netrattaya – Ichalattaya – Putraya – Pangunaya – Udupa – Brahmakaranta – six households.
4. Pakshanathas – Mudilaya – Nidamburaya – these two are pakshanathas for thirty – two villages including Karevuru and Kuta grama.
5. Prabhus – Chautas – Bangas – Mudilaya – Nidamburaya – these four people are supporters of Prabhu (king?).
6. Forty Bhattas are : 1. Munnuraya 2. Arinaya 3. Kovinaya 4. Perannaya 5. Koyamegattaya 6.Kuduraya 7. Majjittaya 8. Talattaya 9. Pijittaya 10. Paturaya 11. Induvalittaya 12. Koyakodanaya 13. Simanturaya 14. Punchanaya 15. Muchanturaya 16. Mogeraya 17. Mittantaya 18. Alevooraya 19. Tunga 20. Brahmakaranta 21. Kalluraya 22. Udupa 23. Baipadittaya 24. Atradittaya 25. Appanttadittaya 26. Belannaya 27. Aremanettaya 28. Idapadittaya 29. Shabaraya 30. Uparannaya 31. Korginaya 32. Ametaditaya 33. Shambaraya 34. Kolataya 35.Mudampadittaya 36. Bajittaya 37. Kornaya 38. Shagurittaya 39. Madantilaya 40. Patturaya – forty households.
7. 26 Agnihotras are: 1. Shimanturaya 2. Muchanturaya 3. Munnuraya 4. Alevooraya 5. Kodencha 6. Manjettaya 7. Sharalaya 8. Madapalittaya 9. Kadambalitaya 10. Kunjitaya 11. Naduvantilaya 12. Shagurittaya 13. Tenkiḷaya 14. Putraya 15. Tekudenaya 16. Bayiritaya 17. Kalluraya 18. Baipaditaya 19.Vappantaya 20. Idepadittaya 21. Kornaya 22. Maraditaya 23. Udupa 24.Brahmakaranta 25. Banninjitaya 26. Shivataya – twenty-six households.
8. Smartas are: Nujitaya – Kedenaya – Naralataya – Talantraya – Ayapinaya – Mannakalataya – Alevooraya – Brahmakaranta – Kalluraya – Udupa – Baipadittaya – Korgninaya – Mundapadittaya – Kodencha – fourteen households.

9. 24 Gramanis are: Paturaya – Poyyetaya – Shullannaya – Kidekidenaya – Kotanjittaya – Tennaraya – Kannarannaya – Madantilaya – Naduvantilaya – Kunjittaya – Herala – Karanta – Narittaya – Edabettanaya – Hebbara – Sampigettaya in Niravara – Ambarannaya – Aramanetaya – Madappinaya – Putrannaya – Kakarannaya – Kinakalattaya – Udupa – Urambali – totally 24 gramanis.
10. Adhivasis are: Alevooraya – Pagampinaya – Taretaya – Annakunjitaya - Bashakannaya -- Kedatiraya – Arbiraya – Peladitaya – Kannaraditaya – Kambarannaya – Uliyaraya – Kabekodinaya – Malampadittaya – Erinkataya – Bartoditaya – Punjukannaya – Kuduraya – Ninjuraya – Iravatturaya – Nambunittaya – Jatodittaya - twenty-one adhivasis.
11. Chinnas are: 1. Madikudilaya 2. Shidikudilaya 3. Tinakalataya 4. Madumannaya 5.Kapunjaya 6. Vailaya 7. Manjittaya 8. Kemmundenaya 9. Vodambaditaya 10. Kabetodinaya 11. Hebbara 12. Ungarapalli 13. Yedabettinaya 14.Kakodenaya 15. Raipattaya 16. Koditillaya 17. Babetilaya 18. Madilaya 19. Urala 20.Kudurettaya 21. Tenkzhattaya 22. Kuntaraya 23. Marataya 24. Ammannaya 25. Bayattaya 26. Pudenaya 27. Mulataya 28. Ardundaya 29. Ambarannaya 30. Ulitaya 31. Paddilaya 32. Edepulitaya 33. Uraya 34. Padilaya 35. Irakaditaya 36. Ponettaya 37. Udupa 38. Herala. Totally thirty-eight chinnas.

Ballalas are four: Talepadi – Manjanodi – Nidumburu – Mudila

Dores are six: Kunda Heggade – Muda Heggade – Maramba Heggade – Bidaresha Omanjuru – Ramanatha – Boladadeshingattaya – hundreds of Heggades – Ballalas – all these were the dores.

Savantas are two: Iravattura Basava Savanta – Mulike Kinnika Savanta.

Nadus are two: Nalvattanadu – Kelanadu.

Bidus are two: Bainduru, Battakala.

Divana are two: Kadari, Karkala.

Simhasana (throne) are two: Barkur, Mangaluru.

Raja sthanas (courts of kings) are four: Barkuru – Mangaluru – Kadaba – Honnavara.

Chavadis are two: Kadari – Karkala.

Six villages were given sixteen *maryades* (customary salutations). These six villages are: Haratatta – Karatattu – Kodatattu – Handattu – Karukala. In this way Sanketa system was established.

The region lying between Sita river, western ocean, Sahya hills and Neleshwara river was divided into brahmin villages and the brahmans were given the right to worship in the temples. The rights were divided into *prabhutva* and *gramanitva*. The brahmans were expected to follow the instructions of Bhattacharya. These brahmans who were brought from Ahicchatra were given new names. These details were incorporated in the *Sanketapaddhati*.

In Gajapura or Kutagrama since Ganapati appeared in the temple of Narasimha and since *ganapati* homa was performed, Brahmakaryavanta was given the duty of performing somayaga and daily pooja and other rituals related to Ganapati. Many brahmanas were given the responsibility to perform various pujas in the temple.

In this way Lokadityaraya established the brahman settlements in the agraharas and appointed the brahmana priests in the local shrines to regularly perform rituals related to gods. The reason that Lokadityaraya continued to live in Tulunadu is that it has been proved that Tulu country was a *dharmadesha*.

In the similar manner in Kerala desha also brahman settlements were established with the existence of trikarmi and shatkarmi brahmans and the brahmans were given the similar duties which were given in the case of Tulu nadu. These details were mentioned in Kerala paddhati.

In this way Lokaditya established brahman families in Haiva, Toulava and Kerala. Bhattacharya was given gift of valuable clothes and jewels and the king worshipped him. In order to know the details of Kerala one has to see *Keralotpatti*.

References

1. The reference to *dauhitra dharma* indicates that in South Kanara there existed the matrilineal type of inheritance. Here Hemanga Raya was ruling the state inherited to him by his father-in-law.
2. Among these Kushastnali and Swasthi can be located in the present state of Goa.
3. This was an agrarian system of South Kanara. According to this system the cultivator was a tenant who gave a particular quantity of agrarian produce to his owner. There was a security of tenure in such agrarian system.

Appendix - II

Gotras in the Inscriptions of South Kanara*

Introduction

In the ancient times, *gotras* played a significant role in determining the social status of an individual in the society. Earlier the brahmans enjoyed the advantage of connecting their genealogy with ancient sages. Later this advantage was extended to non-brahman communities as well, particularly the kshatriyas. The brahman *gotras* were exogamous. Apart from claiming social status, *gotras* were essential to enter into the institution of marriage. *Sagotra* marriage, i.e., marriage within the same *gotra*, was a taboo. As Romila Thapar says *gotras* served a distinct social function and underlined the status of the brahmans and indicated that the knowledge of ritual was a crucial aspect of social status. At the point where it became socially necessary there was a rush to systematize the lists and connections. Further Thapar says that for the brahmans the maintenance of such a system was necessary when new members had to be recruited who were not from the old kinship groups.[1] Thus through *gotras* the brahmans claimed that they were connected to great sages like Vasistha, Vishwamitra, Kashyapa, Bharadwaja, etc. In the rituals the brahmana had to accept the gift after introducing himself to the people that he belonged to a particular *gotra*. As in other parts of India, in South Kanara too one can find large number of land grants that were made to brahmans by kings and rich members in the society with the purpose of

* Published in *Research Bulletin Vishveshwarananda Vedic Research Institute*, Vol. 1. No. 1.

legitimizing their position in society. However, only few inscriptions mention about the *gotras* of the grantees and grantors. Here we inquire as to why only few land grants mention the *gotras* of brahmans. The content of the inscriptions would help us to know that when a detail was left out, this was done deliberately so as to fulfill a particular objective of the land grant.

Land Grants in South Kanara

Several land grants were made to the brahmans of South Kanara. These grants were made both by the king or his subordinates and sometimes by rich members of the society like traders and rich agriculturists. The inscriptions refer to Settis, who were both rich agriculturists as well as well to do traders. They belonged to both Jainism and Brahmanical religion. Land was either given to the brahmans or it was given to temples which would be administered by important members of the society. Land that was given to brahmans was called *brahmadeya,* while the land that was granted to temples was called *devādanas.* Some land grants of South Kanara mention the arrangement made to provide food to a particular number of brahmans. In most of these cases names and *gotras* of these brahmans are not mentioned.[2] This is because the people of the locality were not unaware of these usual arrangements and there was no need to elaborately give all details of grantees.

Reference to *gotras*

In South Kanara inscriptions mention *gotras* when land grant was made to a brahman who was newly introduced to the region. In order to make the people of the locality to adjust with him, his details were given in the inscriptions. The Mangalore inscription belonging to A.D. 1420[3] states that Karanika Hariyarasa of Mangalore made a land grant to some brahmans. Hariyarasa originally belonged to an *agrāhara* of Harihara and he belonged to Bharadwaja *gotra.* Here the grantor is introduced to the locality by mentioning his *gotra.*

A Jain inscription belonging to Mudabidre mentions that the Salva king belonged to Kashyapa *gotra.*[4] Thus not only the brahmans, but kshatriyas (or ruling class) also claimed that they belonged to a particular *gotra*. By the medieval period the need of the kshatriyas or kings to claim a particular *gotra* had become an all India phenomenon. South Kanara was not an exception to this development. The Barkur inscription belonging to A.D. 1431 mentions the grant given by Vishnu Bhatta and Shankara Bhatta who belonged to Haive rajya. It is stated that they belonged to Kashyapa *gotra* and Yajur branch.[5] Haive rajya now comprises the present North Kanara district of Karnataka. Haive was known for the Havyaka brahman settlements. During the later period, many Havyakas migrated to South Kanara and they participated in arecanut cultivation.

The Barkur inscription belonging to A.D. 1434 mentions the grant made by Devarasa Upadhya who belonged to Harita *gotra* and yaju branch.[6] Another Barkur inscription belonging to A.D.1440 mentions that Annappa Odeya, the governor of Barkur, made a land grant to Timire Dandana Ayya who belonged to Harita *gotra* and Yajur branch.[7] Yet another Barkur inscription belonging to A.D. 1440 mentions that Annappa Odeya made a land grant to Joyisa Ramanna who belonged to Maudgalya *gotra* and Rig branch.[8]

One inscription discovered near the Kundeshwara temple, Kundapura dated A.D. 1451 states that a gift of 48 *honnus*, which was the income from salt pans in Kundapura, was made to Joyisa Hariyappa of Maudgalya *gotra* and Rik *shakha*.[9] Hariyappa belonged to Hemmadi. This shows that not only land was given as grants to the brahmans but also sources of income like taxes were given as gift.

Another Barkur inscription belonging to A.D. 1499 mentions the land grant made by sons of Sovanna of Vasudhare to one Narana deva. They belonged to Vishwamitra *gotra* and Ashwalayana sutra.[10] Another Mudabidre inscription belonging to A.D. 1515 mentions Ratnappa Odeya as belonging to Dandadhipa *gotra*.[11] Thus, even the Jains claimed to belong to certain gotras. This shows that it was difficult for Jains to remain in seclusion independent of developments in a brahmanical society. The Paduva Panamburu inscription[12] belonging to the reign of Devaraya II mentions the land grant made by the local Banga Prince Pandyapparasa to Govindadeva's sons who belonged to Kolaturu. The inscription mentions that they belonged to Atreya *gotra*.

An inscription found near Krishna Matha Udupi belonging to A.D. 1614 mentions that Lingappaya made grants to the Krishna *matha*. It is stated that Lingappaya belonged to Sankuvali *agrāhara* of Kolapi *grama*. He belonged to Bharadwaja *gotra* and Rig branch (*shakhe*).[13] Another inscription found in the same place belonging to A.D. 1614 mentions that Damarsa Prabhu, the son of Dama Prabhu belonging to Mathagrama made a grant to the temple. It is stated that Damarsa Prabhu belonged to Kaushika *gotra* and Rig branch. Mathagrama was a part of Sashashtigrama of Goa. Mathagrama was one of the important eight villages of the locality. It is possible that Damarsa Prabhu belonged to Saraswat brahman community and he maintained contact with Krishna temple and gave offerings to the *Matha*.[14]

Significance of reference to *gotras*

The above references to *gotra* suggests that when land grant was made to the brahmans of the locality there was no need to specify their details which were known to the people. Thus *gotras* are mentioned to introduce the person to the society and thereby get legitimacy. There are references to brahmans from Harihara, Haiva rajya and Goa.

Secondly, all these references belong to the Vijayanagara period and post Vijayanagara period. During this time there were many land grants which were made by the kings either directly or indirectly through the governors at Barkur and Mangalore. It was this encouragement given by the kings and officials which was responsible for the creation of brahman settlements in South Kanara. In fact, it was during this period that the brahmanical traditional chronicle *Grāmapaddhati* was written and became popular in the brahman households. Thus, Vijayanagara and post Vijayanagara period represented the expansion of the brahman settlements in South Kanara. This suggestion is also supported by the fact that not only brahmans but also there was migration of traders, artisans and other communities to South Kanara. Therefore, when the gotras were mentioned in the inscriptions there was a specific purpose in doing that.

References

1. Romila Thapar, *Ancient Indian Social History: Some Interpretations*, New Delhi, 1979, pp. 289-290.
2. For instance, see *South Indian Inscriptions* (henceforth *SII*), Vol. VII, Nos. 270, 296, etc.
3. *SII VII*, No. 187.
4. *Ibid.*, No. 207.
5. *Ibid.*, No. 311.
6. *Ibid.*, No. 382.
7. *Ibid.*, No. 313.
8. *Ibid.*, No. 318.
9. *SII*, Vol. IX, Part II, No. 455.
10. *Ibid.*, No. 364.
11. *Ibid.*, No. 212.
12. *Ibid.*, No. 265.
13. *Ibid.*, No. 301.
14. *Ibid.*, No. 302.

Appendix - III

Interpreting Paraśurāma Tradition*

A prominent aspect found in historiography of ancient India has been imposing greater importance to the alliance between the two upper categories in the society, namely, brahmans and ksatriyas. However, a study of Paraśurāma tradition as presented in the puranas and epics of ancient and medieval period shows that the nature of relation between the two upper categories was not so cordial. In addition to this it is attempted to show that there are evidences to prove the hostility between brahmans and ksatriyas. In other words the story of Paraśurāma extinguishing ksatriyas for twenty-one times does obtains importance in the context of the tension that existed between these two *varnas*. This article attempts to narrate and analyse the Paraśurāma tradition both in greater and local puranic tradition.

In the Puranic literature of ancient India, one can find the narration of Paraśurāma as the *avatara* (incarnation) of Viṣṇu and one who fought against the ksatriyas. He is represented both in greater and lesser puranic traditions. In other words references to Paraśurāma are found both in the greater and ancient puranas like *Skanda Purana*, in the epic literature and also in the later local puranas like *Sahyādri khanda*, while discussing the traditions of temples of western coast of India. There are some temples on the western coast of India connected with the Paraśurāma tradition.

Nature of Puranas

The Puranas can be considered as a part of "Itihāsa-Purāna" tradition. Romila Thapar has analysed the salient features of "Itihāsa-Purāna

---

* Published in *World Hongming Philosophical Quarterly*, March, 2003.

tradition".[1] This tradition included Vedic literature, epics and the various puranas. The Purānas represented the changes in the polity and the society. The changes in the society and social structure were represented in the form of changes in the literary tradition. For instance, the process of transition from oral tradition to written tradition is a significant development. Certain sections of brahmans found it necessary to preserve body of knowledge in the form of sacred texts. Purānas consisted of political, social and geographical details. We find the narration of different myths in the Puranas.[2] Some scholars have tried to analyse myths by the study of structure of the myths and to discover symbolic meaning of this narration.[3] This methodology of study of myths seems to be more appropriate for the societies which did not leave enough records to write about their social history. In this context we should mention that many myths were incorporated into Purānas by the brahman authors. It is suggested that hymns uttered in the *yajnas* made it easier for the brahmans to gain control of the tradition.[4]

Theory of Brahmana-Ksatriya Alliance

Scholars who studied ancient Indian social structure suggested that when there was final evolution, during the end of later Vedic period, of four *varnas*, viz., brahmana, ksatriya, vaisya and sudra, initially even though there existed competition among brahmans and ksatriyas for domination in a pre-state society, later there emerged alliance between brahmans and ksatriyas. This alliance between two *varnas* can be seen in the form of marriages between brahmans and ksatriyas. This was permissible according to ancient *sastras* (law books composed usually by brahmans and scholars belonging to elite categories in society) since both these two *varnas* belonged to elite groups in the society and they were allowed to participate in the *yagas*. It is only during the later Vedic and post Vedic period that the social structure of ancient India must have become more rigid in character. The scholars who studied early medieval and medieval society of India also argued that there existed brahmana-ksatriya collaboration.[5] Another form of collaboration between these two *varnas* is found in the case of *yagas* or sacrifices performed by the brahmans and sages, who received sacrificial fee called *dana* and *daksina* in return for legitimising the dominant position of ksatriyas.[6] The other form of collaboration between the two *varnas* is found in the historical tradition itself. Through various forms of literary expression like origin myths, *gathas*, *akhyanas*, genealogy, *kathas* and *upakathas*, *caritas*, *vamsavalis*, the brahmanas tried to protect the interest of the ksatriyas. Scholars argued that state formation itself was the result or the reaction of the brahman-ksatriya collaboration. This is found not only in North India but also in South India, wherein the south Indian ruling lineage are connected with North Indian ruling families like Surya *vamsa* and Candra *vamsa* or Solar race and Lunar race. This kind of alliance is supported by the discovery of large number of land grants that were given during the early medieval and medieval period to brahmans who replaced the ksatriyas as the rulers in the peripheries. It is also suggested that by giving land grants to brahmans an attempt was made by the state to increase the land under cultivation and thus to increase agricultural production. Thus it was found that brahmans and ksatriyas decided to co-operate and collaborate to exploit the economic resources. For instance during the earlier times they shared the cattle wealth[7] while during the later period, they shared the ownership of land. There is a need to study the real nature of relationship between brahmans and ksatriyas during the ancient period. One has to ask the question as to whether the relation between brahmans and ksatriyas was as simple or as cordial as represented in some of the works.

Evaluation of Brahmana-Ksatriya Alliance

Above we have seen that there are many concrete evidences to prove that brahmans and ksatriyas collaborated to exploit the other sections in the society. However there are certain instances to suggest that there existed constant tension between brahmanas and ksatriyas. For instance Visvamitra, who was a ksatriya king to begin with, tried to compete with brahman sage Vasistha to acquire vedic knowledge and other branches of knowledge which had become the prerogative of the brahmans. This shows the existence of this tension between the two communities. Another evidence of this tension between two *varnas* is found in the Paraśurāma tradition.

Narration of *Paraśurāma* Tradition in the Greater Puranas

The word '*parasu*' meant axe which was carried by Rama. It is said that since he used *parasu* for attack and defence he was named Paraśurāma. Another name given to him is Rama Jamadagnya. Since he was a descendent of Bhrigu family, he was also known as Bhargava.

According to Puranic legends Paraśurāma was born on earth to control the atrocities of the ksatriya kings. According to one myth, once god Agni went to Kartaviryarjuna and begged for food. The king allowed him to take as much food as he wanted from anywhere he liked. Agni started burning forests and mountains. Fire burnt the *ashrama* (cottage or residence) of one sage called Apava. The sage cursed that Kartaviryarjuna is at the root of this havoc. The arrogance of ksatriyas has increased beyond limits. Mahavishnu therefore would be born as Paraśurāma to destroy this arrogance of ksatriyas.[8] Accordingly Mahavishnu was born as Paraśurāma in the Bhargava race.[9]

According to another myth mentioned in Brahmanda Purana, Viṣṇu promised Bhumidevi (mother earth) that he would be born on earth as Paraśurāma when Bhumidevi went to him in the form of a cow and complained to him about the atrocities of the wicked ksatriya kings. It is said that Paraśurāma was born as the son of Jamadagni and Renuka on the banks of Narmada River. Renuka was the daughter of king Prasenajit. The family of Paraśurāma was connected with ksatriya families and ksatriya art of warfare. Rama was described as a great warrior, skilled in all weapons, especially archery. Pargiter says that though a brahman, he is generally spoken as virtually a ksatriya, combining two characters, *brahma ksatra.* The battle-axe is mentioned as special weapon. It is in the later writings that he is termed as Paraśurāma to distinguish from Rama, the king of Ayodhya.[10]

Paraśurāma spent his boyhood with his parents in the *asrama.* He did not give much importance to Vedic learning. He showed interest in learning archery. For obtaining proficiency in archery he went to the Himalayas and did penance to please Siva for many years. Lord Siva gave him certain boons including axe. According to tradition Paraśurāma gave instruction in archery only to those who belonged to higher *varnas.* In fact, Karna had to utter a lie that he is a brahman and only then he could get the instruction from Paraśurāma though he came to know that Karna was not a brahman and cursed him for this crime.

The most important event of life of Paraśurāma was the total extermination of the ksatriya race. It is said that Paraśurāma fought against ksatriyas twenty-one times. Here we shall enumerate the circumstances which compelled Paraśurāma to take spiteful bearing towards ksatriyas. The ancestors of Paraśurāma faced the atrocities of the ksatriya kings belonging to Hehaya (or Haihaya) family. It is said that their king Kartaviryarjuna went for hunting in the forests and feeling exhausted after sometime went to the *asrama* of Jamadagni with his retinue. Jamadagni received them well and with the help of the Kamadhenu (wish yielding cow) named Susila, Jamadagni gave a feast to king and his followers. Chandragupta, a minister of Kartaviryarjuna brought to the notice of the king the superior powers of the Kamadhenu. The king expressed his desire to carry Kamadhenu with him to his palace. The sage refused to donate the cow to the king. The officers of the king forcefully took away Kamadhenu and the king's soldiers beat the sage to death. Jamadagni's wife Renuka wept beating her breast twenty-one times and by that time her son Paraśurāma came there and he declared that he would travel round the world twenty-one times to kill and exterminate the ksatriyas from this world. He left for the city of Mahismati where Kartaviryarjuan stayed. In the battle Kartaviryarjuna was killed. The enmity between Hehaya family and Paraśurāma continued afterwards. Puranas mention that Paraśurāma killed the kings of Cola, Cera and Paundra. To stop the birth of ksatriyas in the future Paraśurāma even destroyed the embryo in the wombs of the ksatriya women. To atone for the sin of slaughtering even innocent ksatriyas, Paraśurāma gave away all his riches to brahmins. He invited all the brahmins and conducted a great *yaga*. The chief priest of the yaga was sage Kasyapa. Paraśurāma gave all the land the lands he conquered till that time to Kasyapa. Now Kasyapa said that Paraśurāma should not live in the land donated by him to Kasyapa and that Paraśurāma should go to a southern region and live on the shores of ocean there. Paraśurāma walked south and requested the ocean to give him some land to live. God of ocean, Varuna then asked him to throw an axe. Paraśurāma threw the axe and the ocean receded and gave the land to Paraśurāma. After giving this land to brahmans Paraśurāma went and started doing penance at Mahendragiri.[11]

We have the following observations to make regarding the Paraśurāma tradition mentioned in the Puranas:

1. The family of Bhargavas was known for their enmity with ksatriya dynasty of the Hehayas. Thus when Paraśurāma was born this enmity continued.
2. Paraśurāma had connection with ksatriyas. His mother belonged to a ksatriya family. His uncle was the famous sage Visvamitra, who was a ksatriya and who became a sage after penance. This shows that during this time a ksatriya could become a ksatriya and a brahman could pursue in warlike activities. Change of varna status was permissible. Paraśurāma showed immense interest in acquiring the art of archery.
3. The brahman authors of Paraśurāma tradition used the rhetoric of enmity towards ksatriyas, particularly Hehaya dynasty. This in reality shows the power struggle going on between brahmans and ksatriyas in the actual social structure. The tradition actually states how Paraśurāma gave away all his land to brahmans and he is presented as a protector of brahmans against the atrocities of ksatriyas.
4. In the later tradition it is stated that Paraśurāma came down to the south. Also it is mentioned that Paraśurāma killed the kings of Cola, Cera and Paundra. This may indicate the invasion of South India by

the North Indians or people of Narmada region since it is said that Jamadagni was living on the shores of River Narmada. In South India we also find the tradition of invasion by the North Indian kings. There is reference to the destruction of South Indian polity and culture by the *Kàli arasar* or *Kalabhras* or kings from northern region. It is suggested that invasion of *Kalabhras* led to destruction of some dynasties of South India. This led to the emergence of what is called, "Kalabhra interregnum".[12]

5. The reference to iron axe can be taken symbolically to suggest use of iron in exploiting economic resources of western coast. There was a need to clear forests and create settlements of peasants and brahmans. Scholars have debated regarding the use of different implements to clear dense jungle in early Indian history.[13]
6. It would be problematic to place this tradition in time and space.[14] This tradition should be taken as an indirect way in which we are informed regarding the covert and overt tensions between brahmans and ksatriyas. Even in the local puranic traditions we find the repetition of story of Paraśurāma annihilating ksatriyas. The brahman authors in the localities used this tradition to strengthen their position in the society.

Pargiter argues that the enmity between Paraśurāma and Haihayas ended with the killing of Kartaviryarjuna. After Rama's time Hehayas or Haihayas recovered their power and extended their conquests into North India, making ceaseless raids, overthrowing kingdoms. Pargiter says that ksatriyas must have perished by thousands. The Haihayas conquered Kanyakubja and Ayodhya, but were arrested by the Vaisali kings and later Sagara destroyed all these enemies and rescued India from those evils and re-established peace. Thus according to Pargiter all these events were turned by the brahmans into the fable that Paraśurāma destroyed all the ksatriyas off the earth twenty-one times. The brahmans attributed the killing of all ksatriyas to Paraśurāma, even though there were other rulers who were responsible for killing these kings.[15] Here Pargiter has tried to give an explanation regarding the Paraśurāma tradition. Pargiter has indirectly accepted that there existed show of strength between brahmans and ksatriyas. However, it is necessary to investigate into the attempts made by brahmans to use this tradition to further their interest in the then society. Surprisingly this tradition was used by the brahmans belonging to early period and also later medieval period.

Paraśurāma Tradition in the Local Puranas

In the two later local Puranas, *Grāmapaddhati* and *Sahyādri Khanda,* there is repetition of the Paraśurāma tradition mentioned in the greater Puranic traditions. These local puranas mention how Paraśurāma exterminated ksatriyas on earth and created brahman settlements on west coast. We have seen elsewhere how the brahmans used the Paraśurāma tradition to further their interest in the local society.[16] In these local traditions it is even stated that Paraśurāma converted the fisher folk into brahmans and they were later cursed by Paraśurāma to become degraded in society. This led to the migration of brahmans on the western coast of India. Thus these traditions, both in the greater puranic traditions and lesser puranic traditions, represent Paraśurāma as the protector of brahmans. There must have existed considerable amount of tension between the brahmans and ksatriyas even though at a particular point or points both the upper *varnas* must have decided to cooperate with each other to dominate other *varnas* and *jatis* in society. Significantly, another person chosen by the brahmans as their protector was Mayūra Varma, the Kadamba king who was supposed to have been a brahman to begin with but later he had confrontation with ksatriya kings of Pallava dynasty of South India and this forced Mayūra Varma to become a ksatriya. In the tradition of Mayūra Varma tradition also we can notice the transition of the *varna* status. This tradition also indicates the tension between brahmans and ksatriyas. Both Paraśurāma and Mayūra Varma traditions indicate the complex relations between the two *varnas* – brahmans and ksatriyas in ancient India.

Notes and References

1. Romila Thapar, "Society and Historical Consciousness: The Itihasa-Purana Tradition", in, Sabyasachi Bhattacharya and Romila Thapar (eds.), *Situating Indian History for Sarvepalli Gopal*, Delhi, 1986.
2. D.D. Kosambi suggested that Puranas were written or rewritten to order generally between the sixth and the twelfth centuries. Kosambi stated that Puranas record specially fabricated myths. See D.D. Kosambi, *The Culture and Civilization of Ancient India in Historical Outline*, New Delhi, 1989, p. 49. However dating of the texts of the Puranas has been a constant problem for the Historians and Philologists alike. This is particularly so because during the course of many additions were made in the Puranas by the brahman scholars. For instance, there has been a debate among the historians whether *Arthasastra* was a Mauryan document or a post-Mauryan document. See Romila Thapar, *Asoka and the Decline of Mauryas*, Delhi, 1998, pp. 292-296. One has to ask the question as to why so many additions were made in the ancient literature. We can say that this was done to accommodate emerging new caste groups in the then society. This indicates that authors of Puranas were responding to changing needs of the time.

3. Beane Wendell, *Myth, Cults and Symbols in Sakta Hinduism: A Study of the Indian Mother Goddess,* Leiden, 1977.
4. D.D. Kosambi, *The Culture and Civilization of Ancient India in Historical Outline,* New Delhi, 1989, p. 92.
5. MG.S Narayanan suggests that the evidence of Sangam literature of South India and the land grants of the post-Sangam period indicate brahman-chieftain (ksatriya) alliance. See MG.S. Narayanan, *Foundations of South Indian Society and Culture,* Delhi, 1994, p. 117.
6. Hermann Kulke (ed.), *The State in India 1000-1700,* Delhi, 1997, p. 41.
7. R.S. Sharma, *Material Culture and Social Formations in Ancient India,* Delhi, 1983, pp. 22-36.
8. Vettam Mani, *Puranic Encyclopaedia,* Delhi, Reprint, 1996, p. 568.
9. Pargiter finds reference in the Vedic literature to Jamadagni and his son Rama as belonging to Bhargava family. This is one of the earliest references to Bhargava family in the ancient Indian literature. In the later works like epics and Puranas we find more reference to achievements of Paraśurāma. See F.E. Pargiter, *Ancient Indian Historical Tradition,* Delhi, Reprint, 1997, p. 8.
10. F.E. Pargiter, *Ancient Indian Historical Tradition*, p. 199.
11. Vettam Mani, *Puranic Encyclopaedia*, pp. 568-571.
12. Rajan Gurukkal states that, "Historians have associated this period of discontinuity with the inroads by a predatory groups known as *kalabhras* who belonged to the uplands of Karnataka. They are said to have swept through the domains of the Tamil chieftains and caused their eclipse. This has led to the construction of an interregnum labeled after the *kalabhras.*" See Rajan Gurukkal, "Characterizing Ancient Society: The Case of South India", *Proceedings of the Indian History Congress, Fifty-Ninth Session, Patiala, 1998*, Aligarh, 1999, p. 44.
13. Romila Thapar, "The First Millennium B.C. in Northern India (Upto the end of the Mauryan period)", in, Romila Thapar (ed.), *Recent Perspectives of Early Indian History,* Bombay, 1995, p. 90.
14. On the basis of Puranic references, Pargiter believes that Paraśurāma belongs to interval between the Krta and Treta ages. See Pargiter, *Ancient Indian Historical Tradition* 1997, p. 177.
15. Pargiter, *Ancient Indian Historical Tradition*, pp. 270-271.
16. Nagendra Rao, 'The Making of Local Puranas in South Western India: a Study of Brahmanical Traditions', *Pondicherry University Journal of Social Sciences and Humanities,* Volume 3, Number 1, January 2002, pp. 75-86.

Appendix IV

Analysing Brahmana Settlements in* South Kanara[1]

The emergence of the brahmanas in the history of South India during the early medieval period led to far reaching consequences. The brahmanas played an important role in standardizing the social structure, with the emergence of the *varna* order and evolution of *jati* hierarchy. They also played an equally important role in state formation in the region where there existed pre-state features. The acceptance of *varna* system in the social structure meant the transition from tribe to caste on the one hand and transition from pre-state to state situation on the other.[2]

The practical value of the brahmanas was realized by the kings particularly during the post-Gupta period and they invited the brahmanas to come to their territory and settle there. The brahmanas were expected to legitimize the position of the kshatriyas by connecting their genealogy with the genealogy of the great kings of North India like, e.g., the Ikshvakus. Vedic rituals were another means of the legitimization of the kshatriyas.

Later the brahmana authors in the court of the kings wrote the biographical histories of the kings. One of the popular biographies or *caritas* was the one written by Bana Bhatta regarding the life and times of Harshavardhana of Thaneshwar.[3] Such biographical attempts are made at lesser level when we find the writing of the *vamsāvali* (genealogy) of Mayara Varma. This obviously pressurized the king to grant lands to the brahmanas.

---

* Published in *Research Bullatin Vishweshvaranand Vedic Research Institute*, Vol. 2, December 2003.

The *brahmadeyas* led to two consequences. Firstly, the land grants led to creation of the agency through which the state could express its ideology. Secondly, the state was able to extend the land under cultivation. This led to creation of surplus production on the one hand and creation of resource base for the state on the other. The tax concessions given to the donees helped in attracting the migration of productive and non-productive classes to those regions where there still existed primitive forms of cultivation like swidden or slash and burn cultivation. This explains the reference to both brahmana and non-brahmanical groups in the brahmanical traditions.

The patronage of the kings was expressed through two means. Firstly, the kings issued inscriptions, where in, they assured the rights of the brahmanas over the villages or plots of land that were given to them as land grant. Secondly, this was expressed through the brahmanical tradition though they had the single purpose of establishing the credentials of the brahmanas over the villages or the land grants that were made to them. On certain occasions, this led to creation of spurious land grants and brahmanical myths. Thus in a purely agrarian economy the importance of fertile agrarian tracts were noticed by the brahmanas. It was these brahmans who gave a linkage to the puranic traditions of North India. Thus the caste Purānas of South India, which claim great antiquity, in reality, may not belong to remote past. By doing this, cultural symbols like Vedic rituals remained uniform throughout India.

Thus, all over India one can see a uniform pattern of brahmana settlements. They in fact exhibited more or less similar features. Most of brahmana settlements were found in the form of clusters of villages around important river valleys.[4] They had their assemblies that met in important brahmana settlements. For instance in the case of South Western India, the brahmana settlements are found on the riverbanks like Sita and Netravati. Most of the times one can notice assimilation of the aboriginal culture.

Thus, on the one hand there was worship of brahmanical gods, while on the other there existed the small shrines of non-brahmanical *daivas*. The role of the brahmanas in the previously non-brahmanical society was very significant since the brahmanas possessed the knowledge of agrarian seasons and weather through their knowledge of astronomy and astrology. They were able to suggest remedies for the ills of the people. Thus, it was easy for them to impress their ideology on the people. This pattern of creation of brahmana settlements was a phenomenon one can notice all over South India. South Western India, a coastal region of modern state of Karnataka, was not an exception to this development.

R.S. Sharma argued that the land grants that were given to the brahmanas led to the emergence of Indian feudalism since along with the land grants several administrative and judicial rights were delegated by the kings to the landlords. This led to the creation of conflict between two classes, brahmanas and peasants[5]. B.D.Chattopadhyaya argued that the brahmana settlements led to the expansion of agricultural production.[6] Herman Kulke believed that brahmana settlements were created due the need for validation and legitimacy of the post-Gupta kingdoms. He says that the brahmanas played an important role in the process of legitimization of the rule of the local kingdoms. The brahmanas also integrated the divergent local cults into the greater Sanskritic culture[7]. Burton Stein stated that the brahmans were the authoritative interpreters of the ideological framework. They lived with the peasants in the rural settlements.[8] The studies made by above scholars have revealed certain important aspects of the relation of the brahmanas with the society during the different points of time.

Above details show certain general pattern of development related to brahmana settlements. Some of the above features can be found in South Western India as well. Even though the earliest inscriptions of South Western India mention the brahman communities and brahman settlements like Shivalli, it is in a caste purana, *Grāmapaddhati,* wherein we find important details regarding the establishment of brahman settlements in South Western India. In *Grāmapaddhati* there are details about brahman families in thirty-two villages. The fact that this was a caste purāna enables us to assume that this work was written with a purpose. By preserving the tradition in a written form attempt was made to maintain traditional rights over land and villages.

The brahmanas attempted to claim ownership rights through two ways. Firstly, by composing and preserving the traditions they claimed ownership rights. The tradition regarding creation of Parashurāma *ksetra* belongs to this category. Through the myths, which could not be placed in specificity of time and space, it was attempted by brahmanas to dominate fertile agrarian tracts. The second way of claiming ownership right was through the land grants which were issued in the form of inscriptions by kings, governors, traders, rich members of the society, etc. who needed the support of brahmanas to legitimize their position in society.

Discussing about the first type of brahmanical attempt to claim land ownership rights we may present the data available in the brahmanical traditional chronicle, *Grāmapaddhati.* Through this brahmanical tradition the brahmanas who were obviously the authors of this work, tried to claim ownership rights over large tracts of land in the western coast. The tradition discusses the creation of land by Paraśurāma out of sea by the use of his arrow and by the use of his axe in two different contexts. Basically, this has to be seen as a myth which was purposely created for the preservation of the rights of brahmans over land. It is said that Lord Parasurama donated villages to brahmanas. Here Paraśurāma may be considered as a cult figure, a figure that represents the migration of the brahmanas from North India. Parasurama is seen in the traditions of North India as found in the Puranas. The question as to why Paraśurāma was taken in the case of the brahmanical traditions in South Western India can be answered by arguing that Parasurama himself represented the aggressiveness of the brahmana, who claimed to have defeated the ksatriyas and extirpated the ksatriyas from earth, which tradition itself may highlight the ongoing power struggle between the brahmanas and the ksatriyas.

In this power struggle eventually there must have been a compromise between the brahmanas the kshatriyas as seen in the acceptance of ksatriya Visvamitra by the brahmana Vasishta. Thus, the motif of Parasurama as the divine power is effectively used in this tradition. Another important incident mentioned in *Grāmapaddhati* is the representation of the temporal figurehead in the form of emergence of Mayūra Varma. For one thing, Mayūra Varma is taken since he himself was a brahmana and he had ksatriyaized himself to become the king, another representation of transformation of brahmans from being merely a priestly class to a dominant ruling class. On the one hand, there was the need for the recording of this transformation so as to legitimize the position of the newly established rule of the brahmana ruler Mayūra Varma. This is a clear example of social mobility in early India, a process wherein there was not only a change of profession but also a change in the *varna* itself, which itself is not a simple development, which must have led to far reaching consequences. On the other hand, there was the need for the brahmanas to claim ownership rights, which was done by claiming land grants by Mayūra Varma. We know that land grants during the early medieval and medieval times throughout India had become common phenomena, a feature of growing feudalisation of the society.[9]

This tradition itself can be considered as the attempt of the brahmanas to establish the *varna* order in the society in a social context where there was simple of division of social classes on the basis of the professions performed by these classes. In fact, after the establishment of the brahmana settlement we may safely argue that there was intensification of social stratification in South Western India. *Grāmapaddhati,* the dating of which is a problematic task, uses the details, which place this work in the early medieval and medieval times. However the details of settlement of *grāmas,* the appointment of non-brahmanas to look after the agricultural activities, the enslavement of previously dominant communities of the non-brahmana peasants called holeyas and the reference to feudal terms of relationship between the kings and the people, suggests emergence of feudal polity and society.

There is reference to the settlement of brahmanas in the thirty-two villages or *agrāhāras* of South Western India. Many of these thirty-two villages can be identified even today. The document even gives the names of all the brahmana families who were made to settle in all these thirty-two villages. What are the activities of the brahmanas? It is said that they have to perform the *yajna, adhyapana* other priestly occupations. However, among the brahmanas we find the reference to two categories: *Trikarmis* and *Shatkarmis*. *Trikarmis* were not supposed to perform puja and they were managers of land and the temples. This categorization of the brahmanas indicates the emergence of one section of brahmanas who were more interested in agricultural activities.

Although *shastra* literature condemned agricultural pursuits to the brahmanas, we find certain brahmanical communities like the Matti brahmins, etc., indulged in agricultural activities. The authors of *Grāmapaddhati* clarify that this is allowed because they were fallen brahmanas, cursed to perform agriculture and horticulture.

Grāmapaddhai indicates the migration of the brahmans from outside regions even though it is contentious issue as to exactly from where these people migrated, historians arguing migration from a place called Ahicchatra which has been identified in various places like one in U.P. and other in Andhra Pradesh, eastern coast of South India. However, recent reference that another name of Badami was Ahicchatra as found in the work of R.Champakalakshmi seems to be more acceptable since it is possible and plausible that there was the migration of the brahmanas from Ahicchatra or Aihole.[10] And we are informed that it was the brahmanas who started the agricultural guild of South India which was known as *mahanadu* and which emerged as the Ayyavole Five Hundred.[11]

There are several references to brahmanas as the owners of the land as we find in the inscriptions of South Western India.[12] An analysis of the inscriptions shows that land grants were given to the temples and the brahmanas for the alleged purpose of gaining religious merit from these pious activities. However, real reasons for the creation of *brahmadeyas* and *devādanas* seem to legitimize the position of the traders, trader guilds which originated from an outside region and they had come to stay in the locality. As far as the kings are concerned, they tried to use the temples as the objects of dissemination of their ideology to indoctrinate the subject population of the local zones or peripheries.

Starting from 8th century A.D. the inscriptions of South Western India refer to the activities of brahmanas and mention the importance of Shivalli which is often compared to Kasi itself, which is most sacred domain of the brahmans and a pilgrimage centre.[13] The inscriptions realize the importance of the brahmanas. Their defiance by other *varnas* in the society is compared with the murder of several cows of Shivalli, which is the ultimate crime of the populace in the society which would have fetched the maximum religious demerit for the offender. It is said that those who harm brahmanas would commit the sin equal to killing of one thousand cows, indication of how both brahmanas and cows were important for the agrarian economy of the times.

There are several inscriptions which indicate the patronage given to the brahmanas by not only the kings but also by other communities like traders, bangle sellers, agriculturists, even Jainas and others. This meant that even in the absence of emporiums the brahmanas continued to receive patronage. Later petty chieftains replaced the king. For instance, we find reference to the brahmana who was the advisor of a sudra peasant who stayed in his residence called *bidu.* One way of improving the economic position of the brahmanas was by giving monetary aid and land grants to temples, which were managed by the brahmanas.

Folklore represents the expression of feelings of the common people regarding various sections of society. In South Western India, there is folk literature like *paddanas*, *kabitas*, proverbs, etc. Among these *paddanas* form the most important source of information. In the folklore of South Western India, the brahmanas are pictured as dominant section and some-times, there is a feeling of contempt among the people regarding this community. But they are considered as a kind of necessary evil in the society, since they are knowledgeable in astrology, seasons and contact with divine forms.[14] The brahmanas had become successful in influencing the non brahmana sections and their customs and practices. This is proved by the fact that it was the brahmana priest who initiates the *bhutada kola*, a ritual of non-brahmanas. During the earlier times, there existed *bidus* or settlement of bunts, the local feudal Lords. Usually these Lords were advised by a brahmana. Thus, traditions, inscriptions and folklore tell us how significant brahmana settlements were in the early medieval and medieval society of South India. However, we would clarify that all the brahmanas did not perform the same role as brought out in this article.

Our intention is not to generalize but to suggest certain trends among dominant brahmanical groups.

References

1. Abbreviation: SII= South Indian Inscriptions.
2. B.D. Chattopadhyaya, 'Political Processes and Structure of Polity in Early Medieval India', Presidential Address, Ancient India Section, *Indian History Congress*, 44th session, 1983.
3. A.B. Keith, *A History of Sanskrit Literature*, Delhi, Reprint, 1993.
4. Nagendra Rao, "The Historical Tradition of South Kanara and the Brahmanical Groups: A Study of *Grāmapaddhati* and *Sahyādri Khanda*", Unpublished M.Phil. Thesis, Mangalore University, 1995.
5. R.S. Sharma, *Indian Feudalism*, Calcutta, 1965.
6. B.D. Chattopadhyaya, 'Political Processes.
7. Hermann Kulke, *The State in India*, Delhi, 1997.
8. Burton Stein, *Peasant, State and Society in Medieval South India*, Delhi, 1994, pp. 6-9.
9. M.G.S. Narayanan, *Foundations of South Indian Society and Culture*, Delhi, 1994.
10. R. Champakalakshmi, *Trade, Ideology and Urbanization South India 300 B.C. to A.D. 1300*, Delhi, 1996, p. 50.
11. *Ibid.*
12. See *SII*, Vol. VII and Vol. IX Part II.
13. Nagendra Rao, 'Shivalli: A Brahman Settlement of Dakshina Kannada', *Quarterly Journal of Mythic Society*, Volume XCI, Issue No. 3, pp. 72-81.
14. B.A.Vivek Rai, *Tulu Janapada Sahitya* (in Kannada), Bangalore, 1985.

Bibliography

Primary Sources

- *Annual Report of South Indian Epigraphy (ARSIE)* 1929-30.
- *Annual Report of Mysore Archaeological Department for the year* 1943, (Mysore, 1944).
- *Epigraphia Carnatica* Vol. VII.
- *Epigraphia Indica* Vol. VII.
- *South Indian Inscriptions (SII)* Vols. VII and IX Pt. II.

Holla, Krishniah *Grāmapaddhati*, (Balanadu, 1924). (Referred as GPI in the dissertation).

Cunha, Gerson Da (ed) *Sahyādri Khānda- Skānda-Purāna-ntargata* (Bombay, 1877).

Bhanumati, Y.G. (ed.) *Sahyādri Khānda*, (Mysore, 1984) unpublished.

- Photo copy of *Grāmapaddhati* in the collections of University of Tubingen, Germany, (Referred as GP2 in the dissertation).

Varaha Timmappa *Grāmapaddhati*, No. 79, in Kannada Department Library, Mangalore University, Palm Kannada Department Library, Mangalore University, Palm leaf manuscript collections, (Referred as GP3 in the dissertation). *Grāmapaddhati Kelavu Manetanagalu*, No. 44, in Kannada Department Library Mangalore University, Palm leaf manuscript collections.

Bhattacharya *Grāmapaddhati*, No. 78, in Kannada Department Library Mangalore University Palm leaf manuscript collection.

- Unpublished inscriptions from Ullūru Subrahmanyeswara temple, Kandāvara, by the kind courtesy of Dr. P.N. Narasimha Murthi, Karkala.

Secondary Sources:

Books:

Acharya, Manchi Narayana *Baipādittāya,* (Manchi, 1994).

Acharya, P. Kuppanna *Srimanmadhwācharya,* (Kinnigoli, 1986).

Acharya, P. Kuppanna *Sri Guruvara Vādirajara Charitamrita*, (Kinnigoli, 1983).

Adiga, Venkatakrishna *Nōlavara Mahisha Mardini Suprabhāta Mattu Sri Ksetra Mahātme,* (Nilavara, second edition 1992).

Ahmad, Qeyamuddin (ed) *India by Al-Biruni,* (New Delhi, 1992).

Bhat P. Gururaja *Studies in Tuluva History and Culture*, (Kallianpur, 1975).

Bhat P. Gururaja *Tulunādu*, (Udupi, 1963).

Bhat P. Gururaja *Antiquities of South Kanara (Kallianpur*, 1969).

Bhat p. Gururaja *Aaluparasaru,* (Bangalore, 1976).

Bhat P. Gururaja *Tulunādina Itihāsadalli Sthānikaru*, (Udupi, 1966).

Bhat P. Gururaja *Tulunādina Saptaksētragalu*, (Bangalore, 1976).

Bhatta, Uppangala Rama *Mānasa*, (Udupi, 1990).

Bhatta, Uppangala Rama *Gadinādu Kāsaragōdu*, (Udupi, 1994).

Bhattacharya, Sabyasachi and Romila Thapar (ed) *Situating Indian History for Sarvepaḷḷi Gopal,* (Delhi, 1986).

Bilimale, Parushothama *Koragara Samskriti*, (Bangalore, 1993).

Buchanan, Francis *Journey from Madras through the countries of Mysore, Canara and Malabar*, (Madras, 1870).

Chattopadhyaya, Brajadulal *The making of Early Medieval India*, (Delhi, 1994).

Gopal, B.R. *Minor Dynasties of South India: Karnataka, Vol. I*, (Madras, 1982).

Gopal, B.R. *Vijayanagara Inscription Vol. II*, (Mysore, 1986).

Gowda, K. Kushalappa, K. Chinnappa Gowda (ed). *Dakshina Kannada Jilleya Kaifiyattugalu,* (Ujire, 1983).

Kanakasabai, V. *The Tamils Eighteen Hundred years Ago,* (New Delhi, 1979).

Karanta, Ko. Sa. *Kūta Mahā Jagattu*, (Saligrama, 1958).

Kosambi, Damodar Dharmanand *An introduction to the study of Indian History,* (Bombay, Second edition, 1975).

Macdonell, A.A., *History of Sanskrit Literature,* (London, 1900).

Malavada S.S. *Kāvya Pada Mañjari,* (Bangalore, 1970).

Manipal, Arke Hesarinallenide, (Bangalore, 1989).

Padmanabha Kekunnaya K. *Śivalli Brāhmanara Kulanāmagalu - Ondu Adhyayana*, unpublished dissertation submitted to University of Madras, 1982.

Panditacharya, Narayana (translated by Vyasanakere Prabhananacharya) *Sumadhva Vijaya*, (Bangalore, 1988).

Pargiter F.E. *Ancient Indian Historical Tradition*, (Delhi, Reprint, 1972).

Patterson R.F. *New Websters Dictionary*, (Florida, 1992).

Philips, C.H. (ed). *Historians of Indian Pakistan and Ceylon*, (London, 1961).

Priolkar, A.K. *The Goa Inquisition*, (New Delhi, 1961).

Puttige, Rasika *Kananduru Dharma Arasu Sri Tōdakukkinar Daivasthana Pariñaya*, (Kananduru, 1967).

Ramesh K.V. *A History of South Canara*, (Dharwar, 1970).

Rai, Vivek B.A. *Tulu Janapada Sāhitya* (Bangalore, 1985).

Rai, Subbanna A. *Da.Ka. Jilleya Aitihyagalu*, (Mani, 1994).

Rao, Aigal Ganapati *Dakshina Kannada Jilleya Prachina Itihasa*, (Mangalore, 1923).

Rao, B.K. Gururaja, *The Megalithic Culture in South India*, (Mysore, 1972).

Rao, H. Vishnumurthi, (ed) *Brahmavāni,* (Kasaragod, 1993).

Rao J.S., P. Gururaja Bhat *Archealogical Survey and Research in Temple Workship* (sic), (Bombay, 1976).

Raya, Baik d Venkatakrishna (ed) *Namma Ajapura*, (Brahmavara, 1961).

Saletore B.A. *Ancient Karnataka Vol. I History of Tuluva*, (Poona, 1936).

Sastri, Nilakantha K.A. *The Colas*, (Madras, 1984).

Shenoy, Umanath, Y. (ed) *Sri Vaidyanātha Kripa*, (Kokkada, 1987).

Shetty, Vasanth B. *Brahmāvarada Itihāsa*, (Brahamavara, 1988).

Shetty, Balakrishna *Sheenappa Heggade Samagra Sāhitya*, (Udupi, 1991).

Sircar, D.C. *Indian Epigrapical Glossary*, (Delhi, 1966).

Sundara, A. *The Early Chamber Tombs of South India*, (Delhi, 1975).

Swami, O.L. Nagabhushana *Purāṇa,* (Hampi, Second edition, 1993).

Thapar, Romila *Ancient Indian Social History: Some Interpretations*, (New Delhi, 1978).

Thapar, Romila *The Past and Prejudice*, (Delhi, Third Reprint, 1993).

Thapar, Romila *Interpreting Early India*, (Delhi, 1994).

Vasanthamadhava K.G. *Mūlikeya Itihāsa*, (Mulki, 1988).

Veluthat, Kesavan *Brahman Settlements in Kerala Historical Studies*, (Calicut, 1978).

Veluhat, Kesavan *Aryan Brahman Settlement of Ancient Kerala*, unpublished M.A. dissertation, (Calicut, 1974).

Articles:

Bhat, P. Gururaja, "Udupi Tradition, Antiquity, History and culture" in Vivekananda Kendra Patrika- *Pilgrimage centres of India*, February, 1974.

Dikshitar, V.R. Ramachandra "The Puranas: A study", in Narendra Nath Law (ed). *The Indian Historical Quarterly*, Vol. VII-4, (Delhi, Reprint, 1985).

D Souza, Alponsus S.J. "Economic and Social conditions of the Nairis of Dakshina Kannada", *in Samaja Shōdhana*, Vol. 2, October 1993.

Karantha, K. Shivarama "Jilleyalli Samshōdhanege Sāmagrigalu, in B. Malini Malya (ed), *Shivarāma Kārantara Lēkhanagaḷu* Vol. 2, (Mangalagangotri, 1994).

Sircar, D.C. "The text of Puranic list of Rivers", in Narendra Nath Law (ed), *The Indian Historical Quarterly*, Vol.XXVII-3 (Delhi, 1985).

Vasanthamadhava, K.G. "Pracina Karnātaka Mattu Kāśmira in *Sādhane,* Sanchike-2, (Bangalore, 1974).

Veluthat, Kesavan, "Non-Brahmana Protest in Brahmanical Literary Expressions: The *Grāmapaddhati* From South Canara under the Aḷupās and Hoysalas", *in Proceedings of the Indian History Congress,* (Delhi, 1992).

Index

R

S